To Jane
Love Jim

July 2011

MORE THAN LUCK

a Memoir

James S. Griffin

iUniverse, Inc.
Bloomington

More than Luck
A Memoir

Copyright © 2011 by James S. Griffin

All rights reserved. No part of this book may be used or reproduced by any means, graphic, electronic, or mechanical, including photocopying, recording, taping or by any information storage retrieval system without the written permission of the publisher except in the case of brief quotations embodied in critical articles and reviews.

iUniverse books may be ordered through booksellers or by contacting:

iUniverse
1663 Liberty Drive
Bloomington, IN 47403
www.iuniverse.com
1-800-Authors (1-800-288-4677)

Because of the dynamic nature of the Internet, any web addresses or links contained in this book may have changed since publication and may no longer be valid. The views expressed in this work are solely those of the author and do not necessarily reflect the views of the publisher, and the publisher hereby disclaims any responsibility for them.

Any people depicted in stock imagery provided by Thinkstock are models, and such images are being used for illustrative purposes only.

Certain stock imagery © Thinkstock.

ISBN: 978-1-4502-8993-1 (sc)
ISBN: 978-1-4502-9011-1 (ebook)

Printed in the United States of America

iUniverse rev. date: 6/7/2011

Dedication

To my grandchildren:

Nicholas "Nick" James Griffin

James "Jamie" Scott Griffin III

Tyler Philip Griffin

Malcolm Joseph Griffin

Gibson Scott Collins

Augustus "Gus" Paine Griffin

Wendy Adele Collins

Natalie Torre Griffin

Wyatt Paine Griffin

Cooper James Griffin

Maude Sterling Collins

Gabriela Griffin

Sterling Leraas Griffin

Hope Catherine Griffin

Contents

Preface	ix
Foreword	xi
Acknowledgments	xv
Introduction: Soul Mate: Our Second Life Together	xvii
(1) Early Memories	1
(2) Coming of Age	29
(3) Young Adulthood	50
(4) Alpental: Is Not in the Dictionary	66
(5) Cape buffalo Hunting: An African Safari	104
(6) Namu: The Killer Whale	118
(7) Post Alpental: Of Lumber Mills, Banks, and Other Businesses	153
(8) Nine Lives: Flying a Floatplane	188
(9) Off-Road Racing: The Baja 500	214
(10) Real Estate Development: In Business with My Sons	235
(11) Wendy: One of a Kind	270
Appendix	295
Chronology	334
Griffin/Mathewson Family Tree	338
Paine/Sterling Family Tree	339
Travel Pictures	340

Preface

Grandchildren, I became interested in genealogy in 1988 on a trip to Russia with the board of the Pacific Northwest Ballet (PNB), when your grandmother, Wendy "Nana," one of the ballet's founders, was chairman of the board. Due to the connections of the ballet's co-artistic director, Francia Russell, we had exceptional Bolshoi Ballet theater tickets in Moscow and were able to observe Bolshoi dance classes where principals trained daily. The PNB board received similar VIP treatment from the Kirov Ballet in St. Petersburg.

While touring the Hermitage Museum in St. Petersburg, I couldn't believe the large number of griffin icons displayed on the walls. (The griffin is a mythological beast with the head, wings, and talons of an eagle and the tail and legs of a lion.) I inquired as to their significance and learned they represented Renaissance religious themes brought to Russia by artisans beginning in 1696, when Tsar Peter the Great opened his country to the influences of the West.

When we returned home, my interest having been piqued by the icons, I began researching my Griffin and (on my mother's side) Mathewson ancestors. After discovering that both families played major roles in the development of the Pacific Northwest, I started assembling records for a genealogy, so you would know something of your heritage. After compiling considerable information and family stories, I realized my own experiences would probably be of more interest to you, since you knew me during my lifetime, so I wrote a memoir and intertwined family genealogy into it.

All conversations and events in my book are portrayed to the best of my recollection.

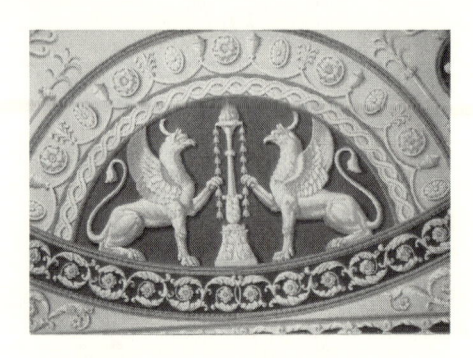

Foreword

"Jim Griffin and I grew up next door to each other. Our friendship has never wavered. If someone was to ask me what comes to mind when I think about Jim, I'd say he didn't let life slide away; he was always available when I needed him and his family came first. Though I was never as conservative as Jim, we were equally compassionate."

~ Booth Gardner, governor, State of Washington, U.S ambassador to the General Agreement on Tariffs and Trade

"Whether you are an African hunter, ride killer whales, race off-road vehicles, fly a floatplane, walk across the Grand Canyon rim to rim in a day, or swim in the Amazon River, you are about to meet a remarkable individual who has survived a number of challenging encounters. You won't want to miss a single perilous adventure, nor James Scott Griffin's tender love at first sight of the woman he would marry, his soul mate. When Jim began researching and writing his family history for his grandchildren, he included a description of his own life. For those privileged to read those stories, it was apparent they should be made available to a broader audience."

~ Lisa Kellogg, family friend of nearly fifty years

"A businessman and entrepreneur with grit and savvy, James Scott Griffin has faced down more than one threat to his life. With an astonishing hunger for discovery, he has experienced firsthand many glamorous and romantic dangers. His curiosity about everything around him pushed him to explore the world and himself, and he's always had a good time, throwing himself fully into every exciting endeavor. This world-class gentleman, with a dash of rogue, is a true adventurer. His resounding good fortune in all areas of his life has come from more than luck. He is guided by an acute sense of the world around him."

~ Charol Messenger, author, book editor

"I have known Jim Griffin since the 1950s. Beginning in the 1980s, he and I became involved in a number of businesses and investments. During that time, Jim published his first book, *How to Make Money in Commercial Land*. I have always been impressed with the Griffin family tradition and the creativity and energy that its members have continually shown. This book should be of great interest to anyone interested in Tacoma/Pierce County history and business."

~ William Riley, family friend and business associate

"Jim Griffin—a free spirit, nothing ventured nothing gained—no mountain too high to climb."

~ George Weyerhaeuser, an old friend

"*More than Luck* is more than a memoir. It is more than a love story. It is more than an adventure tale. *More than Luck* is a gift of love from a grandfather nearing the end of life to his grandchildren, who have yet to live theirs."

~Terry (Greene) Sterling, journalist, author, journalism professor at Arizona State University

"Jim's great love of family has encompassed all of us eastern Paines, much to our benefit. It was Jim and Wendy who reached out to the Peter Paines Sr. and Jr. in the late 1960s to renew contacts between the western and eastern branches of the family, which had lapsed considerably over a couple of decades. As a result, enduring friendships have been created among the younger generations. Both Peter III and Alex lived with Jim and Wendy, and Alex even worked for Whitney for half a year. In Wendy I found not only the western incarnation of the 'Paine gene' (also found in Ashley and little Wendy), but the sister I never had for whom I have the deepest affection. I wish Jim 'tight lines' and 'straight shooting' in the years ahead."

~ Peter S. Paine Jr.

Acknowledgments

I would not have written a memoir if it were not for Lisa Kellogg, a *simpatico* friend of nearly fifty years. Four years ago while compiling information for a genealogy, Lisa happened to read the story of my courtship of Wendy and my terrifying ordeal as an eleven-year-old protecting my baby sister from an intruder.

"Jim," Lisa said, "forget the genealogy. You're a great storyteller. Your grandchildren will be far more interested in your adventures. You can intertwine genealogy into the memoir through what you remember hearing from your parents, grandparents, and your own research."

Unfortunately, Lisa will not be able to read what she encouraged me to write, as she recently passed away. However, her daughters Inga, Susie, and Vivy, who share so many of their mother's physical and mental characteristics, will.

If it hadn't been for my dear friends Bill and Bobby Street, I'd still be struggling to write a coherent sentence. They suggested I take an "online" course, "Writing 101." Bobby also spent hours correcting my spelling and grammar along the way.

In my early drafts—I rewrote my memoir at least three times—I got editing help from Charol Messenger, the writing doctor, and the website Sheila Bender—Writing It Real. Charol and Sheila suggested I read "how-to books," like *Essentials of English* by

Hopper, Fale, Foote, and Griffith; *On Writing Well* by Zinsser; *Creative Writing for People Who Can't Not Write* by Lindskoog; and *The Only Grammar Book You'll ever Need* by Thurman. I did.

My family also contributed. My brothers Ted Griffin and Charlie Spaeth were there for me in times of fading memory; my sister Nancy Hewitt Spaeth and sister-in-law Freda (Zimmerman) Griffin saved me many hours of ancestor research; my sister Beth (Griffin) Farris and my wife Wendy's sister-in-law, Terry (Greene) Sterling continually encouraged me; Wendy's cousin Peter Paine Jr. contributed Paine genealogy; Peter's son's, Alex Paine, company, Web Sight Design, helped bring clarity to massive amounts of material. Wendy's cousin Dotty Paine contributed family stories as told to her by her father, Jordan Paine, and Dottie's sister, Claudia (Paine) Johnson, edited my first chapters, Wendy's cousin, Michael John Evenson, provided information about his father, Admiral Marvin "Chick" Evenson, and my second cousin, Colby Parks, (my grandmother Ada (Parks) Griffin's grandnephew) provided me with Park's family genealogy.

Most importantly, my wife Wendy read and corrected drafts, pushed me when the project became overpowering, and served as a beacon to keep me on track.

Introduction: Soul Mate: Our Second Life Together

We met on a Saturday morning in the fall of 1958, at Stanford University. Rick Prince, a pledge brother, and I were leaving the Phi Delta Theta fraternity when a white, two-door '57 Ford pulled into the circular drive.

Three girls got out and began walking up the driveway. I knew Betsy and Peachy. They waved and I waved back. I didn't know the driver, but I felt a connection, a familiarity. She looked tall, maybe five-foot-eight, with fair skin and blonde hair in a ponytail. She wore a white, short-sleeved blouse, faded Levi's, and sneakers with no socks. Her legs and ankles looked perfectly proportioned, and she moved like a model—which I later learned she was—with full strides and a subtle movement in the hips. Her turned-up nose, full lips, delicate ears, and high cheekbones gave her the look of a Nordic goddess.

My entire body began to tingle, like an arm or a leg when held in one position too long. Adrenaline surged through my veins. *What, what was the connection?* I wondered. Suddenly the memory flashed before my eyes. *I reined in the horses at the brow of a hill overlooking a prairie of grass that stretched to the horizon. Wendy sat beside me, and our children rode in the bed of the wagon.*

Stunned, I turned to Rick and said, "Rick, see the blonde with Betsy and Peachy?"

"Yeah."

"I'm going to marry her!"

"Griffin, get serious." Rick always called me Griffin. "Do you even know her?"

"Yes, but not from this life!" I answered.

"What're you talking about?" he asked. I left Rick and bounded down the steps, taking two at a time.

"Hi, Betsy. Hi, Peachy," I said, trying to remain calm. "You're here kind of early, aren't you? The party doesn't start until seven." I'd dated Betsy Bledsoe, but we'd broken up. I'd known Peachy Williams since meeting her in Sun Valley when we were in junior high. Betsy and Peachy attended Mills College.

"We got a ride down with Wendy," Betsy said. "She's spending the weekend with her aunt and uncle in Atherton. Coming early gives us an opportunity to check in with our Seattle friends."

Betsy turned to Wendy. "Wendy, I'd like you to meet Jim Griffin."

"Hi," she said. "It's Wendy Sterling." *What a beautiful name,* I thought, thinking of Peter Pan.

"Hello, Wendy Sterling." I took her hand. It was soft and warm, not callused like mine from tennis and golf. She had a firm grip, unlike most girls, who shook hands with three fingers. *If she is staying with her aunt and uncle,* I thought, *she probably doesn't have a date.*

"Wendy, any chance you're free tonight?" I asked. I hadn't let go of her hand. I didn't want to break the connection. Her essence flowed into my body like the scent from a rose. "Why don't you come with Betsy and Peachy? I've got a date, but I'll fix you up with one of my fraternity brothers." My grandmothers would turn over in their graves if I dumped my date.

Wendy's smile faded, and she pulled her hand away as if my invitation presented a dilemma. My blood pressure shot up as I waited for a reply. After what seemed an eternity, she resolved whatever had been bothering her, and the sparkle in her blue eyes returned.

"Sure, okay!"

"Great," I said. I escorted the girls to the car, and when I lost sight of it, I started down the driveway.

Rick, still on the fraternity porch, shouted after me. "Griffin! What's going on?"

"I'll explain later." I yelled. *But would I?* I wondered. Rick was my closest friend, but not even Rick would be able to fathom what my subconscious was telling me.

I wandered to Stanford's inner campus, a turn-of-the-century courtyard of low, long, sandstone block buildings connected by arcades that formed a double quad. I sat on the bench in front of the chapel and let my mind wander. I recalled the circumstances of my near-death experience of a past life. My brother, Ted, momentarily fell asleep behind the wheel of a car headed toward a mountain tunnel's abutment, where four lanes funneled into two. Our father grabbed the steering wheel just in time to prevent the car from smashing into the concrete wall, ending the encounter. I wondered whether it could have been a dream.

I'd never given much credence to the possibility of a past life. But now, from the way my "sixth sense" reacted to Wendy's presence, I wanted to believe we were soul mates.

I must have looked at my watch a hundred times before Wendy returned to the Phi Delta Theta house. When I saw the white '57 Ford turn into the driveway, I grabbed my friend Jim Burke, who had agreed to look after her, and introduced them at the foot of the steps. Later when Ann, my date, went to the ladies' room, I caught up with Wendy.

"Would you like to join me on a picnic tomorrow?" I asked. "The view from the hills above campus is awesome. Our cook will fix us a lunch basket." Similarly to when I'd invited her to the party, her smile faded and eyes dulled, which caused my blood pressure to shoot up once again. *Please, God,* I said to myself—even though I didn't believe in prayer—*let her say yes.*

"Yes," she finally answered.

I began to breathe again. "I'll pick you up at eleven thirty," I said. She gave me directions, and we rejoined our dates.

Shortly after Wendy left the party, I walked Ann to her dorm. In celebration of my reconnection with Wendy, I'd had one too many beers and intelligently decided not to attempt coordinating my Volkswagen's clutch and gears. When I returned to the fraternity, it was a challenge to climb the fire escape to the roof where Rick, Bob Parks (another Washingtonian), and I had laid out sleeping bags on mattresses. Normally I would have reached the roof through the third-floor window of another pledge brother, Doug Martin, but he had retired hours before in preparation for a cross-country meet. Bob, Rick, and I preferred the roof's quieter atmosphere, fresh air, and star-studded sky to the fraternity's sleeping porch.

Sunday, on my second pass by, I located the house. It sat well off the road in a grove of oak trees. When I pulled into the gravel driveway, Wendy came out on the porch and waved. She was accompanied by her Aunt Maud, who carried a fancy-looking camera, and Uncle Chick. Last night, Wendy had told me that her aunt was a portrait artist and her uncle a retired admiral. After I was introduced, which included her uncle sizing me up in a manner reminiscent of an admiral or general, her aunt asked us to pose for a picture. I thought that Aunt Maud, like most artists, had a perceptive eye and possibly had recognized what Wendy was yet to discover.

Wendy and me in Atherton (1958)

Wendy looked gorgeous in her plaid slacks, white shirt, button-down sweater, and sneakers with no stockings. I hadn't realized I was staring until Wendy asked, "Is everything okay?"

"Yes, sorry. My mind wandered for a moment." *If only you knew*, I thought.

I drove high into the hills above the Stanford golf course and parked on a bluff overlooking campus.

"Can you see Hoover Tower?" I asked, pointing, before we got out of the car. The tower was framed by the southern tributaries of San Francisco Bay.

"It reminds me of a Van Gogh painting," Wendy said.

We spread a blanket under a giant, crimson-leafed oak. While we ate, Wendy told me she lived in Scottsdale. She said her mother had died when she was eleven. She graduated from Bishop School in San Diego; was an art history major and a sophomore; sang in a touring trio; swam on the Mills synchronized swimming team; and was dating a Stanford student who was away for the weekend—which explained her hesitation in accepting my invitations.

"My father also died young," I said. "He committed suicide when I was a senior in high school."

"Oh no," Wendy said. "I'm sorry."

"I'm over it," I said, wondering if I ever would be. "I'm on the Stanford tennis and ski teams, and my major is philosophy, with a minor in religion. I'm a senior, but I graduate in December and leave in January for marine boot camp followed by flight school." I didn't tell her I was considering giving up my commission because I couldn't risk losing her.

"You're going to be a marine pilot?"

"I hope so," I said. "It's a three-and-a-half-year obligation. The draft is two years, but I prefer a bed to a foxhole."

Wendy smiled. She seemed interested in me but gave no indication of sensing any familiarity between us. While we talked, I tried to think of a way to express my feelings without frightening her. Finally, I just blurted out, "I believe you and I are destined to spend the rest of our lives together." She frowned and looked me in the eye, deciding how to respond.

"Is that a proposal?"

"I guess it is."

"How can you say something like that when we just met? You don't know anything about me."

"I know," I said, realizing I had just embarked on a long uphill battle.

"Please take me home," she said.

"Okay, but I won't be far away." I felt like a horse had kicked me in the stomach. I wanted to reach out and touch her, but I knew better. On the way back to Atherton, my attempt at conversation brought no response. I quit trying rather than dig a deeper hole. I thought, *She must think I'm a complete idiot.*

Monday I phoned her dorm. She refused to talk to me. I tried again on Tuesday, but her roommate said she had gone to the library. *How convenient,* I thought. Over the next few days, I got similar responses to my calls. By the end of the week, my stomach was in knots, and I couldn't study or sleep. Sunday night, while I was having dinner with Rick and his fiancée, Ann, my frustrations, along with tears, poured out. I'd told them it was love at first sight, but nothing about my perceived past-life connection.

"I suggest you become passively aggressive," Ann said. "Hang out at her dorm, but don't confront her. Let her come to you."

Monday morning I drove to Mills hoping to catch her before she went to class. Traffic was impossible crossing the Dumbarton Bridge, and she had left the dorm by the time I arrived. I made myself comfortable in the lobby, in a gigantic cushioned chair with a matching footstool, and pulled out *Plutarch's Lives*, my latest assignment. It didn't take long for Wendy's dorm mates to check me out. They detoured around me to get a look, and I heard lots of whispering. When Wendy returned for lunch, she saw me and ran upstairs, taking two at a time. The dorm's housemother kicked me out at lockup.

Tuesday, and every day for the rest of the week, I "held court" in the dorm. I helped with assignments, gave bridge lessons, and dispensed love advice; I even typed a term paper. Wendy passed me numerous times without making eye contact, as though I didn't exist. The following Monday, as Ann had predicted, Wendy came to my chair. I didn't get up.

"What can I do to make you go away?" She asked. She stood

rigid, as if wearing a corset, with arms folded across her chest.

"Go out with me, and if you don't want to see me again, I'll get out of your life." *There's no way I'm getting out of your life,* I thought.

"All right. When?"

"Are you free Friday night?"

"I can be. What time?"

"How about five thirty?"

"Fine!" she said. Her articulation of *fine* resonated in the air like my father's cigarettes' smoke rings.

"What's the dress?" she asked.

"I'll be wearing slacks and sport coat, no tie." Without another word, she turned and headed for the stairs. She didn't look back. *Not a good sign,* I thought.

Tuesday, my professors gave me curious looks. I hadn't been to class in a week. Luckily, attendance was not a factor in grades. I carried a double load and needed every credit to graduate in December.

Friday evening, Wendy was in the lobby when I arrived, so different from Stanford girls, who kept me waiting. She looked stunning dressed in her plaid skirt, white blouse, and sweater, all set off by a pearl necklace, gold charm bracelet, and high heels. She wore her ponytail wrapped into a bun.

"Where are we going?" she asked in sharp, clipped words, as if she was reluctantly fulfilling an obligation.

"To the opera. *Tannhäuser* is playing. But first we'll stop at the Hungry Eye and catch part of Barbra Streisand's show." (Streisand was a guitar-strumming teenage sensation who became a leading vocalist in the last half of the twentieth century.)

"Streisand! I hear she's great." Then she gave me a curious look. "I can't believe we're going to *Tannhäuser*. I've never been to the opera on a date." The tone of her voice had subtly changed, and the sparkle was back in her eyes.

"I love the opera," I said. "I hoped you'd like it." Actually, I hated opera. An enormous woman pretending to make love to a barrel-chested man half her size really turned me off. Worse, I couldn't understand a word.

Fortunately, we arrived at the Hungry Eye early and got a table on the sawdust-strewn floor near where Barbra sat on a barstool strumming: "Hello, my name is Barbra." I ordered a beer—I'd turned twenty-one—and Wendy a Coke.

An hour and a half later, we arrived at the San Francisco Opera House and luckily found a parking place a couple of blocks away. Once the curtain parted, Wendy's eyes remained riveted on the stage. The few times I tried to make conversation, Wendy put her forefinger to her lips and shook her head, causing a few strands of golden hair to fall over her ear. The soprano's high notes kept me awake.

As we crossed the Bay Bridge on our way back to Mills, I took a calculated risk and put my arm over her shoulder.

She turned and looked into my eyes but made no attempt to pull away, not even when I ground the gears shifting with my left hand.

"When can I see you again?" I asked.

"I'm going out with Bob on Saturday and spending Sunday with my aunt and uncle. Call me Monday evening."

"Okay!" I had to restrain myself from shouting, *Yes!*

We spoke on the phone for an hour Monday, then again on

Tuesday. Wednesday we ate at Mills's hamburger hangout and talked in the dorm's parking lot until curfew.

She let me kiss her at the door. At the touch of her lips, my legs grew rubbery. I had to brace myself against the doorjamb to keep from collapsing.

"How about a movie Friday night?" I asked, as I opened the door. I continued holding her hand.

"I can't. I'm going to Los Angeles with Bob for the Stanford–USC football game."

It took me a moment to catch my breath. "Where … where will you be stay-staying?" I said, stumbling over the words.

Picking up on my distress, she said, "At Bob's house, but don't worry, his parents will be home."

Yeah, I'll bet, I thought. *On the beach in Acapulco is more likely.*

She took my hands and pulled them to her chest. "I like you both," she said, "but I know that won't work." The word *work* hung in the air, like a balloon waiting to be popped. Then she said, "I'll decide over the weekend. Call me Monday."

I was an emotional wreck by the time I got through to her Monday morning. I came right to the point. "Have you made a decision?"

"What do you want to do this weekend?" she said.

I started crying. All the emotion that had built up over the last month came pouring out.

"Are you okay?"

"Yes," I sputtered "*Oh, God!* I wish you were in my arms."

"Me, too," she said.

"I need to tell you something."

"What?"

"I turned down my marine flight commission."

"Why?"

"The deadline to commit passed two weeks ago, and I couldn't take a chance of losing you."

The phone went silent. I wasn't going to mention my conversation with the recruiting officer, who said, "Are you crazy? You'll have your pick of the ladies as a carrier pilot."

"Oh no. What are you going to do?"

"I'll go back to Tacoma and take over the family home-heating business. Hopefully, the draft won't catch up with me now that the Korean War is over. Do you remember what I told you on our first date; about spending the rest of our lives together?"

"Yes."

"And?" I asked.

"Forever," she said. *My God!* I thought. *She's accepted my proposal.*

"I love you," I said.

"And I love you," she answered.

Wednesday night we ate at our favorite burger hangout and then shared dreams until curfew. Saturday afternoon we crossed the Golden Gate Bridge and toured the wine country as the last of the grapes were harvested. Then we went to the Sausalito waterfront and hung our legs over a pier where we could look across the bay to San Francisco and watch the sky fill with stars.

We talked about how many children we would have and what we would name them. She told me about her mother's Frenchman suitor, Pierre Van Laer, who worked with the French resistance during the Second World War, crashing his plane into the Atlantic as the *Île de France* left the shores of France (see Appendix). I told her about my near-death experience and how she had flashed before my eyes in some long-forgotten century. She didn't question me.

"We are soul mates," I said, as I held her against my chest. (It wasn't until some years later after she had read credible accounts of past-life experiences documented under hypnosis that she accepted the possibility of our sharing a past life.)

Wendy came home with me at Thanksgiving. My brother Ted met us on the tarmac at the bottom of the ramp. I had warned Wendy about Ted's inclination to agitate, but neither of us was prepared for his welcome.

"Jim, when did you start taking out girls who wear glasses?"

I don't remember Wendy's exact response, but it was close to, "Ted, I can be just as ornery as you, but I hope we can get along because you are going to be my brother-in-law."

Ted was speechless, and over the last fifty years, I can't recall a time he has not been a perfect gentleman to Wendy.

Wendy and me in Tacoma for Thanksgiving (1958)

Wendy and my mother became instant friends, as did Wendy and my stepmother, Gail, though I hadn't forgiven Gail for her chicanery in attempting to persuade me that my intellect was more conducive to banking than an entrepreneurial pursuit. Gail liked being president of the Griffin Fuel Company.

Wendy had never been in snow, so Friday we drove to Mount Rainier. The road was plowed all the way to Paradise Lodge. We got out of the car and Wendy ran for the snow. We wore street shoes.

"Be careful," I said. "It's slippery." The warning came too late. Wendy's feet went out from under her, and she landed on her butt. Seconds later, we were rolling in the snow and rubbing handfuls of it in each other's face.

We returned to our classes Monday, but we were together or talked on the phone every day. She flew home at the start of Christmas vacation; I waited for my grades to be posted so I could pick up my Bachelor of Arts degree before driving back to Tacoma to take over management of Griffin Fuel Company; I wouldn't be returning for graduation.

The day after Christmas, I flew to Phoenix to meet Wendy's family. Within minutes of arriving, her father asked if he could speak with me privately. Wendy warned me he would insist she finish college before getting married. However, Wendy and I had agreed to get married with or without his consent.

He took me to Jokake Inn, a nearby Scottsdale resort. As Wendy predicted, even before the waitress took our drink order, he said, "Wendy tells me you two want to get married."

"Yes."

"Well, she'll have to finish college first."

"Mr. Sterling, I mean no disrespect, but Wendy and I are getting married in June. If you don't want to put on the wedding, we'll elope."

He looked at me for several moments, sizing me up. Then he said, "I'll put on a wedding."

Wendy returned to Mills after the Christmas holidays. I went back to Tacoma and began working at the Griffin Fuel Company. We talked on the phone every night, and I made the fifteen-hour drive to Oakland every other weekend. We got married June 20, 1959, at St. Luke's Episcopal Church in Phoenix and began our *second* life together honeymooning in Hawaii.

Walter Sterling (Wendy's father), Wendy, me and my mother

Honeymooning in Hawaii

Wendy and me at our home on Steilacoom Lake (June 1959)

****

Ten years after Wendy and I were married, in 1969, we learned of a bizarre link between Wendy's mother's family, Paine, and my mother's family, Hewitt, that spanned the continent and a portion of two centuries. The family connection came to light when Wendy took Whitney, our four-year-old son, to the Seattle Children's Hospital for eye surgery and saw a picture of Alvah Jordan hanging on the hospital wall. Wendy knew her Uncle Jordan had been named after Alvah, so she called him when she got home.

"Uncle Jordan, why is Alvah's picture hanging in the lobby of the Seattle Children's Hospital?"

"He must have left the hospital money. He never married and died without heirs."

"Why would someone from New York leave money to a Seattle hospital?"

"Didn't you know Alvah went to Everett in the 1890s to manage a pulp mill?" Jordan asked.

"No! What was his connection to the Paine family?"

"My great uncle Alvah and my grandfather A.G. [Augustus Gibson Paine Jr.] were cousins and worked for A.G.'s father [Augustus Sr.] at the family pulp mill in Willsboro [New York]," Jordan answered. "Alvah was the son of Augustus's wife's sister."

"Why'd Alvah leave the family business?" Wendy asked.

"He wasn't a Paine and wouldn't be getting any company stock. So when Rockefeller, the owner of the Everett pulp mill, offered him a job, he came west."

"You said Rockefeller?" Wendy asked.

"Yes, John D. Rockefeller, the founder of Standard Oil Company," Jordan said. "Rockefeller's eastern syndicate put up the money to build Everett, and Augustus was one of the investors. A few years later, Alvah and the mill's chief financial officer [William Howarth, grandfather of our good friend Howie Meadowcroft] bought the mill from Rockefeller with a loan from Augustus. Did you know I worked for Alvah at the mill one summer?"

"No."

"Every morning we walked across a bridge he built from his house, over a gulley, to the mill. I also can still see the glass case containing a royal flush porker hand, dealt to him, hanging on his office wall."

When Wendy got off the phone and told me what Jordan said, I thought, *Six degrees of separation* (see Appendix). "I can't believe it!" I said.

"What?" What can't you believe?" Wendy asked.

"Henry Hewitt, my grandfather Ed Mathewson's uncle, founded Everett in the 1880s with money from Rockefeller's syndicate. Tell me about your family," I asked.

"Well, my grandfather, Gibson [Augustus Gibson Paine III], left New York for Phoenix in the mid-1930s. My father followed because he was in love with my mother."

"Why'd your grandfather leave New York?" I asked.

"Supposedly he had a respiratory ailment, but Uncle Jordan said his father was an alcoholic." I remembered Uncle Jordan telling me that the Gibson martini was named for his father because he liked his martini with a scallion rather than an olive.

Continuing, Wendy said, "When my parents married, Daddy's father never forgave him for not finishing college and going into the family business. As you know, Daddy went to work for the Arizona Public Service Company and use to brag about being the only man up a power pole in a Brooks Brothers shirt."

Brooks Brothers was a leading New York men's shop of that era.

"Yeah, and it obviously didn't take him long to become one of the top executives," I then asked, "What was the Sterling family business?"

"Something to do with Wall Street," she replied, "I think the name was Sterling Grace and Company."

"Sterling Grace and Company! That's one of the premier Wall Street firms," I said.

"Whatever! Anyway, Daddy's parents didn't come to my parents' wedding."

"And I thought I had a bizarre family," I said.

(1) Early Memories

My first memory is of my brother, Ted, falling off a pier in the summer of 1941. I was four; Ted was fifteen months older. We were staying at Grandmother Elsie's cabin at Clinton on Whidbey Island. When I heard Ted scream, I looked up in time to see him hit the water. Jack McCutchan, our stepfather, jumped in after him.

"Mommy, Mommy," I hollered. Dropping a starfish back in the tidal pool, I raced for the cabin.

"What's wrong?" Mom shouted as she ran out on the deck.

"Teddy fell off the pier."

"Oh my God!" Mom cried out, looking down the beach. She grabbed a towel from the railing and took off toward the pier. I followed, catching up just as our neighbor, Mr. Roberts, splashed into Puget Sound with his dinghy trailing from a rope behind him.

"Hurry, John!" Jack yelled. Ted thrashed at the water trying to stay afloat but making it more difficult for Jack to keep Ted's head above water. I wondered how they would get into that tiny dinghy without turning it over.

"Grab the back of the boat," Mr. Roberts shouted when he reached them. "I'll tow you." Jack put Ted's hands on the boat's transom and covered them with his hands to keep Ted from letting go.

"What happened?" Mom asked when Jack's feet touched bottom. Jack held Ted in his arms.

"Ted was fishing from that pile of lumber," Jack said, pointing to the end of the pier. "When he got up, the pile shifted, knocking him over." Jack carried my shivering brother out of the water and handed him to Mom, who immediately wrapped him in the towel.

Me at Whidbey Island (1941)   Ted and me sledding (1942)

The following winter was cold with lots of snow. Ted and I couldn't wait for Dad to come home and pull us on our sleds behind the car. As long as I could remember, we had lived with Dad on Gravelly Lake in Tacoma. I had no memory of my parents' divorce in 1940 or of our mother being sick and spending months recovering.

Also that year, I remember racing Ted at Grandma Ada's apartment overlooking Tacoma's Commencement Bay. We called her Adock.

Adock and me (1941)

"You take the elevator, and I'll run the stairs," Ted said.

"Okay, but you have to wait until the elevator starts."

"I will." *Yeah,* I thought. When the door opened, I ran in and pressed the button for floor seven. Luckily, I could see Ted through the window. He saw me watching and smiled. He would have to wait. The elevator started and Ted sprinted for the stairs. Passing each floor, I coached *Come on, come on,* as if this box of steel dangling from a cable had ears. Finally, the elevator slowed and then stopped. As the door opened, Ted streaked by. I ran after him, but not in time to wedge my foot in Adock's door before it slammed shut. The deadbolt clicked. Ted would once again get first pick from the pewter candy bowl, and grandchildren, it was the very one that holds candy for your visits to our house now.

After dinner and a game of "Go Fish"—no television in those days—Adock tucked us into bed.

"What do you want to hear tonight?" she asked. She always told us a story before turning off the lights.

"Tell us about Grandpa," I said. Grandpa Fred died before we were born.

"Your grandfather was born on a farm in Ironton, Wisconsin, after his father Abraham returned from the Civil War." Abraham served in the Wisconsin Volunteer Infantry, and fought in twelve major battles (see Appendix). "In 1888 when the railroad reached Washington Territory, your grandfather climbed on a freight train and hid in a boxcar until the train steamed into Tacoma, the end of the line."

"Why didn't he buy a ticket?" I asked.

"He didn't have enough money," Adock said.

"What did he do when he got here?"

"He worked twelve hours a day with Chinese laborers laying trolley track down Pacific Avenue for a dollar a day. When he saved enough money, he bought a horse and wagon and began hauling freight and delivering wood and ice."

Griffin Fuel Co. wood yard, Fred Griffin, my grandfather, on left (from Tacoma Public Library Archives, circa 1908)

Griffin ice wagon—to provide refrigeration prior to refrigerators—
(from Tacoma Public Library Archives) Library Description:
"Portrait of the delivery truck of the Griffin Ice Company, a branch
of the Griffin Transfer Company…The Griffin Transfer Co. was
organized by entrepreneur Fred L. Griffin. He came west in 1889 to
make his fortune and obtained first a wagon and horse. He started
out delivering fuel wood that he cut himself. After a few years of
grueling work, he had the need for more wagons and employees
and began to do general hauling and transfer. Aside from delivering
coal and wood, the company began the delivery of ice for local
consumption. The company eventually grew into the Griffin Fuel Co.,
in the forties the oldest and largest fuel dealer west of Chicago."

Then Adock said, "I thought I lost him a few years after we were married when the Teamsters Union formed."

"What happened?" I asked.

"Since your grandfather paid his men top wages, he saw no reason to join a union, so he hired shotgun riders for his wagons, like the ones that protected stage coaches. Eventually, some union enforcers caught him alone and nearly beat him to death.

When he recovered, I made him join because I didn't want to be a widow with a young son."

"Dad?"

"No, your Uncle Fred. Your dad was born five years later in 1908. Growing up on a farm, your grandfather had little time for education and after we married in 1900, I quit teaching school and became his bookkeeper."

"Where were you born?" I asked.

"Red Bank, New Brunswick, a small town in Canada. My father, Joseph Parks, was the town's blacksmith."

"Why did you come to Tacoma?"

"To homestead. We came to the Washington Territory in 1886 and settled in Hunt's Prairie a few miles south of Tacoma."

"What's a homestead?"

"Land the government gives settlers to farm."

"Where did the Parkses come from?" I asked.

"My grandfather [William Parks] came to Canada from Ireland and my grandmother [Jane Cowden] came from Scotland."

"Where did Grandpa Fred's family come from?" I asked.

"Your grandfather's grandparents, John and Mary [Chapman] Griffin, emigrated from Lincolnshire, England, in the winter of 1845–46, when your great-grandfather Abraham was thirteen years old." They landed at St. John's, Newfoundland, and then crossed the Great Lakes and bought a farm at Waukegan, Illinois, on *Pottawatomi* Indian land.

Years later, I read an article by Henry Foss, owner of the Foss Tug Boat Company, which appeared in the Tacoma *News Tribune* October 30, 1966:

    Perhaps one of the most admired and friendly characters

on the waterfront during the early period was one Mr. Griffin, the grandfather of the now famous Namu Griffin boys of today.

Mr. Griffin was a very quiet, slender gentleman, and after all these years, I can sense the dignity of his character and his affability.

He operated a wood-yard and transfer company at 15th and Dock Streets, now occupied by City buildings.

On a particular lot he accumulated the four-foot cordwood during the summer, and supplied the demands of the community with dry firewood, cutting it into stove lengths as required, and making deliveries with his various teams of horses, which I can still see pacing back and forth up the 15th Street Hill and 13th Street.

When I say pacing, that means just like a sailboat going up against the wind as the team of horses had quite a difficult time acquiring the summit from the bay to K Street, which now takes only a few minutes by automobile.

Years later, I learned from Mrs. Walter Braget, daughter-in-law of Ole Braget, who homesteaded on the Nisqually Delta, the site of our duck club, where Grandpa got his horses.

"We found out from Walt that the reason your grandfather and Walt's father were friends and business partners was because Pa raised horses and sold them to your grandfather for his business. Ole Braget was a horse lover and in his youth was a Pony Express rider along the St. Lawrence waterway," Mrs. Braget wrote.

After I finished kindergarten in June 1943, Dad drove Ted and me to Everett to visit Mom. Mom had lived with Grandma Elsie and Mr. Irving, my step-grandfather, since she and Jack McCutchan divorced. A few minutes after Dad drove off; Mom put our suitcases in the trunk of Grandma Elsie's Jeep.

My mother, Nancy (Mathewson) Griffin

My father, Ed Griffin

"Get in the car boys," she said. Grandma gave each of us a hug. My face got all wet from her tears. I wondered why Grandma was crying.

"You're sure you're going to be all right?" Grandma asked.

"I'll be fine," Mom said.

"Where're we going?" I asked.

"California!"

"Why?"

"Vacation." We didn't know Mom was running away with us. I preferred being with Mom. Dad was moody. I wasn't old enough to know he suffered from a bipolar disorder.

Mom drove south on Highway 99 to Portland and then turned west. Soon we reached 101 where the highway paralleled the coastline. As we drove through Oregon, gigantic ocean swells smashed into rock cliffs, sending water and foam a hundred feet into the air and sometimes spraying our car. At the top of every hill, she turned off the engine and let the car coast to the bottom.

"Mom, why do you keep turning off the engine?" I asked.

"I'm saving gas. It's rationed because of the war. I can't buy it without ration coupons."

"Where did you get the coupons to get all the way to California?"

"From Grandma, Mr. Irving, and my friends at the radio station," she said. Mom worked at KRKO writing advertising jingles.

Ted and I took turns stretching out in the back seat. I was asleep when we reached Redwood National Forest.

"Jimmy! Mom's driving through a tree!" Ted shouted as he shook me awake. I sat up rubbing my eyes. *What's he talking about?* All of a sudden, it went dark, like someone switched off the lights, and just as quickly, the sun beamed through the windows again.

"Mom, stop!" Ted hollered.

"Why?" she asked.

"I want to look at the tree." Mom pulled into the ranger station lot and parked. While she went into the building, Ted and I ran back to the tree, which grew on a road parallel to the highway. When we returned to the car, Mom gave each of us a postcard picture of the tree.

"The ranger said the tree is a thousand years old." *That's five hundred years before Columbus discovered America*, I thought.

It took three days to drive to Menlo Park. When we got close, Mom stopped at a country store to ask directions. The store clerk was pumping gas into a pickup by pulling and pushing a wooden handle up and down like a teeter-totter.

"You passed the house a quarter mile back. It's in the middle of that cornfield," he said, pointing.

The house sat at the end of a long dirt driveway. When we got out of the car, I noticed bricks were missing from the chimney, and the wood siding had curled up at the ends where the nails had popped out. The porch railings were coated in bird droppings, and the screen looked like somebody had walked through it. While Ted and I unpacked, we heard Mom opening and closing drawers and cupboards in the kitchen. She found a pot, two pans, some chipped dishes, tarnished silverware, and a half dozen odd-sized glasses that looked like canning jars.

"I'm hungry."

"Me too," Ted said.

"Go pick some corn," Mom answered, then added, "the Realtor said there were also artichokes and potatoes growing out back. I'll heat up the water."

"Where's the flashlight?" I asked.

"You have to pick artichokes in the dark," Mom said.

"Why?"

"Light makes them taste sour." She handed Ted the mop pail, and we went out behind the house.

When corn stocks began to rustle, I whispered, "Ted, the boogeyman is after us." Ida, a big-bosomed black lady, who took care of me in Tacoma, told me the boogeyman would get me if I wasn't good.

"It's only a cow," Ted snickered. But I didn't believe him.

When we came back in, water was boiling. While we ate, Mom made up our bed or beds—I can't remember which—with blankets and sheets from the trunk of Grandma's car.

"Mom, where are you going to sleep?" I asked.

"The couch."

It took me a long time to fall asleep because I kept wondering why we'd come to California. In the morning I asked. "Mom, when are we going home?"

"We live here now."

"Does Dad know where we are?"

"I'll talk to you later," she said. "I've got to get to the grocery store." But I knew she wouldn't. I told Ted what she said.

"I think she's hiding from Dad."

"Why?"

"I don't know, but we sure left Everett in a hurry."

In September I started first grade. We left home early because Mom drove the school bus.

"How come you're driving the bus?" I asked.

"It's a private school so parents have to pay, but if I drive the bus, you and Ted get to go free."

"Why can't we go to a regular school like we did in Tacoma?"

"You'll learn to read sooner because a private school has fewer students in a class." When she stopped to pick up some children, I didn't ask any more questions. I didn't want them to know my mother drove the bus. I found out that afternoon that she drove a military van when she wasn't driving the school bus.

Near the end of winter, after my seventh birthday, Mom heard me say, "F–– you," to Ted. She dropped her knitting and flew out of the chair.

"Don't you ever say that dirty word again!" she yelled as she dragged me to the kitchen sink. Then she washed my mouth with soap.

"What's so bad about f–––?" I sputtered, trying not to swallow the suds. I'd heard the word at school, but I didn't know what it meant. When she finally let me rinse out my mouth, I asked her again, "Why is it a dirty word?"

"You're too young to understand."

Ted didn't say anything, but I suspected he knew because he giggled when Mom turned her back. He told me later that f—-ing is how babies are made. I didn't know what he was talking about, and I was afraid to ask Mom for fear she would put more soap in my mouth.

That spring, I had my first exposure to death. Ted and I were playing outside one evening when a car raced past. The driver must not have known about the hairpin turn at the end of the cornfield, because seconds later we heard squealing tires and then grinding metal. We sprinted down the driveway and all the way to the corner. We found the car lying upside down against a telephone pole, across from the country store. The driver lay in a pool of blood next to the car.

The store owner came running across the road shouting, "Go home, boys!" He knew Ted and me. We were his best candy customers, and Mom sometimes used his telephone. I looked back before we rounded the corner. The store owner was on his knees with his fingers pressed against the driver's neck. He turned toward the people getting out of their cars and shook his head. Then he took off his apron and covered the man's face.

I'd seen lots of cowboys and Indians killed in movies, but that was make-believe. As we turned into our driveway, a siren blared. At that moment, I realized I could die and began to cry.

On a Saturday morning in May, a few weeks before school ended, Dad came to the house. Ted and I were surprised because we didn't think he knew where we lived. Grandma Elsie told me later that Dad hired a private detective to find us.

"Boys, go outside and play while your father and I talk," Mom said. Through the open window, we heard them arguing. Later, Dad took us to the San Francisco Zoo. I remember because an elephant squirted us, I suspect because we didn't have peanuts. The next morning, before going back to Tacoma, Dad came to say good-bye.

"Boys, you're going spend the summer with me and then join your mother in Everett in time to start school." I looked at Mom, and she nodded.

"Why do we have to leave?" I asked Mom, after Dad left.

"KRKO wants me to come back to work."

I liked California. It didn't rain every day, and I'd made lots of friends.

I'll never forget the day we arrived in Everett. While we unloaded the Jeep in the alley behind Grandma's house, an unshaven, gaunt, silver-headed black man came by. "Ma'am, could you spare ten cents for coffee and a donut? I haven't eaten in two days."

"I'm sorry. I spent all my money driving up from California." Then she said, "Hold on," and she unzipped a secret compartment in her purse and took out a silver dollar. "I keep it for emergencies—probably the reason that I stash currency. Here, you take it." She put the dollar in his hand.

"God bless you," he said. Then he turned and walked quickly out of the alley.

"Why did you give that man your last dollar?" I asked.

"He needs it more than we do." That was the day I learned about compassion and giving.

Ted and I slept in rollaway beds until Mom found a house.

One night when Grandma was tucking us into bed, I asked, "What happened to Grandpa Ted?"

"Your grandfather died thirty-three years ago, in 1911, when the Snohomish County Commissioners were touring Mount Rainier. The tires bounced out of a snow rut, and the chauffer lost control of the car, which landed on top of your grandfather."

"Where did you meet Mr. Irving?"

"Mr. Irving and your grandfather were logging and sawmill partners. They owned three or four sawmills together."

That fall, when I began second grade, I discovered I had a conscience. Ted and I had taken the bus to town to see a movie. After the cowboy double feature, we went to Kress's ten-cent store to buy candy. As we were leaving, I saw a twin-barreled pirate pistol with cocking hammers that exploded caps. The pistol cost seventy-five cents, and we only had enough money left for bus fare. I looked to see if anyone was watching. Then I put the gun into my waistband under my coat, and we walked out. On the bus ride home, I began to feel guilty. When we got to Ninth and Colby, our stop, I knew I couldn't get off.

"Ted, I'm going back to Kress's and return the gun. I'll never get to sleep tonight if I don't."

"How are you going to get home?"

"I'll walk. Tell Mom not to worry; I know the way."

When I got to Kress's, I made certain nobody was watching, and then I put the pistol on the shelf. As soon as I got out the door, I ran. I turned around every few seconds to see if anyone followed. It started to rain, and a few minutes later the sun dropped below the horizon. When it got dark, I began looking for boogeymen in the shadows. Suddenly, headlights blinded me. The car stopped, and Mom jumped out.

"Jimmy, I'm so proud of you," she said, as she wrapped me in a blanket.

Before bed, Mom usually told Ted and me a ghost story, but sometimes she talked about ancestors. I'll always remember her account of our family's Irish connection. She wrote a newspaper article about it in the ninth grade when she attended the Marlborough School in Beverly Hills, California. Mom told me Grandma took her five children, Edward, Mark, Mom, Nene, and Harriett, to California after Grandpa died because Everett did not provide an atmosphere suitable for young children. I later read that Everett in the 1920s was a wide-open, raucous town, with more taverns than churches.

"So long ago that I can't name her, my fourth-great-grandmother lived in Ireland. Her father was a wealthy lord. She grew up from childhood happily surrounded by all the pleasures that her heart could wish for. Soon came the time for her marriage. Her heart was set. None did she love but her sweetheart in America, a brave and strong man. He had left her with a promise to come back to her and to marry her. Her father's mind was not as hers. His choice was different by far. A young man, a minister, was to be hers. She would not have it. No one could make her marry another than her sweetheart in America. Her father, in anger, shut her up in a high tower in a little room until the minister should come to marry her. She in agony tore fine sheets of linen to shreds and made a rope, with which she lowered herself from the tower window. She could not delay. When on the ground she hastily ran to the landing and onto the ship that was to carry her to America. The wind blew the boat well, and soon the ship was landing its passengers in America. She made her way to find her sweetheart. No lover could she find, for he had died unknown to her. She sought many places and at last in despair decided to accompany a band of immigrants who were slowly pushing their way westward ..."

Before Grandma died, I remember overhearing her and Mom talking about an inquiry from Ireland as to a large inheritance coming from an estate with no direct heirs. Grandmother spent considerable money trying to prove a family connection through her grandmother Sarah Start, but was unsuccessful. Sarah Start's great-grandmother is thought to be the young girl in mother's story. Until the day she died, Grandma never gave up trying to prove her lineage.

Mom also told us about being confronted by a cougar before moving to Beverly Hills. The following is to the best of my recollection.

"One morning, as I was on my way to collect eggs in the henhouse, a cougar limped out of the forest twenty feet in front of me."

"How old were you?" I asked.

"Twelve or thirteen. I knew not to run, because it would chase me down, like a cat after a mouse. I picked up a tree limb and ran straight at it screaming as loud as I could. The cougar turned and slinked back into the woods." It took me a long time to get to sleep that night. I kept thinking about not being born if the cougar had eaten Mom.

Grandchildren, courage is being afraid and doing it anyway. My mother was terrified of the cougar, but she saved her life by assessing the situation, deciding on a course of action, and acting decisively.

In 1945, my sibling rivalry with Ted turned serious. One evening, we fought over a dice game we had learned from a soldier. (During the war, Mom volunteered as a military driver for officers stationed at Pier 91 and sometimes invited them to dinner.) When Mom tried to break up the fight, she hurt her back, and the doctor came to the house. Before school two days later, Dad came before school and took Ted to Tacoma. Though we quarreled constantly, Ted had always looked out for me at recess. And now I didn't have anyone to play games with in the evening because Mom worked nights on advertising jingles for the radio station or writing her novel.

The following year, I got a lesson in accepting responsibility.

"I'll get it!" I yelled, as I watched the ball fly into Mr. Smith's garden. When I ran into the flowers, Mr. Smith came rushing out of the house.

"Get out of my garden," he shouted.

We didn't have another ball, so the game ended. My friend Hartley, grandson of Governor Roland Hartley (1924-1932), and I made a pact to go back that night and get it. After dinner, I snuck out of the house, and Hartley and I tramped through the garden until we found the ball. It lay next to a mushy pile of dog poop. We looked at each other and smiled, thinking the same thing. We scooped up the poop with leaves and sticks and shoved it through Mr. Smith's front-door mail slot. Unfortunately, we admired our work a little too long, and Mr. Smith was out the door after us.

"I know who you are!" he yelled, as we scampered away.

When I got home, Mom was talking to Mr. Smith on the phone. Hartley and I had to go back and apologize and clean up the mess. Worse, my allowance was docked for a month.

Christmas Day 1946, Mom married Bill Spaeth. It was her third marriage. Bill stood six feet, with a wiry, muscular build and curly, sandy-brown hair parted in the middle. If he came home before dark, we played catch. He'd played baseball for the University of Wisconsin. Bill owned a cabin on Whidbey Island where we spent weekends digging clams, netting crabs, and fishing.

In June, after finishing the fourth grade, I flew to Kansas to visit Dad and Sarah (Ferris) Cowles, the woman Dad had married the previous year. Dad was in treatment at the Menninger Foundation. Mom, Grandma Elsie, and Grandma's Christian Science practitioner (a person who heals as Jesus healed) saw me off from Boeing Field in a converted B-29. The practitioner prayed over me while the other passengers boarded. When I got on the plane, every eye followed me to my seat. I couldn't have been more embarrassed.

We lived in Karl Menninger's summer house on the Kansas River, where Ted and I caught gigantic catfish on lines we left out overnight, swam in the river with water moccasin snakes, and skinny-dipped with the sons and daughters of neighboring farmers.

Dad (Ed Griffin), Ted, and me in Topeka, Kansas. (summer 1947)

I returned to Everett before the start of fifth grade. In October, Bill left his position as log manager at the Weyerhaeuser mill and took a job as sawmill foreman in Sutherlin, Oregon.

Sutherlin is where I met the man I call Green Eyes, a disgruntled mill worker; more than a half century later, I'm still haunted by his angry green eyes looking at me through the window.

Thanksgiving weekend, one month after my sister, Nancy, was born, we left for Oregon. We traveled in Bill's gray Buick with a hood ornament that looked like a prehistoric bird. Crumpet, our floppy-eared cocker spaniel, and I rode in back squashed against Nancy's cradle, stuffed with everything that wouldn't fit in the trunk.

Ten hours later, Bill reached back and shook me. "Jimmy, look, you can see the mill's burner." Thousands of golden-orange sparks shot out from what looked like a giant tepee and lit up the night like an erupting volcano. Minutes later we entered Sutherlin.

Sutherlin looked like a ghost town. Soot from the mill's burner had turned all the buildings gray. We passed a gas station with an auto repair shop, a café, a bank, a tavern with a flashing neon Blitz Weinhard Beer sign, and a country store that Bill said sold food and everything offered in a Sears catalog. Houses were interspersed between the businesses. On the side streets, I saw two churches, one with a steeple the other with a giant cross on the roof, and a single-story school house. The mill, Rock Island Lumber Company, sat at the end of town on Highway 99.

Our house and the manager's house were across the street from the mill, next to the woods and away from the ear-piercing racket of a saw knifing through logs. These company houses were separated by a row of leafless oak trees and a lawn strewn with shriveled dandelions. At one time, the houses had been painted green with white trim, but like all the other buildings, they were now gray.

The house was no bigger than a double-wide trailer. The living and dining area faced the mill. Two bedrooms in back looked out at the forest and mountain foothills. A bathroom and a closet separated the bedrooms that opened onto a hall, which connected the kitchen and front room. In Everett, I'd had my own bedroom and bath. Here I had to share a bedroom with my baby sister and a bathroom with my parents.

The house came furnished, but Mom said the furniture looked like leftovers from a garage sale. A yellow, threadbare davenport, with matching cushioned chairs, backed against the front window facing the manager's house. Across the room sat a cedar-plank table and six chairs with missing or broken spindles.

We spent Sunday unpacking, and I mowed the lawn with a push mower I found in the carport storage locker. Monday morning, Mom walked me to school. After registering, I went to the fifth-grade classroom, which shared the room and teacher with the sixth grade.

When I opened the door, everyone stared at me. I hadn't reached five feet or lost my baby fat, and my friends told me I looked like a monk because Mom trimmed my thick, straight black hair under a bowl. However, my features didn't draw their attention; it was my clothes. I wore corduroy pants, a long-sleeved shirt and sweater Mom had knit, and penny loafers. The boys, mostly sons of loggers and mill workers, wore Levi's or overalls, green denim shirts, and high-top, lace-up leather boots. A few days later, my clothes looked like theirs.

Mother and me, holding my sister, Nancy (December 1947)

I first saw Green Eyes—I never knew his name—during Christmas vacation. Bill had given me a job hauling scrap wood to the burner. Green Eyes wore mud-caked overalls with straps that fastened over his shoulders, a faded green denim shirt, and an old bill cap, whose company's insignia was no longer recognizable. His skin looked ink black, and his stubble face appeared to have been chiseled from granite. With gloveless, massive, callused hands that looked like they could crush rock, he pulled eight-inch posts off a conveyor like they were broomsticks.

All work at the mill stopped when the noon whistle blew, and I went home. Mom only let me work half a day. The mill crew, other than Green Eyes, went to a heated enclosure to eat. Green Eyes, who never appeared to have brought a lunch, sat with his back against the burner.

When school started in January, Green Eyes quickly faded from my memory until a Friday night near the end of winter, when my parents and the mill manager and his wife went to Roseburg for dinner, leaving me to care for my baby sister. As soon as they left, I picked up *Gulliver's Travels*, checked on Nancy asleep in her cradle, and joined Crumpet on the davenport. I hadn't read more than a few pages when I heard the hinge squeak on the front screen door. I looked up, wondering why my parents had returned.

It wasn't my parents. It was Green Eyes. His piercing eyes darted back and forth between me and Nancy's cradle, sending shivers cascading down my spine. He pushed his shoulder against the door and turned the handle, but the deadbolt held. Then he spun around and leapt off the porch. I watched through the living-room window as he ran to the corner of the house. I knew he was going to the back door, and I had forgotten to lock it when my parents left. I jumped up and grabbed the baby. I had to get out the front door into the woods before he got in the house.

Nancy started crying when I jerked her out of the cradle. There was no chance to hide now, I thought. *What, what am I going to do?* Then I remembered the shotgun. Bill let me shoot it when we went quail hunting. I dropped Nancy back into the cradle and raced to the closet. In my panic, I knocked the cartridge box off the shelf. It shattered on the floor, and cartridges flew in every direction. I fell to my knees, grabbed a shell and jammed it into the gun's chamber.

A breeze from the hallway brought the pungent odor of sulfur from the mill. *Oh, God!* I thought. *He's in the kitchen!* Crumpet started barking when Green Eyes stepped out of the kitchen into the hall. I slammed the gun bolt closed, disengaged the safety, and raised the widely swinging 20-gauge to my shoulder. Green Eyes heard the safety click and stopped two paces away. Then he began to back up. I got to my feet and followed, staying well out of his reach. He crossed the kitchen, bumped against the screen door, flung it open, and jumped off the porch. I watched him crash through the fir branches into the woods.

I slammed the door behind him, but still shaking, I couldn't turn the bolt. I put the gun down and used both hands. Then I returned to the front room. Nancy had stopped crying. When I looked into the cradle, she smiled, and my mind raced with thoughts about what Green Eyes would have done to us.

I turned off the lights so he wouldn't be able to see into the house if he came back. Clutching the shotgun, I sat with my back against the wall in a spindle-back chair. The mill's burner lit up the night like a full moon, giving me good visibility of the front and side yards. It seemed like hours before I saw the Buick's headlights.

"Jimmy, what's wrong?" Mom screamed, as she came into the house and saw me holding the shotgun.

"A black man," and then the tears came flooding out.

"You're safe now," Bill said, as he raced after Mom to the cradle.

"The black man from the mill tried to get me," I blabbered. "I forgot to lock the back door." Then I completely broke down. When I regained my composure, I sniffled, "I got the gun loaded and pointed at him before he could grab me."

"You did some quick thinking," Bill said, as he gently pulled the gun from my arms. "I fired him yesterday when I caught him drinking whisky during his break. I never imagined he would try to hurt you and Nancy." Then Bill called the sheriff. As they talked, I watched tears run down Mom's cheeks and land on Nancy's head.

A few days later, the sheriff stopped by to tell us an arrest warrant was out for Green Eyes, but he had disappeared.

Not in my dreams has he disappeared, and then I thought, *What would have happened to Nancy and me if Green Eyes had come to the back door?*

In the spring, I won Oregon's safety slogan contest with "Make Caution a Working Word." I became an instant celebrity. A few months later, my slogan hung in every industrial business in the state. I received a congratulatory letter from the governor, a plaque, and a $100 bond.

In July, the mill shut down and we returned to Everett. We lived with Grandma Elsie and Mr. Irving until Mom and Bill bought a house. Most mornings, when we lived at Grandma's, I accompanied Mr. Irving to the Monte Cristo Hotel barbershop for his daily shave—Mr. Irving had owned the Monte Cristo in the early 1900s. Grandma insisted I go with him because he crossed the street in the middle of the block, holding up his hands, like a policeman, to stop cars.

In his late seventies, Mr. Irving was still a giant, with the enormous broad-knuckled hands of a fighter. His white hair had thinned, and his belly hung over unbuttoned, green lumberman's pants held up with brown suspenders, but his eyes missed nothing. *Mill Town*, by Norman H. Clark, University of Washington Press, 1970, described Mr. Irving as "a huge, powerful, roaming terror of a man who could drive four hundred loggers to unprecedented performances." I couldn't believe my grandfather had been a "roaming terror of a man."

Mr. Irving loved telling stories, and the Everett old-timers filled the barber shop every morning to listen. I will never forget his story about an 1890s John L. Sullivan world championship boxing match. According to Mr. Irving, half the male population of Everett was in the Monte Cristo bar. Unbeknownst to his friends, Mr. Irving arranged for a telephone connection to ringside, giving him information ahead of the telegraph recaps (the telephone had been invented in 1876 but remained a rarity). Having his friends find out that he had outsmarted them was far more important to him than winning their money.

Another favorite, a shootout that became known as the Everett Massacre, took place in 1916. A boatload of Wobblies (members of an international labor union) steamed up from Seattle on the *Verona* intending to unionize Everett's mills. To make certain he had everyone's attention, Mr. Irving pulled up his pants leg and showed the scar where he'd been shot. Then he recounted how he'd accompanied Sheriff McRae out on the pier to stop the *Verona* from tying up.

"The sheriff pulled out two pistols and yelled, 'You can't land here!' A voice from the ship hollered back, 'The hell we can't.' Then according to Mr. Irving, three shots were fired from the *Verona*. "McRae and I were hit. When we fell, one hundred guns from the pier opened fire. Before the *Verona* could back out of the harbor, fifty-two were dead or wounded." (Mom, high in a tree on the hillside above the harbor, along with hundreds of onlookers, witnessed the gunfight. She also remembered her Uncle Tom Headlee, the ex-mayor of Everett, running to the house to get his gun.)

Before moving to Sutherlin, I happened to be in Mr. Irving's den admiring a Persian dagger (which I inherited, leading to my antique dagger collection) when he suggested I pick mistletoe in Oregon—mistletoe didn't grow in Everett—and sell it in front of the bank when we came home for Christmas vacation. I did and I significantly expanded my coin collection with the proceeds. Mr. Irving also paid my cousin, Graham Fitch (Nene Mathewson Fitch's son), and me one cent for every weed we pulled. Before paying he dumped out our sacks and meticulously counted each root ball to make certain we hadn't increased the amount by splitting weeds, a lesson that served me well when I got into business.

On another occasion, I asked Mr. Irving, "Why are there so many empty beer bottles in the alleys?" I'd seen the bottles when I took a shortcut home after picking up Grandma's groceries, when she called in an order.

"That's where the drunks and derelicts hang out," he said. "Why don't you pick up the bottles and return them for their one-cent deposit? You can rent my wheelbarrow."

"Why can't I borrow it?"

"Shouldn't I get something for coming up with the idea?" he asked.

"Yeah, I guess so." I returned three hundred bottles and made $2.50—the equivalent of five weeks' allowance—after paying Mr. Irving his rental fee. Two years later, I owned a wheelbarrow and sold mistletoe, Christmas trees, and wreaths door to door. I used that money along with what I made from my paper route to buy twenty-five feet of waterfront property adjoining Bill's cabin on Whidbey Island. (The profit from the sale of the property helped put me through Stanford University.)

Grandma Elsie always looked nice. She usually wore a white blouse with a gray or dark blue suit. The coat reached her knees, and the skirt hung to her ankles. When she took the pins out of her bun, gray hair dropped to her waist.

My grandmother, Elsie (Headlee) Mathewson

My grandfather, Edward Mathewson

One day while visiting Grandma, she asked, "Jimmy, what do you want to do when you grow up?" I don't remember my answer, but I'll never forget what she said.

"You can do or be whatever you want, even president of the United States." Then she said something about setting goals to achieve dreams. "Jimmy, you have big shoes to fill. Your grandfather's uncle, Henry Hewitt"—Henry Hewitt's sister was Grandfather Ted's mother—"founded Everett when Washington was still a territory. He persuaded your grandfather to leave the University of Notre Dame and come west to make his fortune in the timber business. And my brother, Tom Headlee, was elected mayor of Everett at the turn of the century, the same time my Uncle Tom Humes was mayor of Seattle."

"Grandma, where were you born?"

"Iowa. My family came west with a wagon train when I was a teenager. My dad, Ephriam Headlee, homesteaded near the town of Snohomish. A few years later, I moved to Everett to teach school."

"How did you and Grandpa Ted meet?"

"We lived in the same boardinghouse."

"What's a boardinghouse?"

"It's a home with lots of bedrooms that rent by the month and occupants are provided three meals a day, family style, around a big table."

"What about your ancestors, where did they come from?"

"The Humeses, my mother's family, came from Scotland before the Revolutionary War. My great-great-grandfather, John Humes, was a soldier in George Washington's Continental Army." (The family name was originally spelled Hume, but according to a family story a member of the Hume family thought the eighteenth-century philosopher David Hume was blasphemous and changed the name to Humes.)

"I know about the Revolutionary War. We studied it in school."

"The Headlees, my father's family, came to America from England in the mid-1600s. My great-grandfather, John Headlee, also fought in the Revolutionary War. Headlees have been traced back to the 'Baron of Headlee' in the thirteenth century. Did I ever tell you about the 'Richard Headlee Tradition'?"

"No!"

"My ancestor Richard Headlee, a sailor on a British man-of-war, one night off the coast of New Jersey jumped overboard and swam to shore where he married and started a family. British authorities eventually discovered where he lived and sent soldiers to arrest him. However, some years later, sailing at night off the same New Jersey coastline, Richard jumped overboard again and reunited with his family." (Years later I read Grandma's account of Richard Headlee in the "Richard Headlee Tradition," by Richard Bates, published 1888, *History of Greene County Pennsylvania*.)

"Wow!" I said, wondering if I had inherited Richard's gene.

In 1949, after finishing the sixth grade, I moved to Tacoma to live with Dad and Sarah. I loved my mother and grandparents, but I had no close friends in Everett after attending five schools in six years. I had lots of friends in Tacoma where I spent summers.

Also Bill had become an alcoholic, and he and Mom constantly fought. Ted and I were under the same roof again, but we had no more problems. I'd taken boxing lessons and no longer felt threatened because he knew I'd won the Everett championship in my age and weight divisions.

I've never lost thought of the positive influence my grandparents had on me. Mr. Irving introduced me to the world of finance, and Grandma Elsie gave me the confidence to live my dreams. It is my hope, grandchildren, that some of what rubbed off my grandparents onto me will likewise rub off Nana and me onto you.

(2) Coming of Age

"Griffin, what's it like living in a mansion on the lake?" Larry asked during recess, in the fall of 1949.

Gravelly Lake home

If Larry hadn't embarrassed me in front of my new friends, I would have shrugged it off; but I couldn't. I doubled up my fist and hit him in the face. I wasn't big or strong enough to knock him over; but I did give him a bloody nose. At twelve, I was barely five feet tall; Larry was fifteen and bigger and stronger.

He was still in the seventh grade because he had fallen behind, touring with the Ice Follies.

We traded punches until Mr. Gray, the Clover Park Junior High School principal, pulled us apart.

"Since you two want to fight," he said, "you can do it properly with a referee tomorrow at recess."

The next morning when I got off the school bus, janitors were erecting a boxing ring. On the way to class, I caught glimpses of students whispering to their friends. I knew what they were saying: I was the new kid, who was going to get a drubbing. I'd boxed regularly the past three years, so I wasn't afraid, but I had the usual prefight butterflies.

"Stay away from him," Gary said, as he laced up my gloves. "He can't hurt you if he can't hit you." Gary Milgard was my best friend. We met on the school bus the first day of seventh grade.

Larry and I boxed three one-minute rounds. The athletic director called the match a draw. I didn't win the fight, but I won Larry's friendship and the respect of my classmates, who began including me in their social activities.

The winter of 1950 was the coldest on record. The temperature remained in single digits for days on end. Swamps and ponds froze along with Steilacoom Lake, which a century before formed when Chambers Creek was damned to power both a saw and grist mill. I woke up one morning in mid-January to nearly two feet of snow.

After school and weekends we played hockey. When snow covered the ice, we took hockey indoors, playing on the basement lanoline floor of our next-door neighbor, Booth Gardner, who later became a two term Washington State Governor.

I turned thirteen in March 1950 and by summer I entered puberty. Hair had started growing on my arms and legs, and my voice was cracking. Once school started in the fall, I became infatuated with Maura and joined the eighth-grade debate team to spend more time with her. When we passed papers, our hands touched and I fantasized kissing her. My opportunity came a few weeks later at Dianne Jordan's party.

"Do it now," Gary whispered. Dianne's father had just announced that the hamburgers were ready. "Nobody will notice you leaving." Gary had been kissing Georgia since the beginning of summer, and he told me what to do.

"Okay, okay!" I said. After a quick reconnaissance, I saw Maura across the lawn listening intently to Georgia. As I ambled over, I thought, *I hope she is getting the same advice Gary gave me.* It had cooled down after the sun set, but I felt perspiration under my arms, and I had to dry my forehead with my shirt sleeve. Maura and Georgia didn't see me approach.

"Hi."

"Oh, hi," they answered.

"Maura, would you like to take a walk?" My shoulder gently brushed her and, as if on command, Maura's arms, which were folded across her chest, dropped, and our hands touched.

"Sure," she said, as her fingers intertwined into my fingers.

I thought, *This is turning out better than I could have hoped.* Off we went. Neither of us looked back, but I would have bet everyone was watching. On the other side of the house, I turned and faced Maura. We were silhouetted in the moon's reflection off Steilacoom Lake.

"May I kiss you?" Gary had said don't ask, just do it because she might say no.

Before she could answer, I leaned forward. Our lips barely touched, but it was enough to make me feel like a Roman candle was shooting through my veins. Gary hadn't told me about that part. Maura must have experienced a similar sensation because I felt her tremble.

We stepped apart and looked into each other's eyes. She blushed, which caused me to believe it was also her first kiss. Neither of us spoke. I couldn't think of a thing to say and she must have felt the same. Maura took my hand and we started back to the party. Before we rounded the house, she pulled away and ran ahead of me. *How ridiculous*, I thought. *Everyone knows what we were doing. Georgia and Gary would have seen to that.* After Maura joined her friends, Gary came rushing over.

"Did you do it?"

"Yes," I said pumping my fist.

"Good man," he said. Then he slapped me on the back so hard that every head turned. If our kiss had been a secret, it wasn't any longer. I even got an acknowledgment from Larry, who saluted me from across the lawn.

That fall, I learned about the absurdity of war and how fortunate I was to be born an American.

"You did what?" I exclaimed. Fred, our gardener, and I were raking leaves from the lakeside lawn.

"The Americans and Germans declared a truce every evening at sunset. We came out of our trenches and played cards, dice, and drank schnapps together in no-man's-land"—the ground between the opposing trenches.—"At sunrise, we were back in our trench waiting for a German head to pop up so we could blow it off."

Fred was small, possibly five-foot-eight, and couldn't have weighed 130 pounds. When he returned from France at the end of World War I, he killed a man in a bar fight. He said the man was abusing a young woman; however, he wasn't able to convince the jury. When he got out of prison, the only work he could find was gardening. Fred taught me what seasons to plant and dig up bulbs, when and how to trim shrubs, where to find night crawlers, and which lily pads concealed the smallmouth bass.

Also working for my father was a Ukrainian couple, Peter and Jenny. One night when Dad and Sarah went out for dinner, Ted and I ate in the kitchen with Peter and Jenny, and I asked what happened to them during the war (World War II).

"Germany occupied our country and forced me to make war materials in my manufacturing plant."

"How did you get to the US?"

"Jenny and I left the night Russian tanks came. We didn't want to lose our freedom a second time." I knew from history class that Russia invaded German occupied territory from the east and the Allies (Americans, French, and English) from the west.

"You just walked away?"

"No! The Russians had set up roadblocks at both ends of our village. We had to swim across a river. We hid in the woods during the day and traveled by night. A few days later we reached the American lines. After spending six months in a refugee camp, we were allowed to immigrate to the United States."

Also in 1950, Sarah gave birth to my half sister Elizabeth "Beth" (see Appendix), and Mother gave birth to my half brother, Charlie, her second child with Bill Spaeth.

My mother, Bill Spaeth (holding my half brother Charlie), me, my half sister Nancy, and Ted at Whidbey Island cabin

In the spring, I won the Tacoma City Championship 22-caliber rifle, prone, kneeling, sitting and offhand, championship. We learned to shoot at a range in the Clover Park High School basement.

That summer, in 1951, when I was thirteen, Dad told me I had to have a job.

"If you don't want to work in the yard, you might check with Ernie at the 76 station." Dad bought his gas at the 76 station, now the site of Midas Muffler, across from Lakewood Center.

I couldn't believe it when I got hired. I found out later that Dad paid my wages to give me a work experience. I pumped gas, cleaned windshields, fixed flat tires, changed oil, and learned to drive by moving cars in and out of the garage. When my friends biked over to watch, Ernie chased them off.

That fall, I followed Ted to Vermont Academy, "VA," an all-boys college preparatory school in Saxton's River, Vermont, where our friend, Dick Shanaman, and his older brother, Fred, attended. Booth Gardner also joined us. The school had an excellent college acceptance record—though at thirteen, I could not have cared less. I was eager to go because VA had a ski team. I'd learned to ski using my mother's edgeless wooden skis on the hills at the Everett golf course.

Before leaving for school, Dad took me to the bank to open a checking account.

"I'm depositing $900," he said. "It's enough to pay your first semester's tuition, room and board, books, and laundry. You can use the money from your summer job for your personal needs." Writing checks to pay school expenses probably caused me to work harder than I might have. It certainly taught me how to budget.

Adock took us to the train station—I don't remember where Dad was. On the way she asked, "Boys, do you know where babies come from?" Before either of us could respond, she added, "You know they don't come from storks." Ted and I looked at each other and snickered.

"Well, you've answered my question. I won't be concerned any longer," she said.

On the train, which took three days and two transfers, and many times over the years, Ted and I had a good laugh remembering Adock's naiveté. The Victorian atmosphere in which our parents were raised obviously made them uncomfortable explaining human reproduction, because neither my mother nor father ever brought up the subject.

My roommate, John Jepson, and I became immediate friends and skied on the junior-varsity team together. Neither John nor I had been on cross-country or jumper skis, but we quickly learned from our coach, an Olympic Games competitor. We trained for cross-country on pine needles in the forest, before the snow fell. My first jump off a thirty meter-hill was terrifying. After carrying my jumpers to the top of the ramp, more than one hundred steps, I looked down the steep incline over the fifteen-foot platform and down the landing hill to the end of the run out, an eighth of a mile away, and nearly puked. However, after making that first jump—the coach had to push me as I was frozen in place—I quickly became an apt pupil. The euphoria of soaring, with arms spread like the wings of an eagle, produced a "high" I'd never experienced. John's home in Hartford, Connecticut, became my home away from home, and sixty years later, we continue to stay in touch.

Me jumping off Vermont Academy's thirty-meter hill

Me and Ted

When my classmates hounded me for stories about the west, I had no problem convincing them that westerners still rode horses to school, and occasionally marauding Indians scalped somebody. I couldn't believe the gullibility of thirteen-year-old eastern preppies.

Booth was a sophomore, but for some reason he lived in Sturtevant House, a seven-bedroom, one-hundred-year-old farm house, with the freshmen. The first floor was occupied by Mr. Lucy, a teacher, and his wife and one-year-old son, John, John. Booth often amused himself by pulling out the wooden arm rests from his spindle back chair and playing taps on the radiator. The vibration, which travelled to every radiator in the house, infuriated Mr. Lucy, who spent hours clandestinely trying to apprehend the culprit that kept John, John from sleeping. When Booth heard the stairs squeak, he reinserted the arm rests and picked up a book. I was his only confidant and he was never caught. I drank my first beer with Booth. He bought it from day students—we called them townies—and kept it stashed in a creek that ran through campus.

My sophomore year, another childhood friend, Buzz Cain, the son of Washington's US senator Harry Cain, joined us at VA. Buzz and I lived in adjacent rooms on the second floor of a three-story dorm. Somehow Buzz always knew when a package of my mother's chocolate chip cookies arrived. Hiding them was not a deterrent. A teacher-proctor lived in an apartment on each floor. Lights went out at 9:30, and we were awakened at 7:00 a.m. Ties and coats were mandatory for class and meals—students took turns waiting tables and washing dishes—in the dining room, which also served as a theater and place to dance during exchanges.

The food was awful, and the menu rarely changed. Monday we ate stew; Tuesday creamed chipped beef; Wednesday fried chicken, which we called hairy canary because it was seldom completely plucked; Thursday mystery meat, which was unidentifiable; and Friday fish, which we called guppy. Saturday was surprise night, and Sunday featured creamed eggs. Each day I attended five classes, limited to twelve students, not including chapel and two mandatory study halls. Everyone participated in sports.

One incident I'll never forget happened in the spring of my sophomore year. The biggest kid in school, Dave Francisco, who competed in track with my brother, continually tried to pick a fight with Ted. I presume, because Ted not only held the school pole vault record, but was challenging Francisco in field events; javelin, shot-put, and disc. If Ted and I happened to be together, Dave would purposely bump into me, usually knocking me to the ground, trying to get Ted riled. The first time it happened Ted said, "He's not going to hurt you, he's not a bully, he just wants to fight me."

Then one evening after dinner, we were in the basement of Alumni Hall playing pool—there was no TV and radios were forbidden in student rooms, though Ted had built one into his reading lamp. Just as Ted lined up a shot, Francisco happened to come down to the basement. When he saw us at the pool table he came over and picked up the end of the slate pool table, which weighed hundreds of pounds, sufficiently to send the balls rolling. Ted put down is cue and said, just loud enough for me to hear, "Let's get out of here."

As we approached the stairway landing, Francisco came running after us, shouting, "Not this time, Griffin."

"Jim, move over and stay out of my way." Ted said. Ted waited until Francisco reached the landing and then quickly turned and grabbed Francisco around the waist, before Francisco could react, threw him over his shoulder, like a bale of hay, and heaved him to the ground. Francisco never bothered me again. Fifteen years later I read in the Vermont Academy alumni quarterly that Dave Francisco had died in the Vietnam war.

I returned to Clover Park my junior year. I missed my friends and the company of girls. Dad didn't object because he and his new wife, Judy Frasier Bridges (Dad and Sarah had divorced the previous summer), were recovering from an automobile accident and needed assistance at home.

I still get emotional remembering Sarah asking me if I wanted to go with her when she divorced my father. Sarah shared my unhappiness and fear living with an alcoholic who suffered from manic depression.

"Jimmy, come with me to Spokane. I'll adopt you and provide for your education," she said as she held me in her arms—something only my Grandmother Elsie had ever done—on the back stairs landing, which was enclosed, giving us complete privacy.

"I can't," I said. "I can't leave Dad. He needs me." I felt guilty saying it, but I couldn't think of anything else. If I went to Spokane, I'd be, like a fish out of water, in a new environment with no friends.

I missed Sarah and my sister Beth, with whom, more than a half century later, I continue to share a spiritual connection. (Sarah's father, Joel Ferris, president of Seattle-First National Bank, Spokane, now Bank of America, gave me *Gods, Graves & Scholars*, by C.W. Ceram—who visualized archeology as a wonderful combination of high adventure, romance, history, and scholarship—as a Christmas present. After reading the book, at age thirteen, I began searching for Indian arrowheads, which lead to collecting ancient artifacts from around the world.)

That summer, 1952, after finishing the ninth grade, Ted and I worked at the Griffin Fuel Company. I assisted truck mechanics, and Ted helped load and deliver coal. I remember complaining to Adock about having to work when many of my friends hung out at the country club. Adock was totally unsympathetic.

"Your grandfather worked twelve hours a day, six days a week," she said. "One day you'll realize the favor your father is doing for you." As a fifteen-year-old, I didn't think he was doing me a favor.

Griffin Fuel Co., circa 1930s, building on left in background now University of Washington library and building on right now the university administration building (From Tacoma Library archives)

Within minutes of getting home from work, our friends showed up, hoping to go water skiing. We had a twelve-foot hydroplane powered with a twenty-five-horsepower Johnson motor. The hydroplane turned over easily, and at the junior class summer party, Joe Ghilarducci flipped while towing Mr. Gray, Clover Park's principal.

When school started in the fall, 1953, Ted returned to VA for his senior year and I went back to Clover Park. Within days, I was one of the gang again. Other than a few new faces, nothing had changed except I was now the same height or taller than the girls.

Swimming season started in January. Clover Park didn't have a swimming pool, so we were bused to the Fort Lewis pool. The army went out of its way to be a good neighbor. The pool's restroom had a condom machine. Ten cents bought any make or style. A ring formed from the indentation of a condom in a leather wallet was a badge of honor. The looks we got from the teenage carhop waitresses when we pulled out our wallets at Bush's Drive-In were priceless.

In the spring, I fell in love with Pat. She was a senior, class president, and cheerleader. When her parents went out for the evening, I rode my bicycle to her house. My driver's license had been suspended for six months. I'd been stopped by a state patrolman for passing a friend off the road in the gravel. I might have gotten off with a ticket if I hadn't taken a swing at the patrolman.

"Are you Ed Griffin's son?" he asked. He was looking at my driver's license.

"Yes."

"It looks like you're going to turn out just like your dad," he said. Without thinking, I closed my hand and swung. The patrolman caught my fist, spun me over, and put his knee in my back, until I calmed down. I thought it was a real travesty when Judge Johnson, the father of my close friend Judy, revoked my license. I told Judge Johnson what the patrolman had said about Dad, but it didn't do any good. The judge and my father were friends and obviously concluded that I needed a strong message.

Near the end of the school year, Pat told me her father, an army colonel, was being transferred. I was devastated. The night before she left, I proposed marriage.

"I love you," I said. I'd never said *love* to anyone before. "We can get an apartment, and I'll work nights while finishing high school and you can start college."

Pat cupped my chin in her hands and kissed me. "Jimmy, you're seventeen. You'll have many more loves before you marry. Tonight's our last time together. Don't phone in the morning because I won't take your call, and I'm not going to write." Tears ran down her cheeks. I put my arms around her and held her tight. I always wondered if she cried because of my sincerity or my naiveté.

After Pat moved away, Dad experienced a bipolar depression and turned to alcohol to mitigate his pain. Many nights he came home drunk or just didn't come home—I suspect because I'd chained and padlocked the liquor cabinet.

Luckily, that summer I had a very physical job swamping on a coal truck and was too exhausted to feel sorry for myself. The driver and I hauled coal in wheelbarrows from alleys and dumped it through basement windows. If a house didn't have an alley, we carried the coal on our backs in hundred-pound sacks.

Dad must have learned about my broken heart because I became a regular in his weekend tennis games. He even asked if I would like to race the MG.

"Yes!" I said. I couldn't remember ever being so excited. According to Grandma Adock, Dad had always wanted to race, but Grandpa Fred wouldn't let him, nor would my mother or stepmothers.

"Okay, but you have a lot to learn. I'll get Uncle Tom to teach you." Tom Carstens, a close family friend, owned a Porsche dealership and raced vintage cars. I can't remember why we called him Uncle Tom. All his close friends' children called him Uncle Tom.

The next two Saturdays, he drilled me in the basics of cornering, tailgating, passing, accelerating through the gears, downshifting, recovering from a spinout, and most important, watching the tachometer to prevent over-revving the engine.

Race day when the gun sounded, eighteen drivers ran for their MGs, stretched across the runway twenty-five yards in front of us, in what is known as a Le Mans start, after the twenty-four hour Le Mans, France race where when the French flag dropped, drivers ran across the track to their cars, which they would have to enter and start without assistance. By the third lap, I led the field. Dad and Uncle Tom waved and hooted each time I passed. When I crossed the finish line, Uncle Tom and Dad came running over. Uncle Tom wrapped me in his arms, and Dad slapped me on the back.

A few minutes later, I overhead Uncle Tom speak to Dad. "Ed, he has great reflexes and he didn't spin out like most beginners. He's got potential." Unfortunately I burnt up the engine and my racing days ended.

Late that summer, two incidents happened that cause me to chuckle sixty years later. Before picking up Annie (Fisher) Hofius, a childhood friend, for a movie date, I stopped at the B & I pet store and bought a few goldfish. I knew Annie's parents were out for the evening, and like most teenage girls she wouldn't be ready—doing whatever girls do to keep boys waiting. I had plenty of time to dump the goldfish into her parents' bedroom toilet bowl. Amazingly, the Fishers never confronted me. I presumed either they flushed the toilet without looking or were too embarrassed to confront me.

A few weeks later, Annie and I double-dated with Gaye (Titcomb) Pigott, Annie's classmate. I took a bag of pigeons, which I'd trapped, into the movie theater concealed under my coat; they were too traumatized to coo. I released them during a scary scene, causing many to run for the exits.

My senior year, I'd all but forgotten Pat. I turned out for football, but as a slow 155 pounder, I wasn't big enough to play line or fast enough for the backfield. The coach suggested I try another sport. Until swimming season, I spent most afternoons and weekends duck hunting at my godfather's, Art Thompson, farm on the Sound near Key Center. Watching ducks respond to a call and drop into decoys is as good as it gets.

Art Thompson and daughter Kay

Over Christmas vacation, I went to the cotillion ball, the traditional introduction of young ladies into society, held at Seattle's Olympic Hotel and later renamed the Four Seasons. As soon as my date, Anita, and I sat down for dinner, waiters asked what we wanted to drink. I ordered a scotch and water, my father's preferred drink, though I wouldn't be twenty-one for three years. While waiting for our cocktails, we introduced ourselves. When it came our turn, Anita said she attended Smith College. I didn't want to embarrass her by saying Clover Park High School, so I said, "Stanford," though I hadn't applied to Stanford or any other college. Anita gave me a warm smile.

"Do you belong to a fraternity?" a six-foot-five, good-looking escort from across the table asked.

"Phi Delta Theta," I said. Art Thompson had been a Phi Delt at Dartmouth and I didn't know any other fraternity names. He gave me a quizzical look, but said nothing more until his turn came.

"John Ramsey. I'm also a Stanford Phi Delt," he said. *I'm in trouble now*, I thought. Later when John excused himself to go to the restroom, I followed, thinking I'd better set the record straight.

"I'm a senior in high school," I said. We were standing side by side at the urinals. "I didn't want to embarrass my date. Thank you for not calling me on it."

"Well done," he said. "If you come to Stanford, look me up."

Tragedy struck six days after my eighteenth birthday. Mr. Gray interrupted my American history class and spoke quietly to our teacher, Mr. Burkhart, who, although a short-legged fleshy man, came quickly to my desk.

"Mr. Gray wants to talk to you in the hall," he whispered. Curious eyes followed me out of the room. *It must have something to do with class accounts,* I thought. In my student-council position, I was responsible for special event funds. Mr. Gray closed the door and put his arm around me, suggesting a more serious matter than the loss of a few dollars.

"Your father is dead," he said.

"Oh God." I shuddered. "What happened?" But I knew without asking. I'd left the gun room door unlocked. *How,* I thought, *Could I have been so careless?* Dad had been on a bipolar high the last few weeks. Somehow I'd missed the change.

"He shot himself."

As the only hunter in the family, I kept the key to the gun room, which housed my grandfather's shotguns. Five years before, Dad's psychiatrist warned Sarah that Dad's bipolar condition made him a candidate for suicide, so I watched the guns like a hawk.

"Who found him?" I asked, holding back the tears, which must have shocked Mr. Gray. After years of being passed back and forth between parents, like chips in a poker game, with never an "I love you," I kept my emotions locked inside me.

"The gardener. Your father asked him to come to the basement to help move boxes."

Oh, Fred, I thought, what a terrible thing Dad did to you. I'm sure he thought it better for you to find him than Gail or me. (Dad married twenty-year-old Gail Trunkey Thompson when he and Judy divorced.)

Mr. Gray called my friend, John Waller, out of class to drive me home. Fred was waiting on the porch when we arrived.

"I'll see you after school," John said, and then added, "Jim, I'm sorry."

"Are you sure you want to see him?" Fred asked. "It's not pretty."

"Yes." I followed Fred down the stairs.

The gun room door was ajar. Fred stepped aside to let me go ahead. The open padlock hung in the fastener just as I had left it. I knew before looking that one slot in the wall-mounted gun rack I had made in eighth-grade wood shop would be empty.

My eyes dropped to the concrete floor where one leg in a gray-flannel suit pant protruded from behind a wooden crate. Dad always wore a gray or blue suit with a vest. I walked around the crate. Dad lay in a fetal position with his head resting in a pool of blood on the concrete floor, my rifle at his side. I burst into tears; Fred wrapped his arm around me. He didn't say anything. What could he say? The terrible things Dad had said to me no longer mattered. I started to fidget. I needed to take some action. I reached for my rifle.

"No!" Fred said, holding me back. "Don't touch anything until the police arrive. I called them just before you got home. I waited so you could see your dad before they arrived."

"Where's Gail?"

"When she left this morning, she said she would be in Seattle all day." Cell phones were still in the future.

As we climbed the stairs, my foot touched the step where, five years before, Dad caught Ted and me smoking. I began to reminisce, remembering Dad made us smoke every cigarette in the pack. After a few cigarettes we began to retch, but he wouldn't let up. The punishment worked because neither of us ever smoked again. Before we reached the top stair, sirens blared.

John returned after school with Joe Ghilarducci and Gary Milgard. "How are you doing? Are you okay? Anything we can do?" I didn't say it, but I thought, *no, I'm not doing well; no, I'm not okay; no, there's nothing you can do. But you're here for me, and that means a great deal.*

My nightmares returned, but this time, it wasn't angry green eyes looking at me through the window. It was Dad, with the barrel of my gun in his mouth. Dad's psychiatrist told us there was nothing anyone could have done to prevent the suicide. The psychiatrist said the humiliation of bankruptcy (Dad had recently made some unfortunate business decisions) compounded by a severe bipolar depression was more than he could cope. My leaving the gun room door unlocked just made the taking of his life easier. Grandma Adock, who had been in poor health, became so distraught that she died two weeks later.

Tennis season had started, and the team practiced every day, but two funerals in two weeks had taken a heavy toll on me. I turned inward. I didn't want to see or talk to anyone. That's when Art Thompson and Jim March, my other godfather, inserted themselves into my life. Art kept me busy weekends working on his farm and steelhead fishing. I'll never forget the day I plowed a field and broke the main waterline to the farm house. Somehow, Art kept his notorious temper under control.

Jim March developed commercial real estate. When I wasn't with Art, I visited construction sites with Jim. Thanks to him, I had a hands-on degree in finance and real estate development when I finished college.

Ted and I each inherited one-half of the fuel business and were beneficiaries of $25,000 insurance policies. Gail got the house. Life insurance paid enough of the company's debt to keep it out of bankruptcy. Fortunately, Dad's good friend Reno Odlin, president of the bank holding the fuel company's note, agreed to carry the loan until I finished school and had an opportunity to repay the remainder. I never understood how Dad could have so many close friends and not be able say, "Good job, Jim; way to go" or "I love you." I have often wondered how my life would have turned out if my father had not taken his life.

My draft notice came in April, three weeks after Dad died. The letter specified a date, time, and place for a physical examination. When the day arrived, I went to an army barrack in the Seattle port district with a busload of eighteen-year-olds. As we entered the building, a balding uniformed soldier with lots of stripes on his sleeves pointed to a door and barked, "Strip and line up." We were ushered through an examining room like cattle through a chute, less than three minutes per man.

When the last person took his place in line, the elderly soldier shouted, "When I call your name, take one step to the right." My name wasn't called. After observing the athletic-looking group whose names had been called, I felt confident that I would be exempt. Unfortunately it was the other way around. With the Korean War escalating, I would be drafted upon graduation in June unless I had a college deferment. A few weeks later, my Stanford acceptance letter arrived, and I applied for and received a deferment from my draft board.

Dad had collected antique cars. He kept them at our home on Gravelly Lake in four two-car garages: a 1929 J roadster Duisenberg, 1926 Pierce Arrow, 1911 American La France fire engine, 1922 Mercer sports car, 1909 White truck—Griffin Fuel Company's first vehicle—1908 model 660 Palmer Singer and a Stanley Steamer and Loco mobile, whose dates I can't remember (see Appendix).

I'll never forget helping Dad pump out Herb Syford's swimming pool with the fire engine when the Syfords were away for the weekend or backing the Pierce Arrow into the Starlight outdoor movie theater through the exit, with a car load of classmates.

I graduated in June and immediately joined the Teamsters Union so I could deliver coal and oil—Griffin Fuel had a contract with the union—which brought back memories of my grandfather nearly being killed when he refused to join the union in 1903. The irony was that we had to join the union, but couldn't enter the union hall because we were employers of union personnel.

In July, we received an offer of $2,500 for the Duisenberg and sold it. Neither Ted nor I had a passion for antique cars, and $2,500 would pay three years tuition at Stanford. Some years later, I learned that it resold for $1,000,000; if only we had known. Then in 1959, we sold the Palmer Singer, built by Singer Sewing Machine Company and the only one in existence, for $5,500 to Harrah's Casino car museum in Reno. Today it would be worth many millions.

(3) Young Adulthood

In mid-September 1955, John Waller, who had also been accepted to Stanford, accompanied me in the MG to Palo Alto. I couldn't wait to get out of town and away from everyone telling me how sorry they were about my father's death. When I turned off El Camino Real onto Palm Drive, Stanford's principal boulevard, the scent of the eucalyptus trees lining the road permeated the air like incense from a Buddhist pagoda. Golden brown leaves from oak, elm, and maple sailed like gliders in the cooling breeze. We passed the football stadium, which looked like a gigantic earthen dam, and then the track.

I slowed at the tennis center, and my eyes grew big as saucers when I saw the viewing bleachers, where one day I might play. I dropped John off at Encino Hall and then located my room in the new freshmen dorm, Wilbur Hall—we would be the first occupants—where I met my roommate, Kent Kaiser, who remains a friend after more than half a century. After unpacking my footlocker, which I'd shipped, I changed into tennis clothes and went to look at the courts where I would be competing to make the freshmen team.

As I walked through the gate onto center court, a shirtless, hairy-chested upperclassman wearing thongs and a Mexican sombrero rose up from the court bench where he'd been napping. If he hadn't been holding two Jack Kramer racquets imprinted with Stanford logos, I would have thought him a nerd.

"Hey, kid, do you want to hit some?" he asked.

"Sure!" I couldn't believe he didn't bother to put on tennis shoes or take off his sombrero. That was the only time I got to play with Jack Frost, the Stanford all-American who turned professional after representing the United States in Davis Cup competition.

A few weeks later, in my final qualifying match to make the freshmen team—twenty some freshmen turned out. I recalled my stepfather's advice at a boxing tournament. "Jimmy, don't lose. Make him beat you." I'd had minimal instruction and didn't serve or volley well, but hours of hitting against our backboard had made me a retriever. I made the team.

Within days, I could feel myself changing. The veneer that had kept my feelings and emotions locked up for so many years began to peel away in the friendly and accepting campus atmosphere. It was comforting having my high school buddies, Joe Ghilarducci, John Waller, and Buzz Cain, at Stanford, but I was also making new friends, particularly freshman football players who I'd met in the shared gym and athletic facility across from the tennis stadium.

I'd always been mischievous and it continued at Stanford. By the end of fall quarter I was infamously known by most freshman women—three hundred and some entered fall quarter—for hosing down Branner Hall's freshman women's dorm's sun deck. I climbed a drainpipe with a hose wrapped around my waist. When I reached the deck, I signaled my friend Bob Parks to turn on the water.

"Good afternoon, ladies," I said as I raised my head over the porch and sprayed it from one end to the other. The incident caused much gaiety from my second and third floor Wilbur Hall classmates—who I had previously alerted—when topless girls ran for the windows. In a later recap, most observers concurred that a few sunbathers took longer than necessary to exit the roof.

With winter quarter, the two-hundred-year tradition of joining a fraternity, *rush*, got underway. As an unheralded tennis player, I wasn't on any recruitment list. I wanted to pledge Phi Delta Theta, a prestigious jock house where many of my football buddies intended to pledge. Art Thompson wrote a letter of recommendation, but I found out later recommendations went straight into the garbage can. Unfortunately, John Ramsey, the Phi Delt I'd met at the Seattle cotillion, had transferred to the University of Washington.

Though I didn't receive an invitation to the Phi Delta Theta rush party in Palo Alto—Stanford was a dry campus—I tagged along with my new friends. If they hadn't occasionally introduced me, I would have been like a fly on the wall. However, at a follow-up party, an opportunity for recognition came unexpectedly. After a few rounds of beer, the testosterone kicked in, and an arm-wrestling contest got under way. I had an exceptionally strong arm and wrist from hitting thousands of tennis balls and regularly working out in the gym. I bided my time until Stanford's all-American tackle had defeated all challengers. Then, before he could rest his arm, I sat down opposite him and put my elbow on the table.

"Are you serious?" he asked. He stood nearly six inches taller than me and weighed eighty pounds more.

"I'm serious." The vanquished, which included my friends, quickly crowded around the table. I heard chuckling and then Rick Prince, who'd already pledged, spoke up.

"You just watch."

"What's your name?" he asked.

"Jim Griffin."

"Okay, Jim, let's see what you've got." We clasped hands, and an onlooker held our elbows together so neither of us could slide an arm out and reduce the opponent's leverage. While all eyes watched our arms, I reached down and grabbed a table leg to increase my leverage. Then I let my wrist unhinge so my palm paralleled the table. He engaged his powerful shoulder muscle, but most of his energy went to pushing down rather than pulling. When I felt a lessening of pressure, I quickly reengaged my wrist, and before he could reapply pressure, I pulled his arm to the table. His eyebrows dropped and eyes partially closed in a look of amazement. Then a smile slowly spread across his face.

"You've got some arm there," he said.

"Thanks, but you would have easily beaten me had you been fresh," I responded.

As I rose up from the table, someone handed me a beer, and then my football friends crowded around, slapping me on back. Ten minutes later, Rudy Figueroa the rush chairman asked me to join the fraternity. Nearly sixty years later, many of my pledge brothers remain close friends.

Back row from left: Doug Martin, Steve Parkin, Willy Brumder, Phil Burkand, Rick Prince Denny Farrar, Lance Gambel Middle row: Jerry Reinhart, Jerry Bricca, Bob Nicolet, Bob Brazier, Neal Scheidel First row: Jim Sinnerud, Jim Griffin, John Thomas, Bob Parks

That summer, Mr. Odlin offered me a job in the bank's consumer credit department—a fancy name for collections—suggesting I broaden my experience. I'd worked in every department at Griffin Fuel as a mechanic, wood, coal and oil truck driver, phone switchboard operator, salesman, scheduler for automatic oil deliveries, and bookkeeper.

I remember two incidents at the bank that summer, 1956, as if they happened yesterday. On a TV repossession call, a lady opened her door to a room nearly empty of furniture, which I assumed had been repossessed. Half a dozen children, with faces cupped in hands held up by elbows, lay sprawled on the floor watching cartoons. "I'm here to pick up a check or the TV," I said.

She immediately began crying. "My husband ran off with his girlfriend," she sputtered, "and my welfare check barely covers food, rent, and utilities."

I took another look at the children and thought, *I have so much and they so little.* "Don't worry," I said. "I'll figure something out." I quickly stepped off the porch so she couldn't see my tears. Paying off the TV cost me a month's salary.

The second incident was entirely different. A shoeless and shirtless hairy-chested man in his thirties, who wore his long, stringy hair in a ponytail, opened the door cradling a shotgun in his arm. He reeked of alcohol. Before I could identify myself, he snarled, "You're not taking my car. Get out of my yard." As I considered a response, he raised the gun, pointed at my midsection, and said, "Get going."

"Okay, okay, I'm leaving!" I backed off the porch. He lived in a rural area and I thought, *There would be no witnesses if he decided to shoot.* I didn't turn around until the car stood between us. As I drove away, I saw him go into the house and thought, *I'm not going to let him chase me off.*

From his file, I knew he worked night shift and probably would quickly fall asleep. I drove around the bend and parked on the side of the road under a tree, where I'd be out of the sun. I waited twenty minutes, during which time only a half dozen cars passed, and then went back, leaving my car out of sight from the house. After a short surveillance, I went to his car, keeping the car between me and the house, lifted the hood—interior hood locks were then a rarity—opened the distributor cap and extracted the rotor, which transfers spark from the coil to the spark plugs, something I'd learned working in the Griffin Fuel Company's garage. Back at my office, I called the bank's towing company and explained the situation. I suggested they pick the car up after 6:00 p.m., which would give him plenty of time to get a ride to work. His shift began at 4:00.

When I returned to Stanford in September as a sophomore, I along with twenty other pledges moved into the Phi Delt house—freshmen weren't allowed to live in fraternities. Pledges slept together in metal-frame double bunks on a sleeping porch and studied in an upper classman's "big brother" room. Pledge camaraderie was instilled during "hell week," a few days of raucous hazing perpetrated by the previous year's pledges, to supposedly help pledges bond. We suffered a number of humiliating, and sometimes painful, experiences; having to attend class wearing a gunny sack as underwear, with a raw egg inserted so you couldn't sit down—anyone returning to the house with a broken egg received untold hacks from specially crafted hack boards. At meals, our arms were tied to an eight-foot two-by-four to make us eat in unison; all twenty-one of us were locked in a coat closet until we smoked our cigars to a nub; we were paddled for concocted infractions, which often drew blood. Since I was perceived by some as cocky I received more than my share of hacks.

Tryouts for the ski team—a club sport—occurred during a weekend tennis match, but when a member of the team twisted an ankle, the coach asked me to fill in at a multiple school meet of nearly one hundred participants. As I made the top ten in both jumping and cross-country, the coach made me a permanent member of the team.

Stanford was intellectually challenging and exposed me to new concepts and ideas. My maternal grandmother Elsie had started my religious training in the Christian Science church. She paid me twenty-five cents for each Psalm I memorized, which lasted until she died of automobile injuries because she refused to go to the hospital. Pat had introduced me to the Episcopal Church, a condition for dating. However, after taking an introductory course in philosophy, I began to doubt what I'd taken for granted and became fascinated with the meanings of "being" and "morality." I decided to major in philosophy, with a minor in religion and accounting, which would be useful in business.

I read the important philosophers from Herodotus, a fifth-century BC historian, to Nietzsche, a nineteenth-century existentialist, and I studied Christianity, Judaism, Islam, Buddhism, and Hinduism. I concluded that there was no metaphysical right or wrong answer and that no religion was more logical or compelling than any other; all required a leap of faith. I reasoned that environment and indoctrination, not logic, determined what one believed. My thoughts eventually coalesced into a philosophy that worked for me—and still does: God created the universe; man has free will, though his every action is predetermined; prayer is the transformation of energy among the living, not through God; religious doctrine originates from prophets, not God; heaven and hell exist in the here and now, not after our demise; and the soul survives death.

In addition to studies, tennis, skiing, intramurals, and jalopy mud-bowl racing behind fraternity row, with bikini-clad flag-waving starters—my pledge brother Bob Parks drove a 1934 Ford coupé—I dated and partied. I couldn't have been happier. One of our favorite pastimes was hurling water balloons from the Phi Delt roof at the campus cop when he wrote tickets or just happened to be passing the house on his motorcycle. We called him Captain Midnight, We knew we had his attention when he began wearing a rain slicker—sunny days or not.

Me and Bob Parks with Bob's '34 Ford that someone pushed into Lake Lagunita—Bob was a few votes short of winning the junior class presidency

I'll never forget the evening Captain Midnight came to the house. "Is Bill Smith here?" he asked, while standing in the dining room doorway waiving a warrant. I'd never heard of Bill Smith.

"No," the fraternity president said.

"Where can I find him?"

"Don't know."

"Does he live here?"

"No. What's he done?"

"He has fifty unpaid parking tickets. The car registration has the Phi Delt House address." Before the fraternity president could respond, snickering broke out from both sides of the room. I thought, *Jim, you better duck.* Food fights happened rather often because pledges had to clean up the mess. Within seconds, food started flying. If my memory serves me correctly, a deluxe cheeseburger hit Captain Midnight's badge, spraying ketchup from his collar to the top of his head, and when he ran for the door, liberal amounts of fruit and potato salad, baked beans, hamburgers and hotdogs, and milk hit him. Fortunately he got a good rinse off from a bucket of water dumped from the roof as he ran down the steps.

The house got a letter of reprimand from the dean but received fewer than the normal amount of "con hours," detention work at the Children's Convalescent Home. The dean had obviously been amused, and since there was no report of damage or injury—well ... Con hours were allocated by the fraternity president in a most democratic fashion: possibly one hour for a senior, two hours for a junior, and as many as four hours for a pledge. We painted, pulled weeds, raked leaves, trimmed hedges, and pressure-washed, which sometimes led to water fights. Though some of us were experienced electricians and plumbers—plumbing was my forte—the dean, rightfully fearing an even worse situation, prohibited our entry into the convalescent home. The children, many of whom were orphans, looked forward to visits, not only to hear every detail of our latest caper, but for our friendship and encouragement. I was known as an exaggerator of some distinction, and the children flocked to me.

The worst offense, blowing up the SAE fraternity's concrete mascot lions, across the street from the Phi Delt house, brought the FBI as well as the dean to our doorsteps. The explosion, caused by dynamite made from ingredients used in the Chemistry 101 lab blew more than a few windows out of the Stanford Post Office a block away. Though the explosion had all the telltale signs of a Phi Delt ploy, lack of evidence saved the culprits from a summer of con hours and possibly jail.

There were other incidents, like trying to breech the Lake Lagunita Dam in similar fashion and all the intrigue depicted in the World War II epic movie, *Force 10 from Navarone*. Fortunately, looking back, some early riser reported seeing an ever-widening stream flowing from the lake, and the cut was filled before water reached the steps of Roble Hall, the freshman women's dorm.

That summer, while working at the fuel company, my life changed dramatically. My stepmother Gail, who was caretaking the fuel company until I finished school and military service, suggested my aptitude was more suited to banking than an entrepreneurial career. Ted had quit college and bought a pet store. He wasn't interested in the fuel business.

"Jim, I think you should change your major to economics," Gail said.

"Why?"

"I don't think you have the aptitude or personality to manage a business." I knew Gail passionately enjoyed being president of the Griffin Fuel Co., but implying that I didn't have the aptitude deeply hurt, whether it was true or not.

"We'll see," I said. I immediately left the room before I said something I would regret, and the subject did not come up again. By the time I returned to Stanford in the fall, 1957, the hurt had turned to anger, I'd regained my confidence, and I'd come up with a plan to accelerate my education. I'd had enough fun, and it was time to get serious about life.

After hearing my story, the dean, with whom I was now on a first-name basis through dispensing con hours, allowed me to increase my class credits from fifteen units to any amount I could handle. In order to graduate the following December, nearly a year ahead of my class, I would have to take 25 units per quarter plus 3 summer school units. I planned to pick up the three units at the University of Edinburgh the home of the eighteenth-century philosopher, David Hume, my mentor. The overseas adventure would also give me a last opportunity to tour Europe before military service or entering the work force.

With the added credits, my time on the slopes and tennis court dropped substantially; this was no loss, because I hadn't made the traveling varsity tennis team.

Near the end of March on my way to a beach party at Half Moon Bay, celebrating the end of winter quarter, I had a traumatic experience that could have ended my life. When Phil Burkland and I picked up our dates at their row houses, a gentle, midseventies breeze carried the intoxicating scent of spring blossoms. Forty-five minutes later, we left my car on a cliff above the ocean in sight of the Phi Delt bonfire. Faint outlines of stars began to appear in the cloudless sky as we threaded our way through scotch broom down the narrow switchback trail. Then, on a moonlit plateau above the beach, two Hispanics, dressed in black, with chains wrapped around their waists hanging like curtain pull cords, stepped from the bushes blocking our way.

"Give me your beer," demanded the larger of the two. He stood over six feet with shoulder-length, stringy brown hair and a Fu Manchu mustache.

"It's not for—" before I could say, "sale," he grabbed the carton out of my arms. Without hesitating, I sprang forward, knocking him to the ground. With Phil, a six-foot-four Stanford tackle, backing me up, I had no fear. The twelve-pack flew out of Fu's hands and broke open on the trail. Beer cans cart wheeled in every direction.

Fu Manchu lay on his back with me astraddle. I heard the click of a switchblade knife. Then shouts rang out, possibly saving my life. Fu turned to see who was approaching, and I leapt away. Recognizing the voices, he turned back and slashed with his knife, missing my chest by inches. While his cohorts gathered the beer, Fu Manchu made threatening jabbing motions in my direction.

We were trapped. The path to the beach was blocked and shouts of alarm would be drowned out by ocean waves. We huddled together, terrified of what might happen. After collecting the beer, the gang encircled us. Phil and I stood back-to-back, with the girls between us. Fu smiled as he tossed his knife from hand to hand in an intimidating manner. I prepared for a beating and knew the girls feared rape. After a string of obscenities and lewd gestures, the gang turned and disappeared into the thick brush, taking our picnic basket, blankets, and beer.

We sprinted to the beach and joined our friends, many of whom had also been robbed. The early arrivers, who'd had a few beers, wanted to go after the gang. Fortunately, cooler heads prevailed. As most of us were without food and beer, we resurrected the party at Rosotti's, Stanford's favorite local bar. Off by ourselves in a dark corner, we relived our terrifying encounter.

A few weeks later, Fu Manchu's picture appeared in the *San Francisco Chronicle* and Peninsula papers under the headline "Two Stanford Students Hurt in Gang Attack." According to the story, a group of Stanford students partying at San Gregorio Beach (just south of Half Moon Bay) were attacked by a gang of knife-wielding youths. During the altercation, my assailant, identified as a Palo Alto butcher's assistant, struck a student across the forehead with a two-by-four, causing a skull fracture and concussion. As I read the article, I pictured myself with a knife buried in my chest.

One Sunday evening while playing bridge, our house proctor, a Stanford Law School student, mentioned he was taking a class on the Internal Revenue Code of 1954.

"You guys going into business won't believe the hatchet job the 83rd congress did on the 1939 tax code."

"How so?" I asked.

"For starters a progressive income tax with twenty four brackets and a maximum tax rate of 91%. The code book is this thick," he said, spreading his thumb and forefinger two inches wide.

As I planned to take over the family fuel business, I figured auditing a tax course might prove useful. I'd previously sat in on a law school real estate class in the auditorium, where there was less chance of being noticed.

Two weeks into the course, I got busted. The professor after proposing a taxable situation, asked for opinions. As hands went up all around me, I slumped deeper into my chair.

"You there in the back, four seats in next to the lady in the red sweat shirt." Would you care to answer?" *Somebody turned me in*, I thought. After hesitating a moment to regain my composure, I answered the professor's question.

"Correct," the professor said, and then asked "What's your name?"

"Jim Griffin." I knew the consequences of lying—Stanford had an honor code.

He pulled out a folder from the lectern, which I assumed to be a student roster. Everyone was staring. After a few moments, he frowned, raising his arms chest high in a questioning manner. "Mr. Griffin," he said "your name doesn't appear in the law school registry."

"Sir, I'm an undergraduate. I'm here to get a better understanding of what I'll be up against when I start my business career."

"That's admirable," the professor said, "but unfortunately auditing is not allowed. If you have an interest in law, apply to the law school when you graduate," and then added, I'm sorry, but you'll have to leave." I received and equal number of "thumbs up" as supercilious looks exciting the auditorium.

In June, I left for the University of Edinburgh and a whirlwind six weeks of study; interrelating with seventy-some students from twenty-nine countries; playing golf at St. Andrews, the birthplace of golf; undergoing a girth expansion from Scottish ale; and founding lifelong friendships with Colin Campbell and

Hans Solmssen, solidified while winning Edinburgh's intramural flag football championship.

My class work consisted mostly of independent study, for an end-of-term "manuscript," and nightly get-togethers with our philosophy professor. My discourse compared the philosophy of David Hume, a strong empiricist, who believed humans have knowledge of only things they directly experience, to that of Immanuel Kant, who advocated *a priori* knowledge is seated in the mind at birth.

At the end of the semester, Hans and Colin joined me in my Volkswagen "Beetle," which I'd purchased in Amsterdam on my way to Edinburgh, for a tour of Germany. We left Scotland by ferry and landed at Warnemunde, East Germany, where we obtained visas to West Berlin. We ignored our visas' directions and left Warnemunde taking the scenic route.

We also ignored our embassy's warning that East Germany was arresting Americans for minor violations to use as Cold War bargaining chips. Military police stopped us near a munitions factory. Fortunately, they weren't federal police, and we were released after explaining we'd lost our way. With little sleep since leaving Edinburgh, we stopped for an afternoon nap in a hay field, once again ignoring visa instructions not to stop. I woke to the nudging of a bayonet, and I got no licks from the leashed German shepherd. Once again, we were fortunate to have been picked up by soldiers rather than federal police.

The following morning, we made several trips from West Berlin (American, British, and French occupation sectors established at the end of World War II) into East Berlin, hoping to locate information on Hans' family estate in the East Berlin University. His home had been confiscated by Hitler's Third Reich when the family fled Germany prior to World War II. On our third border crossing through the Brandenburg Gate—the Berlin wall wasn't erected until 1961—federal police, thinking we were smugglers, took us at gunpoint to the East Berlin police station. We were strip-searched, and my car was literally torn apart.

After intensive interrogation we were released. Colin and I later got a full report on our interrogators conversation from Hans who did not let on that he spoke German.

Eventually we found the Solmssen estate. Hans and the caretaker, who remembered Hans as a child, had a tearful reunion. The caretaker told us Hermann Goering, Hitler's second-in-command, and Theodor Morell, Hitler's personal doctor, had spent time at the estate during the war.

From West Berlin, we drove to London, this time following the prescribed route through East Germany. In London we stayed at Michael Beecham's home—a castle would be more descriptive. Michael Beecham, nephew of Sir Thomas Beecham, one of the greatest twentieth-century symphony conductors, and Hans's father were friends. I can still picture the banquet room and dinner table where the three of us and the Beechams ate. Without exaggeration, the table would have accommodated sixty people.

I left Hans and Colin, who were on their way back to the States, in London and picked up John Sayre, a high school hunting buddy, and his friend Chuck Alm. During duck season, John, I and others often left for school early and, before class, shot a few mallards at Chambers Bay, where Chambers Creek runs into Puget Sound. In those days, it was acceptable to bring a shotgun to school and leave it in the trunk of your car. If none of the teachers wanted the ducks, we could always get rid of them at a Chinese restaurant in South Tacoma.

John and Chuck's University of Washington eight-man crew, after winning England's prestigious Henley Cup, had just returned from competing with the Soviet national team. Washington's rowers were the first foreign athletes to enter the USSR since the beginning of the Cold War. Two years later, John and Chuck won gold medals in the Olympic Games.

John, Chuck, and I went south, spending an educational couple of weeks visiting Roman ruins and camping out. The highlight of the trip was the Roman Coliseum, where the first Olympic Games were held.

When John and Chuck left for home, I drove to France and visited Jim March, who was vacationing in Nice. A week later, I shipped my Volkswagen to Tacoma and flew home to begin my last quarter at Stanford.

(4) Alpental: Is Not in the Dictionary

Alpental: is not in the dictionary. Bob Mickelson, my partner and codeveloper of the Alpental Ski Area, made up the name. Bob combined the Swiss/German words alpen (alpine), and tal (valley), to describe the mountain valley located north of Snoqualmie Pass summit in Washington State. We'd been in business together for a while; having first met in 1951, shortly after Day's Tailored wear, a Tacoma clothing manufacturer, recruited Bob from Harvard Business School. My father, also a Harvard Business School graduate, invited Bob and his wife, Mary Lou, for an afternoon swim at our home at Gravelly Lake.

From my view as a fourteen-year-old, Bob looked like a Greek god. He stood six feet tall, was broad-shouldered and slim-waisted, and, like all athletes of that day, wore a crew cut. I learned later that Bob played football and track at the University of Minnesota and qualified as an alternate for the 1948 Summer Olympic Games.

I saw Bob only occasionally over the next ten years. Then, in 1961, after I finished college, married, and assumed management of the Griffin Fuel Company, Bob called. After spending a few minutes getting reacquainted, he said, "Jim, will you help me organize a Lakewood tennis club?" I thought,

A Lakewood tennis facility would sure beat driving into Tacoma to play at Tacoma Lawn Tennis Club.

"Sure," I said.

In 1962, after the Lakewood Racquet Club opened, Bob surprised me at our weekly lunch meeting with an offer to go into business with him.

Opening of the Lakewood Racquet Club, from left, Wendy (pregnant with Whitney), Sterling, me, and Scott (1962)

"I'm buying VIP Sports," he said, "Would you like to be my partner?"

I took a deep breath and let it out slowly, trying not to appear too eager. Bob had an impressive business background. He had manufactured ski apparel since 1952, and he'd been elected to the Apparel Hall of Fame. In 1955, he helped organize Ski Industries of America and served as the first president. I thought, *This is the opportunity I've been looking for.* I'd planned to sell the fuel company because gas and electricity were slowly replacing oil heat, and I'd known ever since visiting construction sites with my godfather, Jim March, that one day I wanted to be a real estate developer. This would be a good interim step.

"Why me?" I asked. I couldn't think of anything else to say.

"We complement each other. You're like a pit bull. You grab onto something and don't let go. We'll make a great team."

"Yes" I said. "I'd like to be your partner."

The following week, Bob asked his friend Lou Whittaker, a ski department manager in Seattle, to be our partner and manage the store. It took Lou a few days to make up his mind, because he and his twin brother, Jim, were organizing a Mount Everest expedition. Jim led the expedition without Lou and reached the summit of Mount Everest, the first American to do so.

Senator Barry Goldwater (a close friend of Wendy's parents) on a stopover in Tacoma during the 1964 Presidential campaign (from left, Scott, Wendy, Senator Goldwater, me, and Sterling)

We bought the sporting goods store with a bank loan, and changed the name to Whittaker's Chalet, to take advantage of Jim Whittaker's publicity. A year later, we constructed a building and relocated adjacent to the Tacoma Mall. That same year, 1963, we opened Sport Chalet, a wholesale sporting goods business, to supply retail stores nationwide.

Wendy and I were slowly becoming involved in community activities. We both believed in giving back.

Through Rotary, a businessmen's service club, I met Frank Cooper, chairman of the Pierce County Republican Party. Six months later, Frank appointed me Pierce County Republican Finance Co-Chairman. Then, in the spring of 1964, I became an alternate delegate to the Republican National Convention. When we were not in caucus or on the convention floor, Wendy and I spent time in Goldwater's suite at San Francisco's Mark Hopkins Hotel. The Goldwaters were close friends of Wendy's family, and Wendy and their daughter grew up together. Also Dennis Kitchel, Goldwater's campaign chairman and projected Attorney General, was Wendy's godfather.

While having dinner with the Goldwaters in the Mark Hopkins dining room, which had tables set around a swimming pool, I said, "Eight years ago, I swam nude across this pool."

"What's that all about?" Senator Goldwater asked.

"It happened during hell week. Our fraternity, Phi Delta Theta, had a long list of difficult chores to be accomplished before we could become members."

"Were you apprehended?" Mrs. Goldwater asked.

"It was a close call, with security hot on our heels, but no, we didn't get caught."

"The senator," Mrs. Goldwater said, as she looked over at Barry, "wasn't always so proper." Senator Goldwater smiled but didn't respond.

The convention opened my eyes to the skullduggery and machinations inherent in politics, and when asked to run for Congress and quizzed about my interest in a US Senate seat, I said no, choosing instead to try and effect change behind the curtain rather than on stage, as a politician.

On a Wednesday in December, after the Presidential elections, in which Lyndon Johnson easily defeated Goldwater—Goldwater was too conservative for the times—Mickelson and I met, as usual, at the Bavarian Restaurant. I knew when I came through the door and saw him flipping through a dog-eared yellow tablet that he had a new venture in mind. He smiled when he saw me. I'd seen that sanguine, coy smile before.

"What's it going to be this time?" I asked.

"Am I that transparent?"

"Yes!"

"Let's build a ski area."

"You've got to be kidding."

"I'm serious. Crystal Mountain is the only ski area to open since Stevens Pass in 1955 and skier days"—which are based on the number of ski tickets sold—"have more than doubled. We're already in the retail and wholesale ski business; why not go all the way?" It took me a moment to catch my breath, and then I thought *Bob is speaking from experience. He was co-chairman of Crystal's capital campaign and is one of a limited number of Crystal Mountain stockholders.*

"Do you have a mountain in mind?" I asked.

"No, but I think we should start looking in the Snoqualmie Pass area." When I asked why, he picked up his tablet and began reciting demographics of the six western Cascade ski areas. The following is to the best of my recollection.

"The Summit Ski Area opened in 1937. It has a vertical rise of only 765 feet, bottom elevation 3,000 feet, and top elevation 3,765. Ski Acres, which adjoined the Summit, opened ten years later in 1947. Hyak, located just east of Ski Acres, opened in 1955.

"Stevens Pass opened in 1955. Stevens has a vertical rise of 1,800 feet, bottom elevation 4,061 feet and top elevation 5,845.

"Crystal Mountain opened in 1962. Crystal has a vertical rise of 2,400 feet, bottom elevation 4,400 feet and top elevation 7,012.

"White Pass also opened in 1955. It has a vertical rise of 1,500 feet, bottom elevation of 4,470 feet and top elevation of 5,961. Like Stevens Pass and Crystal Mountain, White Pass is accessed by only a two-lane highway." He looked up at me. "Do you hear what I'm saying?"

"I'm listening."

Continuing, he told me that the Snoqualmie Summit ski areas' base elevations were a thousand feet lower than the base elevations of Stevens Pass, Crystal Mountain, and White Pass, and had less than half the vertical rise of those ski areas, but the Snoqualmie Pass areas had more skier days than Stevens, Crystal, and White combined.

"Jim, the short freeway drive from the Seattle metropolitan area to Snoqualmie Pass more than compensates for Snoqualmie's lower-base elevation, lower vertical rise, and shorter ski slopes." Bob put down his yellow tablet and raised his eyes to mine, waiting for a response.

I thought a moment, then said, "Sounds good to me," and then added, "I assume you've figured out where to get the money."

Bob smiled. He knew financing would be my first question. "We'll find a mountain that adjoins private property and develop lots and condominiums. Bill Janss did it when he bought Sun

Valley from Union Pacific. We can too. We'll raise any shortfall through a stock offering."

Bob's enthusiasm was infectious, and his Harvard Business School training had stood us well in organizing and building a community tennis club and operating successful retail and wholesale sporting-goods businesses.

"I'll contact the consultants that I worked with at Crystal Mountain to see if they have any ideas. Why don't you check out state and railroad property?"

A week didn't go by before Bob called. I could hear the excitement in his voice. "Jim, Sully [Jim Sullivan, Crystal Mountain's hill manager] says there's a mountain just east of Snoqualmie Summit with a base elevation similar to Crystal Mountain's. How about lunch? I'll bring a topographic map."

"Okay, noon at the Bavarian," I said.

The mountain had all the attributes we were looking for, north-facing slopes (which would allow skiing well into the spring) and a twenty-five-hundred-foot vertical rise, with a four-thousand-foot base elevation. Unfortunately, the area required building and maintaining a five-mile access road.

The following week, Sully called Bob with another suggestion; Denny Mountain, located on the northeast side of US 10 (later renamed to I-90) at Snoqualmie Summit. We checked Bob's topographical map along with a sectional map, listing land owners. Denny Mountain had north-facing slopes, a twenty-four-hundred-foot vertical rise, and an access road from the highway to the Sahalie Ski Club (an alpine chalet that housed weekend skiers and hikers), at the foot of Denny. Most importantly, the mountain adjoined a privately owned valley formed by Denny, Mount Snoqualmie, and Guye Peak (famous for its rock climbing). The only negative feature was a thirty-two-hundred-foot base elevation; only two hundred feet higher than Snoqualmie Pass, where winter rain occurred frequently.

On a bright, blue-sky morning in January, Bob, my brother, Sully, Lou Whittaker, and I skied into Denny Valley. After we passed Sahalie, the terrain flattened out, where Denny Creek flowed into the South Fork of the Snoqualmie River, and then rose gradually as we tramped through heavy snow along the west side of the river at the base of Denny. There was no mistaking the boundary between Forest Service and private property. The federal land was heavily treed with fir and some pine and cedar. The private land was barren except for a scattering of saplings; rotted stumps were all that was left of the old-growth timber cut in the late 1800s. The second-growth looked to have been logged in the 1940s. We climbed through the trees and made long traverses across the lower slopes. The terrain was steep, but there were no canyons or ravines.

From the lower slopes, Bob and I looked across the valley and envisioned a winding road lined with alpine chalets. The road would access condominiums on the lower slopes of Mount Snoqualmie and Guye Peak before terminating in a parking lot adjacent to a walking bridge spanning the South Fork.

That same afternoon, Bob called the recreation manager of the Snoqualmie National Forest, Stan Olson, and made an appointment. Olson liked the idea of a world-class ski resort in his district.

"I'll need schematic drawings of the proposed ski terrain and private development and aerial photos of the mountain and valley for my boss, the regional administrator, in Portland. Let me know a week in advance, and I'll set up a meeting."

Bob arranged for his friend Warren Miller, the legendary producer of ski movies, to make a short film. A few days later, Bob picked Miller up at the airport and brought him to Snoqualmie Summit where I waited with a rented G-2 Bell helicopter in the Summit Ski Area's parking lot.

The chopper took us to the top of the mountain where our future Chair Two would unload. Bob, Ted, a female member of the

US Ski Team invited by Bob, and I skied into the bowl on the west side of the mountain, as Miller filmed from the hovering helicopter. The bowl dropped eleven hundred feet to a ridge at the tree line, where our future Chair One would terminate. We named the bowl Edelweiss, after the floral symbol of the high mountains and Bob's ski-clothing line. Then we descended through the trees to the valley floor, dropping another 1,250. On the second run, as Miller filmed, we skied off the northeast side of Denny into a narrow chute that funneled out onto a wide slope too steep for vegetation to withstand avalanches. We named the run Internationale. *Sports Illustrated* later described it as "the nation's steepest ski slope per square foot."

From the tree line, at the bottom of Internationale, we descended to the valley floor, passing over what would become the top of Chair Three, with a vertical rise of 525 feet. To the north of Internationale were a series of bowls. The largest, I named Great Scott after our firstborn son.

Activity generated by the helicopter brought a crowd to the parking lot, and Miller was recognized. The following day, rumors of a new ski area ran rampant. We knew we had to move quickly and tie up the private property before land speculators moved in.

The sectional map showed the valley divided into eleven twenty-acre patented mining claims. Denny Mountain was named after Arthur A. Denny, who filed iron-ore mining claims on Denny Creek in 1869. He was also given credit for founding Seattle. He and his party of homesteaders had arrived at Elliott Bay in November 1851.

Fortunately, Victor Borden, an Indian fish buyer on the Olympic Peninsula, owned all eleven claims. Bob and I met Borden at the Morck Hotel in Aberdeen, two days later. After a few minutes of getting acquainted, I said, "Mr. Borden, Bob and I would like to buy your Denny mining claims to develop a ski area. Would you consider selling?"

"Yes, but I won't sell the mineral rights. I bought those claims because a geologist friend of mine believes they contain valuable ore. I just haven't been able to raise the money to drill the property." An hour later we shook hands.

On February 8, 1965, only six weeks after Bob proposed developing a ski area, we executed a $220,000 purchase agreement subject to obtaining a Forest Service use permit. We took title in a partnership, Alpental Land Company. Bob and I each owned forty percent, and Jim Sullivan, who had agreed to install the chairlifts, twenty percent.

While Miller produced the movie, an architect prepared schematic drawings. When they were finished, Bob and I joined Stan Olson in Portland and made a presentation to the regional administrator. The administrator liked our proposal and agreed to recommend it to the Department of Agricultural, the lead agency of the US Forest Service. A few weeks later, a use-permit application came in the mail. That night, Bob, Mary Lou, Wendy, and I toasted with Champagne. The following day we began our quest.

We spent the spring of 1965 working with a ski-area management consultant and a civil engineer assembling documentation for the permit. Ironically, after submitting our application, Janss decided to sell Sun Valley for $2,400,000, the approximate amount we had budgeted to develop Alpental. The thought of owning a world-class ski resort was intoxicating, but Bob and I were too far along with Alpental to consider abandoning it and buying Sun Valley.

Bob's first call went to Sigi Ingle, the director of Sun Valley's ski school, to get advice on chairlifts. He learned that the Riblet Company in Spokane made the best lift. We met with the owner of Riblet and contracted for preliminary cost projections.

In early December, I sold the fuel business, now named Griffin-Galbraith Fuel Oil Service Company. Three years before, in 1962, I'd called on Jack Galbraith, the owner of Fuel Oil

Service Company, to see if he would consider merging our companies.

Jack greeted me in the reception area and led me back to his office where pictures of fuel oil delivery trucks, some dating back to the 1920s, hung on every wall. He indicated for me to sit in one of the two ribbed-back mahogany chairs situated in front of a matching mahogany executive desk. He sat in a cushioned swivel chair behind the desk.

"Mr. Griffin, how can I be of help?" he asked.

"Please call me Jim," I said. "When I hear Mr. Griffin, I think someone is talking to my dad."

"Okay, and you call me Jack."

"Fair enough," I said. I came right to the point. "I've decided to sell Griffin Fuel Company. As you know, the utility companies are capturing a larger share of the home heating business, and I figure I'd better sell now before I lose more oil volume."

"How does Fuel Oil Service fit in with your plans?" Jack asked.

"If we merge and put the combined firm up for sale, I think either Associated or Chevron would buy it." Associated Oil Company supplied Griffin Fuel, and Chevron Oil Company supplied Fuel Oil Service. "Our combined oil volume would account for more than a day of either major oil companies' refinery output, which neither would want to lose."

As I spoke, Jack clasped his hands behind his head and leaned back in his chair. He made no attempt to interrupt. I thought, *He either thinks I'm an impetuous young man or out of my mind.* Finally, he spoke. "I think you're onto something." Six weeks later we signed merger papers which included Cadigan Fuel Company, owned by his brother Tom.

Griffin-Galbraith Fuel Oil Service Co., circa 1964

Jack agreed to let me be president and manage the business, and I agreed to let him be chairman of the board with final say—Jack had nearly twenty more years of business experience than me—if we had a disagreement. We didn't, and as I'd predicted, when we put the company up for sale, Chevron lost no time in agreeing to our terms. When Chevron's district manager, delivered the check, I thought, *Grandfather, I hope you'd be proud of me. You built this company with your own sweat, starting with an ax and horse and wagon. I'll try not to disappoint you.*

Also in 1962, I went into the insurance business. Our company's broker, John McAloon, happened to mention that one day he hoped to have his own business.

"Why wait?" I asked.

"I don't have enough savings to cover family bills until the business can pay me what I'm making now."

"Would you consider a partnership?" I asked.

"What do you suggest?"

"I'll put up the money, and we'll be equal partners. When I get paid back, we'll adjust the ownership so you'll own two-thirds."

"Why would you do that?" he asked.

"I want to diversify my business investments," I said, thinking, *I can't tell him that I'm planning on selling the fuel company.*

"That's a fair offer," John said. "You've got a deal."

After selling the fuel business, I took my family to Klosters, Switzerland, for the winter. It would be months before the Forest Service processed Alpental's "use permit," and I wanted to visit European ski areas to learn the business and get a better understanding of the *gemütlich* atmosphere of the Tyrolean and Bavarian architecture Bob and I intended to replicate at Alpental.

My brother Charlie, me, Wendy, Whitney, Scott, Sterling, Joan Griffin (Ted's wife) and Nancy Holt, our Au Pere, at SeaTac Airport

Wendy in Klosters, Switzerland (1966)

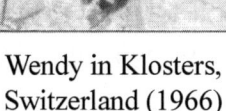

Whitney, Sterling, and Scott (Klosters)

I returned to Tacoma in January to obtain a line of credit to rezone and plat the valley. Our bank granted the line and agreed to loan the necessary funds to construct the valley road and three bridges over the South Fork of the Snoqualmie. The chairlifts, day lodge, and utilities (sewer, water, and power) would be constructed the following summer.

In February, King County approved the rezone and Alpental made the front page of every newspaper and aired on all TV channels.

Two months later, Bob called with wonderful news. "Jim, the Forest Service issued a temporary permit to cut trees."

"Fantastic! Does it include the ski runs, parking lots, and day lodge site?"

"Yes, all three, and Stan Olson said the full permit won't be far behind," Bob said.

"I wish we were with you to celebrate."

"We'll celebrate when you get home. And when might that be?"

"Early June. We're going to spend a couple of months at the beach and explore southern Spain and France. It's a family opportunity we may never have again, but if King County approves the preliminary plat, I'll come right home." The bank required lot sales contracts to collateralize the loan to build the road and bridges. After we hung up, I thought, *Timing will be critical.*

A few days later, Wendy and I flew south looking for a home on the ocean. We first visited Torremolinos on Spain's Costa del Sol.

When we entered the Pez Espada (swordfish) Hotel, where we were staying, we noticed some intriguing impressionistic paintings in the hotel's art gallery.

"Jim, while you check in, I'm going to take a look at the art."

"Okay, I'll get our bags to the room and come and find you."

Shortly after I rejoined Wendy, Gino Hollander, the artist (see Appendix) arrived. The gallery attendant, thinking we were friends of the Hollanders, called him while Wendy wandered through the gallery. Wendy grew up near the Mexican border, but her rudimentary Spanish had obviously been misinterpreted. Wearing riding boots, tattered blue jeans and a poncho, Gino appeared to have just come from the stable. With black hair over his collar, a dark weathered face, and a long-ago broken nose, he looked like a Spaniard, that is, until he spoke. He hadn't lost his New York accent. Though he stood only five-foot-eight, his larger than life demeanor and air of confidence permeated the room. We took an immediate liking to each other.

After a short history of why the Hollanders lived in Spain, Gino said, "Let's get your bags. You're staying with Barb and me." Wendy and I looked at each other in utter disbelief. A moment later, Wendy's eyes brightened, and I knew she was thinking,

What an opportunity to get to know the country. So after a token protest, we were on our way to Casa la Chopera, the Hollander home overlooking the Mediterranean. Over the next few days, we looked for a potential rental, visited the outdoor market to buy ingredients for Barbara's incredible meals prepared from scratch, took in the sights, swam in the ocean, and napped before touring expatriate bars where Gino sketched or played running games of chess, which sometimes lasted weeks. This was all in between Gino using Wendy as a model—painting her twenty-six times. We also spent two glorious days exploring Seville, where I witnessed my first bullfight—Wendy had seen bullfights while growing up in Arizona—and Gino sketched Wendy while we drank vinto tintos at the Hollanders' favorite haunts.

Gino Hollander in Torrmolinos, Spain

Wendy, Whitney and Dandy at Cap Ferrrat

After leaving Spain, we spent a few days recuperating at the Negresco Hotel in Nice before renting a four-bedroom home, perfect for our family and visiting friends, on Cap Ferrat, a peninsula in Villefrance, between Nice and Monaco. Each morning we'd walk to the bakery for fresh bread and the *Herald Tribune* and then spend afternoons building sand castles, swimming, and scuba diving in the Mediterranean.

One afternoon while I was diving with my brother Charlie, the j-ring, a rubber washer between my air tank and regulator, failed and the remaining air quickly left the tank. From our depth, I risked getting the bends if I ascended too quickly, so Charlie and I leisurely raised to the surface, taking turns breathing from his tank—another "more than luck" experience.

Evenings we visited local fish bars where I often ate Blue Point oysters on the half shell and Wendy bouillabaisse. Some nights I walked to the well-known Beaulieu casino, usually alone because Wendy didn't like to gamble. The other men wore white dinner jackets; the women, formal gowns and spectacular jewelry. I never lost more than fifty dollars, my limit, and sometimes won a few hundred. One evening I met the British actor and Academy Award-winner David Niven, who, in celebration of something or other, continued filling my glass from Champagne bottles, one in each hand, while never taking his arms from around the shoulders of two bejeweled young ladies.

Before leaving France, we spent a day at Pierre Van Laer's villa. After spending a romantic few months in 1932 with Wendy's mother in Paris, Pierre flew out to the *Ile de France* (see Appendix) to say good-bye and crashed his biplane in the Atlantic. It was fortunate that he was rescued before drowning because of the time involved; it took three miles to turn the ship around.

By the time we returned to Tacoma, Bob had resigned from Day's Tailored Wear, opened an Alpental office in Lakewood, and sought bids on the valley road and bridges. A few weeks later, we were desperate. King County still hadn't approved the plat, and snow could shut the valley down before Thanksgiving.

Finally, in mid-July, preliminary approval came. The following day, we sent out invitations for Warren Miller's movie. Receptions were held a day apart in Tacoma and Seattle. I'm certain few people came with intentions of buying, yet within two days, 80 of the 123 lots (40 hillside lots needed additional engineering) and nearly all 48 condominium units were reserved, most with backup offers. Lot prices ranged from $5,000 to $10,000 and condominiums from $11,000 to $30,000, with Alpental retaining ownership of the land under the condominiums and receiving an annual fee.

I took the lot-reservation agreements to the bank and obtained the additional line of credit to construct the road and bridges. However, lot sales couldn't be finalized until King County approved the final plat, and that couldn't happen until we constructed the road and bridges and put up a bond guaranteeing the installation of utilities. We worked from dawn to dusk, determined to finish before snow closed the valley.

To provide interim access for logging trucks, backhoes, and Caterpillars, we built a temporary bridge over the South Fork and a temporary road along the base of Denny Mountain. Unfortunately, installation of the bridges' footings to support the concrete T-beams, which held up the bridges' decks, discolored the river's crystal-clear water. County, state, and federal protection agencies were inundated by complaints from downstream residents and flooded Alpental with citations, which we ignored.

Me looking across river at temporary road.

In July, my brother Ted joined our partnership. We needed Ted's mechanical skills; he could fix or make anything. Bob and I each gave up 5 percent of our partnership interest so Ted could own 10 percent. Sully's partnership interest remained at 20 percent.

On August 4, Bob, Sully, Ted, and I met with Forest Service department heads to review locations for the day lodge, parking lots, chairlift towers, and Heidi Hut, a warming enclosure at the top of Chair One, named after Bob's daughter. All locations were approved. Sully's mountain crew immediately started cutting trees. Logs from the parking lots and day-lodge sites were picked up with artificial claws attached to flexible booms that truck drivers operated from platforms atop their cabs. Trees cut from the lift lines and ski slopes were left where they fell; the Forest Service would not allow motorized equipment on the mountain. They would be picked up by helicopter the following summer, in conjunction with installation of the ski lift towers.

A few days later, I met with Puget Sound Power and Light and Cascade Telephone. Both utility companies were prepared to install overhead lines, on poles, at no cost. However, Bob and I were adamant about protecting Denny Valley's pristine views, and we agreed to pay the additional cost to bury the lines.

By late August, surveyors had completed lot staking, and we notified reservation holders they had ten days to approve their lot choices or we would return their deposits, because we had backup offers. Only four of the eighty decided not to buy.

In October, the Forest Service issued a permit to remove pit-run gravel from the lower parking lot, which we used for the valley road sub grade, saving thousands of dollars by not having to haul rock from a commercial gravel pit.

I will never forget our dispute with the Forest Service about a stand of trees near the bottom of Edelweiss Bowl. We contended that skiers would have difficulty avoiding the trees, but the Forest Service wouldn't let us remove them. After the first snow, Bob and a ranger skied to the site where, as expected, the ranger crashed into the trees. When he regained his composure, he said, "Bob, cut down the damn trees." The incident was typical of our relationship with the Forest Service. It reminded me of grade-school show-and-tell.

In November, I met with the Kittitas County and Summit Sewer Commissioners. They were in the process of combining their systems and forming a new sewer district. It would be a huge financial burden if we had to build a sewer-treatment plant. After a heated debate, the commissioners voted to allow Alpental to join their district when completed the following year. That night, the Griffins and Mickelsons celebrated overcoming another hurdle.

Fortunately, snow didn't shut the valley down until Thanksgiving, giving us time to complete the road subgrade, bridges, and timber cutting. The twelve-hour days came to an end, but not the constant pressure and worry. We had only five months after the Christmas holidays to complete the engineering, prepare construction documents, bid out the work, and, most important, borrow or raise $1,650,000 to erect three chairlifts, build the day lodge, and install utilities. A savings bank had committed to making a condominium construction loan.

Alpental needed $320,000 immediately—$100,000 for architectural and engineering and $220,000 to bond completion of the sewer and water systems—to obtain final subdivision approval from King County. The bank agreed to increase our line if we pledged the hillside lots and got an additional loan guarantor.

Bob and I were not surprised at the bank's request. From the beginning we knew a financially strong partner would be necessary. Our first choice was Booth Gardner, stepson of Norton Clapp, a principal stockholder and president of the Weyerhaeuser Timber Company. Booth and I had been friends since childhood, and Booth had worked for Bob at Day's Tailored Wear after graduating from Harvard Business School.

In December 1966, Booth and I met in Boston, where Booth worked as assistant dean of Harvard Business School. Booth couldn't have been more excited about getting into the ski business and agreed to make a substantial investment and guarantee Alpental's bank loan. When I returned home with the good news, the Griffins and Mickelsons celebrated once again.

After the additional bank loan and Booth's investment, Alpental still needed $1,000,000 before summer construction, so we put together a stock offering. Unfortunately, we couldn't find anyone interested in investing in a ski area that didn't include revenue from lot and condominium sales and retail businesses. Our banker suggested I try to get a loan from an insurance company, but none were interested. Insurance companies didn't make loans to a start-up seasonal business.

By mid-May the snow was nearly gone, and contractors were

preparing to move into the valley. We were desperate. I went back to the bank and pleaded for additional funding, but we had reached the bank's lending limit. Our banker said he would try and find a correspondent bank to participate. I had my first good night's sleep in weeks.

In preparation for the summer's activity, Bob moved a trailer into the valley for a temporary office and a place to sleep when too tired to drive home. He began interviewing potential department heads for the ski school, professional ski patrol, volunteer ski patrol, ski shop, snow removal, maintenance crew, ski ticketing, volunteer ski patrol, first aid, chairlift operation, and a host of other positions, including a food-service contractor. The first department heads to commit were the ski school director and assistant director, two Sun Valley ski instructors who had been on the Swiss Olympic ski team. Also from Sun Valley, Bob hired the professional ski patrol director and assistant director.

While Bob interviewed, I worked out of Alpental's Lakewood office, to be close to the bank and accountants, pay bills, and be available for government agency conferences. We learned quickly there were fewer delays when Bob or I attended an agency review meeting.

By early June the last remnants of snow were gone, and rumors began circulating that Alpental had financial problems. When contractors threatened to pull out, we had to begin construction or declare bankruptcy. Booth, Bob, and I met and decided to move forward without a commitment for financing. It was a gutsy decision because on August 10, in just six weeks, contractors would expect their first payment.

Overnight Denny Valley became a beehive of activity. D-8 Cats, cranes, backhoes, and logging and cement trucks snaked their way in and out of the valley like a trail of ants. Work halted only when dynamite charges blasted rock from the roadbed or chairlift tower footings. Shutdowns were costly because our leased Sikorsky 58 helicopter, the Vietnam War workhorse, cost $10 a minute, whether it flew or sat on the ground. (Shortly after construction began, a private plane crashed into Guye Peak. The pilot was flying under the clouds, following US 10, and lost sight of the highway when it entered the snow tunnel. All occupants died on impact. It was a gruesome sight for our hill crew, the first to reach the plane.)

We hired a management consultant, John Beyer, to oversee construction. It did not take contractors long to discover he was an experienced engineer, and they began coming to him with cost and time-saving suggestions. Taking Beyer's recommendation, we hired one utility contractor to install all utilities, thereby avoiding contractor coordination problems.

Bob was not as lucky dealing with Forest Service personnel. They constantly cited Alpental for river discoloring, dynamite blasting, and timber cutting violations. Also bored teenagers kept Alpental's surveyors busy replacing road alignment and contour stakes. We installed a gate, at the valley entrance, and hired Wolf Daub, a Germanic, no-nonsense, King County deputy sheriff to patrol the valley. After Alpental opened, Wolf often stopped by our condominium in the evening and played chess with Scott and Sterling.

Fire season came early, and the consequences were disastrous. Alpental's Sikorsky and G-2 Bell helicopters were conscripted to fight fires. Worse, because of fire danger, the Forest Service substantially limited the number of workers on the mountain, forbid the use of dynamite, and prohibited any mechanical equipment on the slopes. We had no choice but to ignore the Forest Service's mandates. Under cover of darkness, Sully blasted footing holes for the chairlift towers. Surprisingly, the sheriff's department never investigated the nightly explosions. Bob and I assumed Wolf had intervened. We didn't ask because we didn't want to know.

After weeks of badgering, the Forest Service relented and let Alpental's crew back on the mountain. However, they required us to use electric Copco drills, rather than the more common gas drills, and electric caps, instead of lighted fuses.

Everything, dynamite, drills, rebar (steel rods to reinforce tower footings), even food and water—had to be hand-carried up the mountain.

A few days after the crew returned to the mountain, Puget Sound Trade Council, an association of unions, picketed Alpental. Our contractors were union shops, but the mountain crew was not. Bob and our attorney met with the Trade Council. They insisted we hire union personnel and provide eating and sleeping facilities on top of Denny. The first grievance went away when no union member would carry a hundred-pound load up the mountain. The second grievance became moot the night that Bob erected a tent; a bear smelled food and clawed through the tent as the workers slept.

As soon as we solved one problem, two others popped up. Bob and I were beginning to feel like Odysseus returning to Ithaca. The next bomb to drop, a phone call from Sully's foreman, Burl Pierotti, came when Bob was out of town at a national ski area meeting.

"Sully's missing," he said. "He hasn't been on the mountain since Friday."

"Is this the first time?" I asked.

"No."

"Do you know where he is?"

"I heard a rumor he's installing a T-bar [a type of ski lift] in Eastern Washington, near Twisp."

"I'll come right up," I said.

I was able to reach Bob before I left. "My God," Bob said. "Sully and I have been friends for years. Jim, you'll have to take over."

"I'm on my way." One hour and twenty minutes later, I drove into Alpental and parked next to the construction trailer, alongside

Sully's red Dodge pickup. As I got out of my car, the day-lodge foreman came out of the trailer onto the elevated porch. His eagerness to greet me indicated he knew why I was there. "Where's Sully?" I asked.

"On the mountain," he said. "Half hour ahead of you. What are you going to do?"

I didn't answer. I opened the car trunk and got out my hiking boots, canteen, and rain slicker. After lacing my boots, I headed for the temporary bridge spanning the South Fork of the Snoqualmie.

As I crossed the river, I saw framers constructing footing forms for the day lodge foundation. All hammering stopped when I passed. They recognized me but had never seen me on the hill. Bob and Sully were the visible partners. Every few hundred feet, I passed gray-streaked rock, the telltale sign of dynamite. An hour later, I reached the top of Chair One. Two crewmen were setting steel rebar in a lift tower footing hole.

"Sully around?" I asked.

"On top," they said, almost in unison.

I began climbing. Chair Two was shorter but steeper than Chair One. An hour and forty-five minutes after leaving the parking lot, I stopped under a rock overhang below the summit. I needed to catch my breath before confronting Sullivan.

Five minutes later, I topped the ridge and saw Sullivan, with bare-chest Popeye-muscles rippling, thrust a two-inch, thirty-pound steel maul into a granite fissure. As he pulled the maul out, he saw me. He couldn't hide his look of surprise.

"What's up?" he asked.

I gave my speech. I can't remember the exact words, but it went something like "I hear you're installing a T-bar near Twisp." When I got to the part about "our partnership has to end," I kept my eyes on the maul.

"I contracted to install the T-bar before joining Alpental. I thought I could handle both jobs. Obviously I can't." Without another word, Sully dropped the maul, put on his shirt, and started down the mountain. That was the last time I saw him. Sullivan's and our attorneys negotiated a buyout of his partnership interest.

I was now hill manager. I spent the rest of the day with Burl, checking tower locations and meeting with the hill crews. Time was critical; we couldn't afford to lose one day. We operated two shifts, one beginning at daylight, and the other at 1:00 p.m., ending just before dark.

The following morning, I arrived before sunrise, at 4:45, in time to accompany the crew up the mountain. It took only a few days of me carrying a load equal to that carried by crewmen for me to gain their respect.

Forty years later, Wendy still tells the story about my Mickey Mouse stenciled lunch pail. One night after falling asleep—I retired early because I left for Alpental at 3:30 a.m.—I awoke to Wendy's scream. Not knowing what to expect, I grabbed my baseball bat and ran to the kitchen, where the scream originated.

"Look," Wendy shrieked, pointing to my lunch pail lying on the floor. Two red-fused sticks of dynamite, exposed like Fourth of July Roman candles, lay alongside the open lunch pail. I thought, *She must have dropped the pail when she saw the dynamite.*

"It's a joke," I said, as I watched tears run down her cheeks.

"Some joke," she stammered. "We could have been killed."

"No, dynamite is harmless until the fuse is lighted. The crew is just playing a trick on me." It took half an hour, while holding her in my arms, to convince her that someone wasn't trying to kill me.

Good news came at the end of July. A correspondent bank

agreed to loan two thirds of the $1,000,000, with our bank taking the remaining one-third. That night we drank a fifth bottle of Champagne.

Alpental's borrowing now totaled nearly $2 million and required personal guarantees from all partners. As a 10 percent partner, Ted didn't want to be liable for the entire Alpental loan and asked us to buy him out. We did. Bob, Booth, and I were now equal partners.

In August, before King County would sign off on the completed sewer and water systems, which were public utilities, they had to be checked for leaks. County engineers inserted water, under pressure, into the sewer line. Aghast, we found water bubbling to the surface all along the line. When a backhoe dug down, county engineers found that the pipe had not been bedded in the required amount of sand to keep rocks from crushing the pipe during backfilling.

Sand was expensive; it had to be hauled from a gravel pit some distance away. It cost $200,000 to replace the pipe. Even though Alpental prevailed in a lawsuit the following year, the extra expense at the time was devastating. Fortunately, there were no leaks in the water line, which was installed in a separate trench on the opposite side of the road. Power and phone cables were laid together in a third trench alongside the water line.

Shortly after King County approved the water system, an insurance investigator came to check hydrant flows. The day lodge and condominium were nearing completion, and our insurance company wanted to make certain the hydrants were operational. When the investigator opened the valve, only a trickle of water came out. After a frustrating few minutes, Burl, happened by.

"What's going on, he asked?'

"There's no pressure," Bob said. "The line had plenty of pressure yesterday."

"Damn," Burl said. "I closed the reservoir gate valve to connect the river intake pipe and forgot to open it."

The investigator must not have believed Burl's story because a few days later the insurance company made a significant premium back-charge. Bob had to do some fast talking to get the hydrants retested and the surcharge reversed.

Bob Mickelson and me (fall 1967)

The Sikorsky and G-2 helicopters returned in September. I witnessed their first flights. It was surreal. While lumber, cement, and logging trucks darted in and out of the parking lot, the Sikorsky swooped down from above the trees, like a hawk after its prey, to a waiting truck, with a log dangling from a fifty-foot cable. Simultaneously, the G-2 lifted straight up from the parking lot, like a hot air balloon, ferrying a twirling bucket of cement toward a chairlift foundation footing. I shuddered as the helicopters crossed paths. *My God*, I thought, thinking of the disaster tangled lines would cause. Minutes later, the G-2 returned and hovered above the parking lot while crewmen held the oscillating bucket to receive cement churned out of the truck's spigot.

Then my gaze shifted back to the parking lot where the Sikorsky hovered, waiting for the ground crew to unhook the choker cable, which encircled a log like a hangman's noose. When the log was free, the Sikorsky lifted skyward while a giant claw, protruding from the self-loading truck, grabbed the log. Seconds later, the Sikorsky was back above the ski slope waiting for two men in yellow hard hats to wrestle a choker cable around another log.

The loop was broken only during refueling. The pilot set the Sikorsky down next to a fifty-gallon gas barrel. When the rotor quit turning, the pilot climbed out of the cockpit and stood on the landing skid. An attendant handed him a hose leading from the fuel drum. Before inserting the hose into the helicopter's tank, the pilot carefully wiped it clean with a rag from his pocket. If dirt clogged the fuel line, the engine would quit, and the helicopter would drop like a falling rock.

Time was running short, which was dramatized in an October 8 *Seattle Times* interview. "But the challenge now is man versus mountain and a December 2 target date. 'Opening-day ceremonies are set, and the deadline will be met,' Griffin said, surveying a scene of hundreds of uprooted trees, unfinished buildings and near-impassable roads."

Before the end of October, the sewer pump station, septic tank, and drain field were approved by all government agencies; a temporary solution until we connected to the sewer district being formed the following year.

After the Sikorsky cleared the slopes of trees cut over the summer, it began setting chairlift towers. Dropping a swinging tower over four bolts imbedded in concrete protruding from a two-foot-square steel plate equated to threading a needle in a windstorm. From the day lodge balcony, I watched two men struggling to position a tower. They wrestled with the gigantic steel tube until jerry-rigging it over a bolt, jutting out from one of the four holes in the tower base plate. Before they could screw a nut over the bolt, a wind gust caused the chopper to sway, raising the tower off the bolt. After a number of attempts, they managed to secure a nut on a bolt, and seconds later positioned the tower over the remaining three bolts.

Concrete on way to a lift tower footing

Chairlift tower erection (fall 1967)

Every day presented a new crisis. The latest was how to winch Chair Two's electric motor and gearbox up the hill. It was too heavy for the Sikorsky, which had a load limit of 3,500 pounds, and the Forest Service remained adamant: no motorized equipment on the mountain, which prevented our crew from towing anything up with a D-8 Cat. Totally frustrated, Bob went to the Forest Service office in North Bend to work out a solution with the assistant district ranger. As Bob explained the problem over lunch, a logger overhearing the conversation said, "That's no big deal. I bet you a fifth of whisky I can winch it up before the day is over." And he did. I didn't witness the winching, but Bob talked about it for days. We later found out the logger had learned his art during the construction of Crystal Mountain.

When the motor and gearbox were in place, the crew dragged a small diameter wire rope down the hill and attached it to the chairlift tower cable, which was wrapped, like a spool of thread, around a giant roller. As the electric motor pulled the cable off the spool and over the second tower, the pulley frame broke. As there were no welders in the valley, I called Ted. Two hours later, he was scrambling up the tower with a portable welder on his back and within minutes the crew was back pulling cable.

Crises always seemed to come in pairs. The following day, the wire rope, where it was attached to the cable, broke causing the cable to fall back off the carriage pulleys and fly down the mountain, leveling every small tree in its path. Two teenagers, who had ignored Alpental's "Danger, No Trespassing" signs were struck as the cable snaked its way down the hill. Medics took them to the hospital in North Bend. Fortunately, neither sustained serious injuries.

With ski season rapidly approaching, we arranged for our Swiss Olympian ski school directors to give a demonstration on an artificial grass ski ramp at the Seattle Ski Fair. The *Seattle Times,* Sunday addition, featured the demonstration and made Alpental a household word.

In early November, I nearly lost my life. I'd hitched a ride in the G-2 to the bottom of Internationale to verify that enough trees had been cut from the trail funneling skiers across the ridge to the top of Chair Three. If more trees needed to come out, it had to be done before the Sikorsky left the valley. As the G-2 descended to the ridge, a gust of wind blew it against the face of a cliff. I was standing on the landing skid preparing to step off when the rotor blade struck rock. As the rotor disintegrated, boomeranging off the rock wall, I dove to the ground beneath a rain of shrapnel and took cover behind a granite outcropping. The helicopter's rotor blades tore into the cliff causing a cloud of sparks, like a bomb in a Fourth of July fireworks display.

The rotor finally stopped spinning, and the air grew still. I heard raindrops bounce off my slicker. I stepped from behind the outcropping expecting to find the pilot cut to pieces. Surprisingly, he remained strapped in his seat with his hands firmly gripping the cyclic control lever. Bulbous veins protruded from his arms and neck. His eyes were expressionless. Pieces of the Plexiglas bubble, fuselage, tail section, and rotor lay scattered across the ridge.

"Are you hurt?" I asked. He didn't respond. *He's in shock,* I thought. I unbuckled his seat belt and helped him to the ground. He lay on his back, eyes expressionless. A few minutes later, the heavy breathing stopped and he sat up.

"I couldn't let go of the cyclic," he said. "I would have been disemboweled. I flew two tours in Korea and took some hits, but nothing like this."

As he spoke, I realized that my chest and arms were throbbing. I reached under my sweater and felt something sticky. My hand came away bloody. I slipped my rain jacket off and pulled up my sweater.

"My God!" the pilot exclaimed. "You're bleeding." I pulled off my jacket, sweater, and T-shirt, which I ripped apart and wrapped around my chest, thinking, *Had the shrapnel sliced an inch one way or the other, I might not have walked away.* The pilot, a licensed instructor, had been giving me flying lessons. A few more hours and I would have soloed. I never got in a helicopter again.

A few days before Thanksgiving, the Forest Service tested the chairlifts. I felt like a teenager before a final exam as I waited for the motor to engage. The chair began to move. It rounded the bull wheel. The attendant grabbed the chair to prevent it from swinging, and the assistant district ranger took his seat. The chair swung forward. Bob and I locked eyes. He smiled and raised his thumb, and it hit me that despite losing the helicopters for more than half the construction season, we had erected three chairlifts in one season, a feat never accomplished before.

The following week brought more bad news. The Washington State Liquor Control Board denied Alpental's application for a keg-beer license. According to the liquor inspector, our application had received numerous protests because keg-beer patrons often cause a rowdy atmosphere. The inspector suggested we reapply and ask for a bottled beer license.

When I informed Bob, he said, "I can't believe it; nobody seems to get what we are trying to create." We reapplied, and Bob and I made the presentation to the liquor board. We showed slides depicting the Tyrolean village *gemütlich* atmosphere that we intended to replicate. Before leaving, we invited the board to the opening ceremonies and of course mentioned that Governor Dan Evans, who had appointed most of them to the board, would be cutting the ribbon. The license was unanimously approved. As with other major milestones, the Griffins and Mickelsons celebrated that night with Champagne.

On December 6, twenty-four hours before opening ceremonies, a contractor accidentally severed the telephone line to the trailer office. Bob raced between the trailer, the day lodge, and Summit's public phone coordinating last-minute details; cell phones were still in the future.

Snow began falling as the sun dropped below the Cascades. Spotlights rigged to illuminate the uncompleted work refracted off the snowflakes like rays from a many-faceted diamond. Simultaneously, a crane set the lift operator's hut at the bottom of Chair One where carpenters waited to apply shingles; Alpental's electrician hung lights beneath the roof of the walking bridge; cement churned out from a truck's spigot at the base of the "Welcome to Alpental" sign at the valley entrance; an eighty-foot flagpole was being erected in front of the day lodge, a gift from Mary Lou and Wendy; electricians hung from the rafters attaching light fixtures in the bier stube (similar to a European ski area tavern); and cafeteria table-and-chair sections were passed hand to hand, like a fire brigade, from a delivery truck into the day lodge.

After unloading the truck, Alpental's furniture representative exclaimed, "I forgot the screws!" Workers who heard his outburst watched him dash across the walking bridge, jump into his truck and peel out of the parking lot, with rock and snow flying out from behind his tires. Forty minutes later, he called the lodge from North Bend.

"I've got the screws, but the pass is closed," he said. A snowstorm was raging.

Having worked three years under the shroud, *if something can go wrong, it will,* finding screws to assemble the dining room tables and chairs didn't even register on the crisis scale. Bob scrounged screws from ski bindings that hadn't been mounted on rental skis. Then he, the hill foreman, and others who weren't engaged in last-minute jobs assembled the furniture, while Mary Lou cleaned the restrooms. Bob and Mary Lou didn't finish washing windows until after midnight.

Seven hours later, as the sun peeked over Mount Snoqualmie, the road grader and snow plow headed for the barn. At 10 o'clock, the governor cut the ribbon as a crowd of friends, family, employees, Forest Service personnel, and government dignitaries watched. Then Mary Lou, Wendy, and Jean, Booth Gardner's wife, broke a bottle of Champagne on a chair pylon, after which everyone went into the day lodge to celebrate. There wasn't enough snow for skiing.

Two weeks later, with stumps still poking through the snow, Alpental opened (Tye Rice, a pro-patrolman, broke his leg when his ski caught a stump). Bob had a payroll to meet and couldn't wait any longer. Alpental had used up its bank line of credit.

The winter of 1967–68 was the worst snow year on record. Our consultants had estimated that 75,000 skiers would visit Alpental; only 10,000 came. Without an infusion of capital, we would have been bankrupt by April. Fortunately, Jack Galbraith, my partner in the fuel business, and two of his close friends (also our friends), Sam Brown and Tom Murphy, joined our partnership and put up enough capital to keep us operating.

The following ski season was equally devastating; too much snow. Some weekends we couldn't clear snow fast enough to keep the lifts operating or we had to turn cars and buses back because the snow was too deep to get them into the parking lots.

In 1977, after operating for ten years, Westours, an Alaskan tour bus company, offered to buy Alpental. All partners eagerly accepted. Being owners of a ski area had ceased being fun.

Bob and I agonized over what went wrong. We concluded we had convinced ourselves that Alpental's resort ambiance would motivate skiers frequenting the other Snoqualmie Summit ski areas to switch to Alpental. That did not happen because Alpental's very limited beginner and immediate terrain could not compete with their larger and better-groomed slopes. Also we had expected many Stevens Pass, Crystal Mountain, and White Pass advanced skiers to switch because Alpental had a similar vertical rise and a much shorter commute. That did not happen either. Advanced skiers preferred the lighter snow and fewer rainy days offered by the higher elevation ski areas.

In August 2005, forty years after conceiving Alpental, I had breakfast with my old friend Bob Mickelson, now in his eighties. He moved to Sun Valley shortly after we sold Alpental. I contacted him because I wanted to include his thoughts and memories in my memoir. "Bob, what comes to mind when you think about Alpental?" I asked, after we'd caught up on each other's children.

He chuckled, which accentuated his forehead's frown lines. He looked over my head and out the window, deep in thought. "I had to be up at four every morning to call in the weather report. It always seemed to be thirty-five degrees and raining. Oh, and the track came off the Tucker Snow Cat when your brother took it for a test drive after the opening ceremonies."

Then he lowered his head and looked into my eyes. "Jim, I will never forget watching Ed Holmes"—Alpental's pro-patrol director—"through the day-lodge window, ski down Chair One with a chain saw, slicing off the tops of fir trees that poked through the snow. And when Pat Bauman"—another pro-patrolman—"tried it, he cut off the end of his ski boot." Bob laughed. He was on a roll.

"Remember when Holmes and Bauman fired the Forest Service's 75-millimeter recoilless gun trying to knock cornices off the top of Edelweiss Bowl?" he chuckled. I began to laugh. I knew the story. "They misaligned the gun's sight and sailed the shell over the top of Denny Mountain," he said. "Only by the grace of God did it miss the freeway."

Continuing, Bob said, "Remember when Rhody Lee and Bill Dempsey were building their chalet and asked our dynamite crew to blast a hole for their wine cellar?"

I nodded. "A boulder from the explosion went through the roof of your trailer and landed on the bed's foam mattress," I said. Bob grinned. His smile spread from ear to ear.

"Which exploded, covering the entire inside of my trailer three inches deep with tiny white particles," he laughed. "Of course, it wasn't funny at the time. Jim, were you there when Rockefeller"—a chairlift crewman and later a pro-patrolman—"tangled his arm in the cement bucket's cable and was pulled fifty feet off the ground?"

"Yes!" I said, "Thank God he hung on."

"Oh, and my chalet caught fire. Frank Pattison installed a metal fireplace but forgot to insulate it. I went to sleep with a fire burning and woke up with the cabin full of smoke," he said.

"Speaking of the chalet," Bob said with a chuckle, "Burl Pierotti plowed the snowbank away from my front door, so I wouldn't have to crawl through a snow tunnel to get in. With the weight of the snow gone from one side of the cabin, the other side rose up like a teeter-totter. Until the spring thaw, I had to block up one end of my bed to keep from falling out."

Bob quit laughing and once again looked out the window. "One of my biggest rewards was the Alpenbees," he said. Bob had put kids to work building trails, like the CCC camps. (Grandchildren, during the great depression, President Roosevelt appointed Gibson Paine, your Grandmother Wendy's grandfather, to head the CCC.)

Then Bob's smile faded. "How our lives would have changed if Alpental had been selected to host the Winter Olympic Games," he said. I remembered how excited we had been when Alpental was selected as Washington State's representative at the Olympic selection committee meeting in New York in 1967. Had Alpental been chosen to host the Olympic Games, the Swiss Von Roll Company would have installed and financed aerial trams from the day lodge to the tops of Mount Snoqualmie and Guye Peak.

After three hours of reminiscing, Bob and I were emotionally drained. We shook hands and departed.

As I drove away, I thought, *Would I do it again?* It seemed like we had been in a maze for two years bumping into one blind alley after another. The heartaches, frustrations, disappointments, and unrelenting stress had taken a heavy toll on our families. But we had removed three million board feet of timber; built three miles of road; constructed three bridges; installed water, sewer, electrical, and phone systems; built parking lots for a thousand cars; developed 123 lots and constructed 150 condominiums; erected three chairlifts without motorized equipment; built a day lodge and a walking bridge; and raised $2,500,000, the equivalent of $18 million in 2010.

Yes, I would do it again, I thought. The experience led me to a successful forty-year career in land development.

(5) Cape buffalo Hunting: An African Safari

Forty-five years later, my heart still races when I look into the eyes of the Cape buffalo mounted in the entry of our home and remember the feel of those deadly horns.

From age sixteen, when I shot an antelope in Montana, I'd dreamed of going on an African safari. I'd grown up in a hunting environment; both my stepfather and godfather were avid hunters.

In September 1969, when I was thirty-two, my dream came true. Wendy and I went to the African Portuguese colony of Mozambique, on the Indian Ocean. Chico, a quintessential African safari white hunter, met us at the Beira airport. Chico stood just under six feet, had broad shoulders, curly black hair, and a sun-bronzed face.

The following morning we flew inland over the savanna to the base camp of our outfitters, Safarilandia, on the southern border of what was then Rhodesia (now Zimbabwe) near the Sabi River. Similar to the summer American western plains, the terrain was flat, arid, and covered with grass. As I looked down on a massive herd of wildebeests, I knew what early American pioneers must have experienced when they saw buffalo darken the prairie, like the shadow of a giant cloud.

Before landing, the pilot buzzed the dirt airstrip to chase off grazing impalas, and on the final approach we flew alongside a family of giraffes eating leaves high in the trees. A khaki-colored van and topless jeep that looked like relics of some desert war, waited at the end of the runway along with half a dozen Bantu natives.

When the pilot opened the cockpit door, desert heat engulfed us. "It's a sauna out there," Wendy gasped.

Safarilandia base camp, Wendy behind tip of right wing

"You'll be used to it soon enough," Chico said. Ten minutes later, he parked the jeep in front of a whitewashed mud-brick hut with a thatched roof. Seven similar cabins circled a central compound that Chico said contained a kitchen, dining area, and lounge. He carried our duffel bags inside the hut and dropped them on a bench across from a clothes pole with hangers. At one end of the room, a table and lamp separated twin beds. At the other end, a door opened into a bathroom with a toilet, sink, and shower. I flicked the light switch, but nothing happened.

"The generator comes on at dusk," Chico said, then added, "I'll see you in the dining room at noon. We'll sight in your guns this afternoon." I looked at my watch. It was 11:15. After Chico drove off, we changed from our sweat-drenched clothes into shorts and T-shirts.

The camp manager and his wife joined Wendy, me, and Chico for lunch at a large rectangular table. Others at lunch were a German father and son, who, like us, had just arrived; two Frenchmen stopping over between bush camps—hunters stayed at various camps depending on the animals being hunted; two jubilant Australians heading back to Beira with many trophies; and the other's white hunters.

The cook and waiters were Bantu. They stood barely five feet tall, with short black hair and dark brown skin, unlike Zulus, who were black-skinned and a foot taller.

After lunch and a siesta, Chico took me to sight in my guns, which could have been knocked out of alignment during four plane changes and numerous custom inspections. I brought a 7-millimeter telescoped Mauser for long distance shooting and a larger caliber .340mm open-sighted Weatherby for Cape buffalo and short-range brush shooting. Both guns' sights had to be adjusted.

Over cocktails, while watching the sun dip below the horizon, Chico asked, "What's number one on your trophy list, Jim?" A trophy is an animal with horns large enough for mounting.

"A Cape buffalo," I said.

Chico looked into my eyes as if measuring my resolve or maybe my courage. Frown lines deepened the creases in his weathered face. Then his smile returned, as if he had come to some conclusion. "I expected as much," he said. "But I must warn you, Cape buffalo are extremely dangerous. They rank right along with hippos and poisonous snakes at the top of the man killers." Then he said, "A few weeks ago a buffalo butted and flipped a Japanese movie-crew's jeep and then gored and trampled the occupants."

"Any survivors?" Wendy asked.

"No."

I looked at Wendy. Her face was ashen. I knew she was thinking it could happen to us. If Chico was trying to scare me, he had succeeded. Wendy and I drank another rum and Coke—a double—before joining the others for dinner.

After an early breakfast, we left for the first bush camp, nearly one hundred miles away. The tracker rode in front with Chico. Wendy and I sat in back, and the skinner stood on the jeep's rear platform, between a spare tire and two five-gallon gas cans. Bantu staff followed in a van with our luggage and supplies. There were no roads, only traces of tire tracks not erased by wind and sand. The dry season had come early, turning the grass and leaves golden brown.

The savanna had large patches of what looked like dwarf scrub oak and scattered umbrella-like acacia trees, with massive trunks that grew from ant and termite knolls. Periodically we passed a Bantu family compound. Their huts were made of two-inch-thick wooden poles arranged in circles and topped with grass.

Bantu native hut   Me with Bantu natives

When the sun was high in the sky, we stopped at a water hole. While the Bantus made preparations for lunch, Chico circled the water looking for animal snares. Within minutes he held up a camouflaged wire noose.

"I hardly ever stop at a water hole without finding a snare," he said. While disassembling the noose, he said, "Snares are illegal, but that doesn't keep the natives from using them."

"How about guns?" I asked.

"Mozambique is in the middle of a revolution," Chico said. "If a native is caught with a gun, he'll likely be shot on the spot. So far, there have only been isolated attacks against farmers." (Mozambique didn't win independence until 1975.)

Something else to worry about, I thought.

Two hours after leaving the water hole, I heard what sounded like a two-cycle gas engine and thought, *What's a motorcycle doing in the middle of the savanna?* A few seconds later, I smelled the intoxicating aroma of baking bread.

"It's the camp's generator," Chico said, answering my questioning look, "for lighting and refrigeration. Can you smell the bread?" he added. "The natives bake it in ground ovens."

As Chico directed us to our tent, I thought, *Hundreds of miles from civilization and we'd have ice in our cocktails tonight.*

"Chico, how does he heat the iron?" I asked, pointing to the young native ironing Levi's.

"They insert coals from the fire in the iron," Chico replied. "When we return from hunting tomorrow, the clothes you're wearing today will be washed and ironed, even your underpants."

Twin cots separating a miniature table just large enough for two glasses, a pitcher of water, a pan for washing, and an oil lamp, left little space in the tent for maneuvering. A bath and face towel lay neatly folded at the end of each cot, on sheets still warm from ironing. Netting hung over the tent openings to keep out mosquitoes and tsetse flies. A private privy and shower, made from reeds and thatched grass, sat on either side of the tent, the privy some fifty feet away because it attracted hyenas. While we unpacked, a boy poured water, heated over the cooking fire, into an elongated bucket that hung from a branch above the shower. Pulling a cord attached to the canister opened a spigot and sent hot water cascading down.

Shower, sleeping tent in background

Over twelve days, Wendy and I visited three nearly identical bush camps, except for terrain and vegetation. We were in the jeep by daybreak scouting for fresh tracks. Wendy didn't shoot; she enjoyed hunting birds but not animals. Unless we were too far from camp, we returned for lunch and a siesta, and then went out again in the late afternoon, after the temperature dropped. In early afternoon, animals stayed in wooded areas, in refuge from the hot sun.

I shot a trophy kudu, nyala, impala, water buck, reed buck, wildebeest, and sable. They were all old animals that had been driven from their herds by younger and stronger bucks, who through successful challenges had taken over the harems. Mostly, we found them in dense thickets, where lions and hyenas couldn't get at them.

Wendy and me with Greater Kudu

After skinning, the capes and skulls were stretched out on the hot sand so ants could remove any remaining flesh, and the sun could cure the hide. At the end of the safari, they would be shipped to Jonas Brothers Taxidermy in Seattle. No meat was wasted. What our camp couldn't use went to Bushmen, who mysteriously appeared whenever an animal was butchered.

We put many miles on the jeep scouting, but hadn't seen buffalo horns large enough for mounting. On one hunt, while checking for tracks at a water hole, we found leopard prints. While the natives built a brush blind, Chico took me to shoot an impala some distance out in the savanna so as not to frighten the leopard, if it was still in the area. Chico dragged the impala, in outward concentric circles, around the water hole where the leopard could pick up the scent. Then he hung the impala from the branches of a tree located between the water hole and blind. We returned late afternoon, before dusk. Chico hid the jeep well away from the water hole and then we waited motionless in the blind without bug spray—any movement or strange odor would have alerted the leopard. After a defenseless two hours exposed to marauding tsetse flies, there was no mistaking the horrifying sound of cracking bones.

Chico flipped on the spotlight, which he had hooked up to the jeep's spare battery, and I fired my open-sighted Mauser just as the leopard leapt from the tree—there would have been no time to get a sighting through the scope. I knew my aim was true when I heard what sounded like a hand slap, however the leopard landed on its feet and scrambled into the brush.

"I hit him."

"A gut shot," Chico said. "We'll come back at dawn. There's nothing more dangerous than a wounded leopard at night. Hopefully, the hyenas won't get to him first." The following morning, as the sun filled the sky, circling vultures led us to the leopard.

Wendy and me with leopard

A few days later, an incident occurred that alerted us to the possibility of becoming victims of Marxist guerrillas. It happened just after we left camp. Chico chambered a shell, which he always did prior to a hunt, and ashes filtered out of the chamber.

"My God!" Chico cried out. Then he sank into the jeep's seat, laid the gun across his knees, and bent forward from the waist, cupping his head in his hands. His breath grew short.

"What, what's wrong?" I asked.

He took a few moments to regain his composure and then said, "Someone's trying to kill me. My gun's barrel is packed with charcoal." He opened the breach and slapped the gun's stock. A handful of ash flittered to the Jeep's floor. "If I'd pulled the trigger, the breech would have blown up like a hand grenade. We both could have been killed."

"Why would someone want to kill you?" I asked. Chico treated the Bantus like animals, but I couldn't imagine someone trying to kill him. I looked at Wendy. Her suntanned face had turned white.

"One of the camp boys must be sympathetic to the guerrillas," he said, as he stared out across the savanna to the horizon.

When we returned to camp, Chico went to his tent and came back with a pistol for me and a shotgun for Wendy.

"Sleep with the guns within reach and loaded," he said. Wendy and I got no sleep that night and little sleep the remainder of the trip, though no more incidents occurred.

The next to the last evening before we were to depart, the tracker ran into camp screaming gibberish. He and Chico spoke for a few minutes, and then Chico translated, "He found fresh buffalo tracks, one set was gigantic, at the edge of that swamp we passed a couple of days ago. We can take a look in the morning if you want, but it'll be tough going. The swamp runs for miles and in many places is near impassable. We could be tracking for hours. The brush is so thick we may not see the buffalo until we are on top of them. You'll have to shoot quickly, because they'll charge or spook, and be gone in seconds."

"I'll let you know before we turn in," I said.

"You're not going, are you?" Wendy asked a few minutes later.

"It's my last chance to get a buffalo, and Chico wouldn't take me if he thought it too dangerous."

"Well, I'm not going!" she said.

That night, I dreamed a buffalo caught my scent and circled behind me. When I heard the sound of breaking branches, I turned and watched a giant albino come out of the brush and charge. I took aim and pulled the trigger, but there was no bullet in the chamber. I woke in a cold sweat as the buffalo picked me up on its horns. *Was the dream a warning*? I wondered.

We left at sunrise with plenty of food and water. I knew Wendy would be happy staying in camp, but she would worry. Minutes after we entered the swamp, my arms and legs were covered with scratches and welts. An hour later, we followed buffalo spoor out of the swamp into dense woods. Instantly monkeys, high in the trees, began howling.

"The buffalo slept here last night," Chico said. Then he told me that buffalo and monkeys often stayed together for mutual protection, because monkeys saw predators during the day and buffalo smelled them at night. He told me we would try and intercept the buffalo when they returned to the woods to get out of the sun, or when they went out to feed in late afternoon.

We followed their tracks back into the swamp for another hour, before coming out on the savanna some miles from the jeep. Seeing my confusion, Chico said, "They move in circles so they can smell predators no matter which way the wind is blowing."

We continued along the edge of the swamp until the Bantus stopped and began waving. "The wind has shifted. Now it's coming from behind us," Chico whispered. "We have to get downwind from them."

We reentered the swamp, perpendicular to the way we'd come. I followed directly behind Chico, as he soundlessly pulled aside stalks twice as high as pussy-willow stems and four times as thick.

Two hours later, the buffalo returned to the woods to get out of the sun. It was now midafternoon. The heat and humidity were oppressive. I lifted my canteen to my lips. It was empty. As the tracker made a short survey of the area, I wrung a few drops of moisture from my shirt, to wet my mouth, but it immediately turned to mud. Then the tracker trotted off into the brush. Chico jerked his head indicating for me to follow. I struggled after them.

They finally stopped in a grassy clearing of scattered trees adjoining the swamp. I was near exhaustion. I sat down and braced my back against a tree, watching Chico and the Bantus study the ground. After a few minutes, they huddled.

When they finished talking, Chico came to where I was sitting. "The buffalo fed here minutes ago," he said. "Their dung is still warm. We'll have to be quiet. Make certain you don't step on a branch."

I dragged myself to my feet and followed. We were nearly across the clearing when Chico pointed to a tree full of birds. "Tick birds," he whispered. "They ride on the buffalo and dig ticks out of the hair. We're close."

A moment later, all hell broke loose. Buffalo stampeded through the thicket ahead of us, leaving a trail of broken branches. Over the thunder of pounding hooves, I heard Chico shout. "Jim, off to your left! A trophy bull!"

I raised my .340 Weatherby and looked down the V-sight just as the largest bull disappeared behind a tree. Then I heard branches break behind me. I turned and felt a rush of adrenaline. A giant buffalo, with horns four feet across and as thick as my legs, bulldozed out of the woods thirty yards away. He stopped, lowered his head, and pawed the ground, creating a cloud of dust. Then he charged—just as in my nightmare.

"Shoot, for God's sake!" Chico shouted.

I fired. The bullet ricocheted off the bull's thick head cartilage, with the sound of breaking glass. As I chambered another round, I caught sight of Chico moving off to my right and the tracker and skinner scrambling up an acacia tree. The bull took no notice of them. I was its primary threat.

I fired again and heard a whop. The bullet struck flesh, but the buffalo didn't slow. I chambered a third shell and pulled the trigger. The bull tumbled to the ground, a few paces away. I breathed a sigh of relief, but, before I exhaled, he was up and coming straight for me.

I chambered my last shell, aimed at his exposed chest, and fired. The buffalo collapsed, spewing blood from its nose and mouth. Thinking the bull was dead, I moved forward.

"Get back!" Chico shouted. "He's not dead!"

Horrified, I watched the bull get back on his feet, two paces away. I was close enough to see the rage in its bloodshot eyes. In panic, I fumbled for a bullet from my shirt's web cartridge-holder. Too late! As the bull lowered his head to impale me, the image of a matador being gored in Seville flashed before my eyes. I dropped the gun and reached for the horns, hoping I could throw myself out of its path—as I had seen picadors do—and make a run for the acacia tree.

"Chico, shoot!" I screamed. As my hands touched the horns, the sound of Chico's .458 Winchester Magnum exploded in my ear, and then exploded again. The buffalo plummeted to the ground.

The next few moments were a blur. When I could finally speak, I hollered, "Chico, why did you wait so long to shoot?"

"I couldn't. The bull's horn was shielding its shoulder until he was perpendicular to me. If I had shot before the shoulder was exposed, the buffalo would have killed us both."

Me with Cape buffalo

Euphoria replaced terror. I had a trophy buffalo—which, in fact, turned out to be just short of making the record book. We took pictures before the sun dropped below the horizon, and then Chico went for the jeep. Dehydrated and physically and mentally exhausted, I lay on the ground—oblivious to the evening mosquitoes and tsetse flies—and watched the skinner, with a surgeon's skill, gut and skin the buffalo.

Chico returned as stars began to fill the cloudless sky. Then we left for camp, planning to retrieve the buffalo at first light. I couldn't stop wondering how Chico would have explained my death to Wendy.

At sunrise, after packing our duffels—a bush plane was coming for us at 11:00—Wendy and I went with Chico and the Bantus to pick up the buffalo. On the way back, Chico shouted, "Look out." He turned the jeep sharply to the right, flinging me violently against the roll bar, as the tracker and skinner leaped off the back. "Holy Mother of Christ!" Chico gasped. "That was close."

"What was close? What happened?" I asked.

After catching his breath, Chico said, "A green mamba snake.

It rose three feet out of the grass and would have struck you if I hadn't swerved and knocked it over."

"Go back! I didn't see it."

"No," Wendy shouted. Wendy was terrified of snakes.

As Chico circled to pick up the Bantus, he said, "Mambas are deadly, especially the green mamba. Two years ago one bit my partner. He died within minutes."

"How did it happen?" I gasped.

"The mamba came through the jeep's floorboard clutch plate and bit him in the ankle."

"Oh my God!" Wendy said, causing me to think how close I'd come to death once again.

"A Cape buffalo and a green mamba in consecutive days," Chico said. "You'll have a fascinating story to tell your grandchildren.

(6) Namu: The Killer Whale

In February 1962, my brother Ted sold his pet business and leased a warehouse at the end of Pier 56 on Seattle's Elliot Bay, intending to open an aquarium. After remodeling the warehouse, he and his friends from the "Mud Sharks" diving team collected specimens throughout Puget Sound. Four months later, June 22, 1962, during the Seattle World's Fair, Ted opened the Seattle Marine Aquarium.

A few weeks later he nearly lost his life in an underwater encounter. While making nightly rounds, before crossing the sound in his speedboat to his home on Bainbridge Island, he discovered that seawater had stopped circulating in the fish tanks. The pump was running but no water flowed, he got into his diving suit, strapped on an Aqua Lung, and followed the water intake pipe to a depth of about forty feet. Then he groped—visibility was less than two feet—for the intake pipe's protective grill to see if it was plugged. His remembrance of the terrifying next two minutes comes from his book *Namu: Quest for the Killer Whale*.

"Suddenly a mass of thick, suction-cupped tentacles grabbed my arm and held firm. From its strength, I judged the devilfish to be enormous. My struggling only made its grip tighter. I relaxed; the hold slackened. I jerked my arm, breaking free. Cautiously,

I reached ahead, toward the foot valve. I sensed him near again. In the darkness, I discovered one of his thick arms was snagged in the suction line. I drew my knife from its scabbard, and with several brisk, sawing hacks, cut through the tentacle, but the octopus wrapped his arms about my head. He climbed onto my back. I nearly panicked trying to avoid his poisonous beak. With both arms stretched overhead, I took a grip on his torso. It was massive; I could reach only part-way around. Still holding the knife, as a last resort, I pressed my fingers inside his gill openings and squeezed violently. The octopus's grip slackened a little, then a little more. When I no longer felt his encircling arms, I released the hold."

Ted fighting octopus under Pier 56, from *Namu: Quest for the Killer Whale* (Drawing by Paul Taylor)

Ted's fascination with killer whales started with a childhood interest in tropical fish. In 1944 when he was nine and I was eight, our grandmother gave us a bowl of guppies. For Ted, that was the beginning of a hobby and ultimately his career.

In 1945, when I joined Dad and Ted in Tacoma for the summer, Ted had moved to Tacoma the previous year and I stayed with my mother in Everett, I couldn't believe the number of buckets, large jars, wash tubs, and steel frame glass aquariums he had set up in the basement. I remember being fascinated watching a mother swordfish give birth while the daddy gobbled up the babies dropping from her womb.

By the time Ted entered high school; he was exploring the bottom of Gravelly Lake with a borrowed makeshift diving helmet, while I pedaled a bicycle, set in a frame, to power a pump that was getting air to him through a rubber hose. Later, when the Aqua Lung became commercially available, he carried air in a tank strapped to his back. I dove with him only once. A four-foot carp under water looked like a great white shark. Several years later, Ted learned welding from the truck repair foreman, Doyle Cox, at Griffin Fuel and was then able to fabricate his own fish tanks out of angle iron and used glass he found in building supply salvage yards.

Ted was athletic. He attended Colorado College, where he played ice hockey and participated in track and field. His hockey team won the 1955 National Championship—Ted started on the freshmen team in 1954 and played junior varsity in 1955. He also set pole vault records at many colleges where he competed and was Colorado College's decathlon champion.

Ted pole vaulting

The year following our father's unexpected death, Ted quit college and went to work at a fish hatchery, and later a pet store. By 1959, he was part owner of two pet stores and a fish tank manufacturing businesses.

In 1961, at age twenty-five, Ted married Joan Holloway. They lived in a rented cottage north of Seattle, at Richmond Beach on Puget Sound. Ted dove at every opportunity, searching for octopus and eels. His first encounter with a killer whale happened in a kelp bed in front of their house. Ted recounts, "The few seconds we stared at one another were to have a profound effect on my life." The World's Fair closed in the fall of 1962 and the aquarium's attendance dropped to a few visitors a day. Ted desperately needed publicity, so he and his "Mud Shark" diving buddies went looking for a record octopus. At the sewer outlet off Alki Point, at the south end of Seattle's Elliott Bay, they captured an eighty-four-pound monster, eleven and a half feet in diameter. The largest officially recorded octopus was only seventy-two pounds. Advertisement of a tag team match between the octopus and two "Mud Shark" divers brought record crowds.

Ted never gave up on his dream of capturing a killer whale. He read every whale book he could find, hoping to get a better understanding of what he was up against. Unfortunately, the books mostly contained legends or sketchy accounts of human confrontations. What he did learn, he shared with me: killer whales lived in all oceans, but frequent colder water where there is an abundant food supply and their preferred diet of salmon. They have a thick layer of insulating blubber that keeps their body temperature at 98 degrees Fahrenheit. Their skin serves as a cooling system so in warmer water their blood flow is redirected to the skin's surface, where excess heat discharges into the water. They don't spout water; the plume, which can be seen for miles, is water trapped over the blowhole that vaporizes when they expel their breath. The orca has the largest mammal brain next to man in proportion to body weight and dominates its environment, even though it is one of the smallest whales, less than twenty-eight feet in length and weighs a maximum of eighteen thousand pounds. Orcas can eat up to six hundred pounds of fish and small mammals a day.

Each sighting presented Ted another opportunity to study the whale's behavior. Ted writes, "I went out in my boat to be near them, watching for hours, trying to understand what they were about and imagining ways to capture one. People were learning about my efforts. A phone call from Portland, Oregon, offered me a chance to participate in a killer-whale-capture trip with a veterinarian, a gunsmith, and an entrepreneur who offered to pay most of the expenses."

At the next sighting, while the team made their way up from Portland, Ted went out in his twenty-three-foot open runabout, *"Pegasus,"* named after the flying horse from Greek mythology, to scout the whales. After locating the pod at the mouth of the Duwamish River in Seattle's Elliott Bay, he returned to the aquarium and picked up the team. When Ted couldn't get the *Pegasus* close enough for the gunsmith to fire the syringe dart, Ted called the Seattle Police Department and talked them into sending their helicopter.

Ted put it this way, "The helicopter climbed high above Puget Sound. Swooping like a hunting falcon, the chopper dropped out of the sky just as several whales rose to the surface. A red-tasseled dart flew to its target. To our great disappointment the muscle-relaxing drug had no apparent effect."

When Ted called me that night, he told me they eventually caught up with the mildly sedated whale, but while trying to get ropes around it, the whale's mate surfaced, swept its head against the dart, and dislodged it. Then the whales dove deep and they didn't see them again.

Several weeks later, they tried again and successfully harpooned a whale from a chartered G-2 Bell helicopter. They followed the red buoy, attached to the harpoon line, in the *Pegasus,* but each time the whale rose to breathe, two other whales surfaced, one on each side, deliberately screening the harpooned whale, preventing them from getting a shot with the syringe dart containing sedatives. Just before dark, the harpoon worked its way loose and pulled out.

Ted knew he wouldn't be able to keep the aquarium doors open much longer without media attention. He visited a number of marine aquariums to get ideas. After watching a California animal trainer, Homer Snow, entertain a large audience with a troupe of seals and sea lions, Ted talked the trainer into coming to work for him. A month later, with two sea lions, Gertrude and Gus, who Homer helped acquire and train, attendance increased.

Ted's continuing research on killer whales eventually led him to the US Fish and Wildlife Service, which loaned him a shoulder-fired, small-shafted, harpoon rifle. At the next whale sighting, in Clovis Passage at the north end of Vashon Island, Ted found three pods of whales. He knew from previous capture attempts that the whales would surface three times to breathe, at fifteen second intervals, before diving deep. In a leased helicopter—the police helicopter was only available that one time—the pilot positioned the G-2 over the whales as they came up the third time. Ted was ready. He had removed the door from the helicopter and dropped it off on the beach at Point Richmond. He said he leaned out, straining to the limit of his safety harness, and fired just as a pod bull broke the surface. The 1,000-yard buoy line attached to the harpoon immediately began uncoiling as the orca dove.

Ted describes it this way: "Absorbed in watching the giant orca, I forgot to pay attention to the buoy line … Suddenly the craft dropped sharply to starboard. The line was drum tight. The buoy was caught near my feet, too late to throw it out. The helicopter was falling from the sky; the diving whale was dragging us to our doom! I fumbled for my pocket-knife in near panic but couldn't reach it. *Twang!* The snagged buoy suddenly broke free and flew out the open copter door, disappearing underwater. Instantly Bob recovered the falling craft. When I could draw a breath, I glanced at Bob … The look in his eyes told me how close to death we had come."

Ted called the next day. I could hear disappointment in his voice as he told me what happened. He said it took fourteen minutes for the whales to reappear, and by the time they caught up with them in the *Pegasus*, just north of Gig Harbor, the tide had turned and the whales were running back north. He said the helicopter dropped him off on Vashon Island's south shore where one of his aquarium employees picked him up. As they followed the whales north, they rigged a canvas funnel, like an airport wind sock, and attached it to the buoy, hoping to tire the bull. When the sun dropped below the horizon, he attached a marker light to the buoy so they could follow the whale in the dark. Hours later, off Alki Point, the buoy quit submerging. At first, it appeared the whales had turned back south with the change of tide. However, when they began pulling in the slack nylon line, Ted knew the capture attempt was over. Hours of buoy drag had loosened the harpoon until it finally pulled out of the whale's blubber.

When I asked him about finances, he said, "We're okay at the moment." I didn't press, but I knew leasing a helicopter was costing a bloody fortune.

By mid-September, tourist traffic along the waterfront had dropped substantially, and Ted's neighbor, Harbor Tours, a significant catalyst of aquarium visitors, shut down for the winter. Ted couldn't close because his fish and animals had to be fed and cared for. It was two weeks before I heard from him again.

Ted recounts his financial distress: "On several occasions my brother had asked about the growing seriousness of my financial condition, but I was avoiding the issue. Finally Jim confronted me: 'Ted! You are in real trouble; any one of your creditors could force you into bankruptcy.' ... When I resisted his recommended restrictions on my free-wheeling style, he snapped, 'Do you think I take pleasure in this?' ... Jim's anger quickly turned into a smile. I felt a strong resentment for what I considered his interference and myself for getting into the predicament. I applied for a bank loan, which Jim guaranteed, then arranged a rent deferment, laid off most of the aquarium employees, and reluctantly promised I would curtail whale-capture attempts."

The following spring, 1964, Ted received a call from a fisherman who had rescued two Alaskan fur seal pups in Puget Sound. Ted told him to bring them to the aquarium.

"One look at the nearly dead sacks of flesh, fur, and bones in a garbage pail and I couldn't refuse. The babies quickly thawed under a twenty-four hour heat-lamp. After several weeks of good food and vitamins, they grew fat and sassy ... A photograph appeared in the *Seattle Times* newspaper of the 'father'—holding his 'twins.' The human-interest story of the orphaned fur seal pups brought an overwhelming number of aquarium visitors."

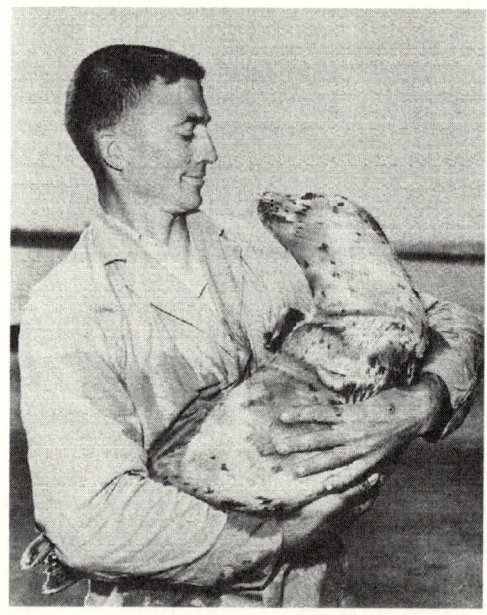

Ted with orphaned harbor fur seal, from Namu Inc. brochure (Seattle Times photo – Bruce Mc Kim)

Two weeks passed before I heard from him. "Did you see my picture in the *Seattle Times* this morning?" he asked. I hadn't, we only subscribed to the Tacoma *News Tribune*.

"No. What did you catch this time?"

"You're not going to believe it," he said.

He told me he had been baiting hooks with slabs of bacon and turkeys and throwing them off the end of the pier at night, hoping sharks might be hanging around the fish-processing plant on the adjoining pier. One morning he couldn't pull up the fish lines and assumed they were snagged on pilings. He and Dell Rossberg, his diving friend who had helped catch the record octopus, happened to have stopped by the aquarium. The two of them put on wet suits and Aqua-Lungs and followed the steel cables, hand-over-hand, down to the chain leaders.

The lines weren't snagged. Ted had hooked two sharks. He signaled Dell to wrap his legs around one of the shark's body and pull the snout back so Ted could pry out the hook without being bitten by the shark's multiple rows of teeth.

"How the hell could Dell hang on?" I interjected. "Aren't they slippery?"

"No, their skin is like sandpaper," he said. "I jumped on behind Dell and we rode the shark sixty feet to the surface."

"Why would the shark surface? I asked.

"Sharks have gills and have to keep moving to breathe. With Dell keeping the snout pulled back, the shark couldn't bite and spiraled right to the surface."

Ted wrestling a twelve-foot mud shark, from *Namu: Quest for the Killer Whale* (drawing by Paul Taylor)

"Oh my God, you're nuts," I said.

"Well, it was a little scary," he said. "By the time we got him secured, the pier was crawling with spectators and reporters, so we went back down and rode the other one up. You wouldn't believe how long the line is. People are waiting a half hour to get in."

Ted recounted that his press agent, Gary Boyker, gave the best explanation for the aquarium's visitors' fascination with sharks: "'Something in all of us shudders and screams at the mention of sharks; they're sinister and dangerous,' he suggested. However, 'greater than a fear of the beast is the curiosity of it.' This was borne out by the visitors' reactions. Fear both attracted and repelled them, but once near the creature, fear faded, and their interest and questions were endless."

Keeping the sharks alive was more difficult them catching them. When they quit eating, Ted force-fed them with herring and mackerel. Unfortunately, they didn't live long.

In October, I read that the Vancouver Public Aquarium had harpooned a killer whale. I called Ted to find out what he knew.

"Joan and I just got back from visiting the whale. We went up in the *Pegasus*," he said, then added, "We got caught in the act."

Here's Ted's description of the episode; "A fin broke the surface of the muddy water. A fifteen-foot killer whale drew a shallow breath and sank out of sight. To get closer, I climbed down to a small float inside the enclosure; the whale circled … The whale looked gaunt, skin pocked without a sheen, its movement lethargic. Though I couldn't see the eyes, I sensed they were lifeless. In light of the whale's traumatic capture, it was pure folly to have expected anything else.

"From a distance, I recognized the director of the Vancouver Public Aquarium. 'You're doing a naughty thing,' he began … but of course I never expected the unauthorized visit to merit a warm reception. I realized he probably felt as possessive of his whale as I would have. Joan and I departed … Unfortunately

Moby Doll succumbed to her injuries and died the following month ... Though Moby Doll lived but a short time in captivity and was never on display in the Vancouver Aquarium, she nevertheless created considerable interest in whales ..."

All winter long Ted hung out near the phone waiting for a whale sighting. Then late one June evening in 1965 he got a call at home.

"May I speak with Ted Griffin, please?"

"Speaking."

"Are you the fellow who owns the aquarium?"

"Yes."

"My name is Walter Piatocka. I have two killer whales for sale."

"*Killer whales!* Are you sure?"

"No doubt about it."

"Alive? Where? How have you got them? I mean, how are you holding them?"

"In nets."

"*In nets?* Are they tangled? They must be injured."

"No. They're perfectly all right."

"Where are they?"

"In Warrior Cove, near a little cannery town north of Vancouver Island. Do you know Port Hardy?"

"Yes—yes."

"It's about seventy-five miles north of there."

"That's five hundred miles from here. How do I drive there?"

"You can't. Boat or plane."

"What are you asking for the whales?"

"Come up and make an offer, but you better come quick or they will be sold to someone else." *Click ...*

Ted carries on the tale: "I was numb. Finally, whales, but in a foreign country. At any moment they could escape, die, be sold to someone else: *Marineland? Vancouver Aquarium? The Portland group? They all have money, manpower, expertise.* Joan interrupted my thoughts, 'Ted, how would you get two whales back to Seattle?'

"'I don't know, but I have to go, at least see them. There might even be a way to buy them.'

"'Where will you get the money?'

"'Maybe I can pay the fisherman when I get the whales home, earn the money from putting them on display.'"

Ted called the next morning. He told me two killer whales were trapped in gill nets two miles south of the cannery village of Namu, British Columbia, on the mainland north of Vancouver Island. When I started to ask questions, he said he wouldn't have any answers until he flew to Namu and assessed the situation. He said he just wanted me to be thinking about how he could finance the acquisition of a killer whale.

"I've got to go," he said. "I'll call you when I know something."

Ted called that evening. "Where are you?" I asked.

"Home."

"What happened?"

He didn't stop talking for five minutes and when he hesitated, I knew he was wiping away tears. He told me on his way out to see the whales in the gillnetter's boat, the fisherman asked him how much cash he had. When he said none, but would give them a letter of credit, they turned the boat around and took him back to the wharf. They told him Vancouver Aquarium and Marineland were coming with cash. Before he boarded the floatplane home, Ted said he gave his business card to one of the fisherman and told him to call if a sale didn't work out.

"How did the whales get caught?" I asked.

"William Lechkobit, a Canadian fisherman, snagged his net on a reef near where a pod of killer whales was feeding," he said. "The next morning his friend and fellow fisherman, Robert McGarvey, happened by and saw the trapped whales and put his net around the reef. Then another gillnetter, Walter Piatocka, came by and put a third net around the reef."

I didn't hear from Ted for three days. When he called, I could hear excitement in his voice.

"Jim, I made a deal for the Canadian whale," he said. "I've got to get to the cannery by midnight tomorrow with eight thousand in cash, or they're going to let it go."

"What happened to Marineland and the Vancouver Aquarium?" I asked.

"Marineland couldn't figure out how to get the whale to California"—the young whale had escaped—"and Vancouver Aquarium wanted the whale delivered. I offered them $3,000 for their three nets and $5,000 for their lost fishing time, and they went for it."

Sunday morning, Ted cleaned out his cash register and safe, collected the rest of the eight thousand from neighboring businesses (who loaned him money because they would benefit immensely from the publicity), and flew to Namu. Later I learned he had one more hurdle to overcome. After arriving at the cannery, he went directly to where the gillnetters were moored and shouted, "McGarvey?"

"Yeah, come on board. Got the eight thousand?"

"Yes; you still have the whale?"

"That whale's not going anywhere until I say so, but he's not yours yet. Sit down. Some other people want to buy the whale. Maybe I don't know if you're the right guy to have it. Put your hand up here. If you can take me arm wrestling, I'll sell you the whale."

The following is Ted's description of what happened: "The fisherman's hand was rough; his fingers strong. They gripped mine like a vise. The muscles in his stocky forearm bulged as he increased the pressure. Why was he challenging me? If I lost, would he really refuse to sell me the whale? It seemed like a bluff, an after-midnight game of cat and mouse. But I couldn't afford to lose. *I won't lose.* Straining, I watched his eyes. Was he getting tired? My whole body ached. Believing he had reached his limit, I visualized the great bull orca, summoned every ounce of strength, and pressed the back of his hand to the table.

"'You have more under the hood than I would have thought, Griffin. You get the whale.'"

But it wasn't over. Ted wrote: "A few minutes later in the cannery lobby I heard someone say, 'No, they're not here. They turned in for the night.' Two men hovered near the wireless telephone conferring about an expected whale counteroffer from the Canadian fishermen's union. It was rumored they wanted to keep the whale in Canada. How ironic; before last week they were killing the whales, as competitors. I took Homer aside"—Ted had rehired Homer Snow, his animal trainer, after the capture of the sharks. "'You get on the phone. Tie up the line, fiddle around; do whatever is necessary. No calls can be allowed through tonight … You get my drift?'

"Homer's eyes twinkled, 'Don't worry. I'll take care of it.'

"Randy the guard and one of the fishermen counted the money. As if from far away, I heard someone say, 'It's all here, eight thousand.' At long last, I had my leviathan, a killer whale never before tamed, with a bloodline twenty-five million years long."

When Ted got back to Seattle, he told me he left Homer and Don Goldsberry, his friend from Tacoma's Point Defiance Aquarium, at the cannery to take care of the whale. He said he called Marineland to see if they had any ideas how to transport a whale, and they said, "If we knew the answer to that one, we'd have bought the whale."

Biologists at the US Marine Mammal Laboratory told Ted he couldn't use a sling because the weight of the whale would cause its lungs to collapse, which a year later, Ted proved wrong. He said he had decided to build a cage and tow the whale to Seattle. He figured it would cost about $60,000 and wanted to know if I would help him get commitments from the neighboring businesses. I told him I would and suggested he try and secure insurance so he could repay the loans if the whale died. He thought that was a great idea and asked me if I would get the insurance because he would be busy building the floating pen.

A few days later in London, where Wendy and I had gone to try and get Lloyds to insure the whale, we learned from a newspaper article that Ted leased a DC-3 cargo plane and flew a load of structural steel to Port Hardy where it would be shipped to the cannery to build a pen to tow Namu to Seattle— Ted had named the whale after the cannery village. What the article didn't say, because the reporter didn't know, was the pilot landed at an unmanned airstrip near Port Hardy. After unloading four tons of steel rods, the pilot immediately took off to avoid RCMP or Canadian customs officers.

Ted walked out to the highway and flagged down a truck. The trucker gleefully accepted a fistful of Benjamin Franklin bills and accompanied Ted back to the airstrip. After loading the steel in the truck, they drove to the dock in time to catch the weekly departure of the northbound costal freighter. According to the article, when Ted tried to launch the forty-foot by sixty-foot by twenty-foot high pen, supported by fourty-one fuel drums, with two forklifts at one end and an A-frame boom at the other end, it collapsed like limp spaghetti. After making the necessary repairs, he and the two hundred or so spectators picked up the pen, carried it to the end of the pier, and dropped it in the water.

Ted writes, "'Hey, look at that, it floats!' they cheered, and I felt a tightness in my chest. The pen worked just the way I planned, yet in the water it suddenly seemed too small. I was more anxious than before."

Ted called from Port Hardy. "Did you get the insurance?" he asked.

"Yes! Lloyds jumped on the publicity opportunity. Your adventure is running in all the European papers."

"My God, who would have thought ... How much did they write?" Ted asked.

"I tried for $100,000, but Lloyds would only go the $60,000 you estimated to bring Namu to Seattle," I said. "I paid the $5,000 premium. We'll work that out later. Oh, and I made a tour of the waterfront merchants and got all of them to sign a commitment to pay a portion of the $60,000."

Ted describes my actions: "I was reminded of the Dutch boy who plugged the hole in the dike; Jim certainly had plugged the holes in my finances. My nature was to take incredible risks if the potential reward was great enough ... Not so with Jim. He'd get just as excited as anyone about a new undertaking; then he had the remarkable ability to step back and take a hard look. If he decided the deal was okay, my brother would go for it, but hedge his bet and place a limit on his exposure."

"Jim, I'm stuck in Port Hardy until we get a tow. The fishing boats are all working. Any chance you could get your buddy Drew Foss to send a tug?" The Foss family owned Foss Tug and Barge (now Foss Maritime Co).

"I'll give him a call. How'd you get the whale in the pen and then over to Port Hardy?" I asked.

He told me Bob Hardwick, a Seattle radio talk show host, brought his thirty-foot boat, a replica of a New York harbor tug, up from Seattle and offered to tow Namu back to Seattle while broadcasting his show. With Hardwick were two reporters from the *Seattle Times* and Ted's PR guy, Gary Boyker. He said when Hardwick's boat struggled to tow the pen to Warrior Cove; he knew the boat would never make it to Port Hardy, let alone Seattle.

"I used up another of the cat's nine lives when I cut the nets we stitched to the open end of the pen," he said.

"What happened?"

Ted writes it this way, "I sliced my way to the bottom, taut cords parting like butter with the touch of a razor-sharp knife blade. When the opening was almost complete, I felt a sudden chill, then ropes and nets fell on me. They had started too soon! Must have thought I was clear. They were sinking the cork line with heavy weights. I'll drown! The strong current tugged at the nets, ensnaring me. I struggled but the tank held firm. Clamping my teeth on the mouthpiece, I slowly wriggled out of the air-tank harness. By slashing the nets, I finally worked my way free."

Continuing, Ted told me they drew the circle of net tighter and tighter, like a funnel, until Namu could only move forward into the pen.

"I held my breath," Ted said in his book. "Compressed with each moment was the fear of tragedy, the hope for success, and a vision reaching to the end of my life. Please whale, find your way.

"Grim faces broke into uncontrollable joy. The watercraft rooting section raised a cheer, ringing the ship's bells, blowing their whistles and horns. It was a celebration of victory, and more, a salute to the whale, who for now had acquiesced, and entered into a human world."

Maneuvering Namu from nets into pen, from *Namu, The Happy Whale Coloring Book*, produced by Ann and Loren French for Namu, Inc. (*Seattle Times* photo - Bruce McKim)

"Then what?" I asked.

"Hardwick towed the pen back to the cannery, and the next day, I got one of the fishing boats to tow it across to Port Hardy. If we hadn't tied logs under the fifty-gallon drums and constructed a log A-frame in front, the pen would have broken up in Queen Charlotte Sound's ten-foot waves." Then he added, "Namu's cow and calves trailed the pen all the way."

"How'd that make you feel?"

"I don't want to think about it."

While I lined up a tug and called on the merchants, Ted and Don worked day and night in Port Hardy repairing the pen, which had sustained considerable damage crossing Queen Charlotte Sound. They replaced and welded many steel supports, and underwater where they couldn't weld, they tied the pen together with chain and rope. Some of the most dangerous water on the Pacific Coast lay ahead, the narrow channels of Johnstone Strait, the whirlpools of Seymour Narrows, and open stretches off the Georgia Strait.

Then another crisis arose. Namu's publicity had stirred up animal protection societies, who were demanding the whale's release. Ted heard that a private detective had been hired to free the whale. He had to hire a security firm to provide twenty-four-hour protection.

When the tug, *Iver Foss,* showed up, Ted reluctantly agreed to fly back to Seattle and have medical treatment on his infected leg, which had been gouged by one of the pen's steel rods. He returned to the expedition just after a lone bull killer whale tried to run off with Namu's family. Hardwick, in the escort boat, which housed the flotilla's crew, threw Fourth of July cherry bombs at Namu's rival to keep him away.

Leaving Port Angeles with Namu in tow
(Seattle Times photo – Bruce McKim)

When Ted returned to Seattle to make preparations for exhibiting the whale, he described the crossing of Seymour Narrows, between Vancouver Island and Quadra Island in

British Columbia, as the most frightening two hours he ever spent in a boat. He said it was like navigating a raging river. Had Namu not kept moving, he would have been beaten to a pulp against the steel rods. The pen sustained considerable damage, and he sent a diving buddy with a barrel of chain in a floatplane to help Goldsberry repair the damage.

On July 24, sixteen days after leaving the cannery, the flotilla reached Friday Harbor on San Juan Island, where hundreds of well-wishers on the dock and in boats greeted Namu. Ted flew in from Seattle to facilitate clearing Immigration and US Customs and dealing with a government threat to impose a duty on Namu. Though a duty was not levied, Ted later had to pay a state sales tax. (Before Namu left Friday Harbor, Ted received notice from the Department of Fisheries that it was illegal to feed fish that were suitable for human consumption to a whale. Fish were Namu's main diet.)

Following is Ted's description of the flotilla arriving in Seattle: "One mile across Elliott Bay the collection of pleasure craft and commercial boats turned toward Seattle ... Aircraft circled in the cerulean blue sky ... When the whale's pen neared the aquarium, the large tug, *Iver Foss*, released the tow, handing the line over to the escort tug, *Robert E. Lee*. While the band played a rousing melody, Hardwick's jubilant crew eased Namu's pen into the mooring area at Pier 56 ... A flood of tears blurred my eyes. 'This is the greatest moment of my life,' I said, choked with emotion, and found it nearly impossible to speak any more to the assembled dignitaries." They had presented Ted with a commemorative "key to the city."

After barely keeping the aquarium's door open for three years, Ted had to hire another ticket taker. Within a few days of having Namu on display, Ted paid back the money he had borrowed to buy Namu, and he expected to pay all trip expenses before the end of summer. But his problems weren't over.

"Jim, do you have any political muscle?" Ted asked over the

phone. "Namu's losing weight because he won't eat scrap fish, and the State Patrol is watching me like a hawk."

"Maybe," I said. "I've met Senator Magnuson [US Senator Warren Magnuson] a couple of times. I'll see what I can do."

I called Magnuson's office in Washington DC and after a short explanation to a staff member, Magnuson came on the line. I suspect the publicity was irresistible, because he sounded very optimistic about getting a waiver based on Namu's importance to Washington's tourism. An amendment was tacked on an appropriations bill that President Lyndon Johnson couldn't veto. Following my notification of the waiver, I stopped by the aquarium with two fresh salmon I'd picked up at Johnny's Fish Market.

Ted's description of my visit follows: "A few days later, my brother came with friends to visit the whale. 'How's your appetite, Namu?' Jim asked. He removed his suit coat, rolled up his shirt-sleeves, and descended the ladder. 'Come on, Namu, this is fresh caught, not that ole junk Ted is trying to feed you...' Jim casually splashed the fish ... then held it beneath the surface. Namu swam toward him and, without hesitation, took the salmon. That's the first time I'd actually seen Namu swallow a fish. Do you have any more? Jim offered the expectant animal a second, firm, fresh fish.

"I'm glad you got him to eat, but you just broke the law," I remember Ted saying. "Are you on good terms with the highway patrol?"

"Not to worry," I said. "Congress attached a rider to an appropriations bill exempting Namu from existing law." I can't remember Ted's response, but it was something like, "You amaze me!"

After Namu started eating, he became frisky, and Ted figured it might be time to try and interact with Namu. He put a dinghy in the pen, and when Namu didn't tip it over; he climbed into the dinghy with a long pole brush and began scrubbing Namu the way he had seen Marineland's trainer scrub dolphins. Namu liked it so much he rolled over on his back and let Ted scrub his stomach. The aquarium visitors loved it.

Ted realized he couldn't continue to manage the aquarium, keep the books, and put on an hourly Namu dinghy show. He called Don Goldsberry, who was back working at the Tacoma Aquarium, and talked Don into coming to work for him.

With Don looking after the aquarium, Ted had more time to spend with the scientific community. Calls came in from all over the country. Boeing sent a research vessel to record Namu's vocalizations. Their scientists wanted to understand the range and accuracy of Namu's sonar. Dr. Tom Poulter, director of Biological Sonar Research at Stanford Research Institute, compared Namu's voice recordings with those of Ted's and concluded that Namu was trying to match Ted's underwater sounds. Dr. Merrill Spencer, director of Virginia Mason Research Center in Seattle, studied Namu's breath-holding ability, believing it could have significant medical benefits for humans.

Other studies indicated that cetaceans' cardiovascular systems reduce blood flow to nonessential extremities when necessary and that marine mammals utilized four times the amount of oxygen from each breath as humans. A 1962 US Government publication, stating killer whales would attack and kill any human in the water, caused the Navy's Department of Antisubmarine Warfare to ask Ted to visit the Pentagon. Ted's theory that the orca had potential to transport people and equipment long distances led the Navy, in 1968, to purchase two whales from Ted—who by this time had perfected a method to capture them.

On one of my weekly visits, Ted asked if I thought the producer of the *Flipper* TV series might be interested in producing a killer whale movie. Ted was a fan of *Flipper* and watched it regularly to get ideas for his seal and sea lion shows. I told him I had no idea, but I would find out. I called my friend Jerry Zeitman, a

Hollywood documentary filmmaker whom Wendy and I had met while vacationing in Hawaii. Jerry knew the show's producer, Ivan Tors, and put us together.

Ted's account of meeting Ivan Tors in August 1965 follows: "A light breeze swept clean the morning air. Sparkles of sunlight danced across Elliott Bay, converging on Namu. My brother appeared, escorting two men along the public walkway overlooking the whale. I greeted them, 'Hello, Jim, Ivan, Lamar [Boren, Ivan's cameraman].'

"'Good morning Ted, how's Namu today?' inquired Ivan.

"'Fine! Why don't you go down and visit him?'

"Ivan Tors [and] Lamar Boren ... descended the ladder to the whale pen. When they were out of earshot, Jim said, 'They went for it, Ted! We have a deal to make a feature motion picture. They want to start right away, filming in a natural setting. I told them you want to exhibit the whale at the aquarium until the end of the summer tourist season. Oh, one more thing, they insist you swim with the killer whale. They have to show it to the film's backers; otherwise it's no deal.'

"'Sure, Jim,' I gulped, not ready to go in with Namu. 'Maybe in a few weeks.' I shrugged and walked away. Just over a month had passed since Namu arrived in Seattle, yet I didn't feel secure with him ... The movie people returned up the ladder ... I was surprised to see Jim sitting inside the pen dressed in a wet suit, dangling his feet in the water. Namu showed little interest, so my brother slipped in the water. What the devil was Jim doing? Namu circled the pen, eyeing him."

"'Hey, Ted, you sure this is a killer whale?' Jim hollered.

"Darn, my brother was baiting me. I was unprepared but had to make a move. When I joined him in the pool corner he climbed out without a word, the smirk on his face remarkably revealing. I approached Namu with the usual long-handled brush. He allowed me to scrub him, taking no particular notice I was in the water instead of the boat.

"Lamar descended the ladder dressed in a black wet suit. Underwater with his huge camera positioned like a shield, the cinematographer motioned me toward the animal. I swam around Namu in wide circles, finally approaching with brush extended. This time the whale was more accepting, allowing the familiar grooming ... I reached for his dorsal; the tall fin trembled as my fingers gripped tightly over the edge. Namu jumped forward; pulling free of my grasp ... I grabbed his fin again. Instantly the orca surged ahead, dragging me. Mask and snorkel were stripped away ... I gathered the courage to try again. Holding my mask in place, I grabbed his dorsal fin; Namu bolted! Teeth clenched, I hung on with all my strength ... The orca dropped his head and raised his back high above water. I spiraled forward; bucked off again ... I swam to Lamar's corner and saw the excited look in his eyes.

"'You sure have your hands full with that whale. Great footage! How about keeping Namu occupied while I climb out?'"

Scott Griffin, Ivan Tors, and Sterling Griffin, August 1965

Ted called a few days later. He was ecstatic. He said Tors called to tell him United Artists agreed to back the whale movie. Tors offered him $50,000 for movie rights, agreed to cover all whale maintenance expenses, and pay him to be the technical adviser.

Ted and Lamar immediately began searching the lower Puget Sound until they found Rich Cove, a clear-water lagoon near Bremerton, Washington, where strong tidal action would keep the water clean and clear for filming. Then Ted and Don blocked the mouth of the cove with a war surplus Navy cable-ring anti-torpedo net. When Ted towed Namu to Rich Cove, Namu shot out of the pen and happily raced away with a series of flips, before exploring his greatly enlarged new home.

Ted called after the first day of filming. He said he walked into the Sound from shore waist deep, put his face under water, and called Namu with a series of "Eeee, urrh, eh, eeee-urrh-eh" sounds. Namu came to Ted and grounded himself a few feet away. Ted said he moved out to Namu and began stroking him. Then, watched by a growing group of spectators that somehow slipped past the guard, he grabbed Namu's dorsal fin and slowly raised his knees until he could swing his leg over the whale's back. He said he couldn't believe it when Namu backed off the bottom and swam to the middle of the lagoon. Lamar got the entire episode on film.

Ted's description: "On sunny days the crew filmed Namu swimming left, swimming right, swimming upside down, and from every angle in the lagoon. On especially bright days, Lamar worked underwater. As the filming progressed with the actors"—the film starred Robert Lansing and Lee Meriwether—"at Friday Harbor, they sent requests for specific action takes. I generally doubled for the male lead in scenes with the whale. Ever since that first time in the cove, Namu had readily accepted me as a rider."

Ted scrubbing Namu, from *Namu: Quest for the Killer Whale*

When I next heard from Ted, he said, "Ivan Tors exercised his option to film a whale capture."

"That's great, but you've been trying for three years. What makes you think you can do it now?"

"I'm going use a purse seiner and net a whale in shallow water, similar to what happened to Namu."

"How are you going to get a whale into shallow water?" I asked.

"If we can heard a pod bull into a cove with outboards, the cows will follow."

"Let me know when you're on a pod. Wendy and I would like to watch."

"Will do," Ted said.

Two weeks later, in mid-October, Ted phoned from Gig Harbor. After receiving a call that whales had been sighted near Blake Island, south of Bainbridge Island, he and Don Goldsberry flew out to the pod in a charted Cessna 180 floatplane.

I didn't hear from him for three days. When he called, he said the whales disappeared. He was frustrated and exhausted, having kept a twenty-four-hour watch in the *Pegasus* under the narrows bridge while Don searched the sound in the floatplane.

When I next heard from him, he said he'd seen it all. A decoy cow led him on a merry chase away from the pod, near Tacoma's Point Defiance, to the town of Ollala, in Clovis Passage on the west side of Vashon Island.

"We're back on the pod now, and if you want to join us, I'll have someone pick you up in the *Pegasus* at Gig Harbor."

"Great! How about Wendy?"

"I'll send the chopper to pick her up at the Villa Plaza, at noon," He said.

Two hours later with a cigar in my mouth, traveling at thirty knots in the *Pegasus*, I lit and dropped cherry bombs, like a destroyer dropping depth charges, trying to herd the whales into Vashon Island's Quartermaster Harbor. Every time we chased them to the harbor's entrance they stopped, refusing to enter the shallow water.

Ted writes: "'Look at the chart, Don. If you're a whale using sonar, that harbor entrance would appear as a vertical wall. It rises from twenty-five fathoms to three or four. When they get inside the canyon they can't see their way over the top.'" Then the whales dove deep and disappeared. Ted returned to Gig Harbor in Adam Ross's purse seiner, the Chinook, and Wendy and I went home. Lamar shot some good action scenes of the speedboats herding the whales as the helicopter swooped down, but worthless without a capture.

The next morning Adam Ross got a call from his Wollochet Bay neighbor. The whales were traveling west under the Fox Island Bridge.

Ted describes the chase: "An hour later the cold morning air surged through the open chopper doorway ... The whales scattered, sensing the vibration of our aircraft. 'They're going to be tough today. They've got your number,' the pilot said ... We searched for an hour, but failed to locate the bull. A large cow came into view. The pilot made a rapid descent, estimating where and when she would show again ... The big orca surfaced directly under me. At the same instant I fired .... The orca's sudden, unusual maneuver resulted in the harpoon hitting below water in the abdomen. Darn, tough luck; I hoped the animal had plenty of protective blubber there. I threw the buoys out, and we followed their path ...

"At first light the whales swam unhesitatingly into Henderson Bay, quite a contrast from their refusal to enter Quartermaster Harbor. However, this time the water became shallow on a gradual slope. 'What do you make of it, Ted, only two?' Don said.

"'I don't know ... At least we have a chance to catch a companion for Namu.' ...

"'Twelve fathoms,' Don called out; 'let her go.' Steaming at nine knots, top speed for the Chinook, the seiner released its net. The whales, sensing the sudden barrier, tried to outrun the ship ... The speedboats raced ahead and forced the surfacing whales back. With one third of the net out, the seiner heeled over in a ninety-degree turn and headed toward the beach. The whales' escape was cut off in two directions; the buoy indicated they had doubled back. A minute later Adam's six hundred-fathom net was all used up, lying in a giant U shape.

"The skipper on a second seiner"—Peter Babich, who had previously worked for Ted as a backup—"released his net, heading straight across the open end of Adam's, like putting the keeper plate on a horseshoe magnet. Snap, the escape route closed...

"Adam's slow, emotion-filled voice broke over the CB, 'Inside, boys, they're inside the net.' ... Don leaned over the side and cut the harpoon line and buoys away from the cow ... Lamar came up to the nets and called, 'Ted, that was really exciting action. The first capture of a live killer whale and it's all on film!'... Catching the whales had taken all my ingenuity, more money than the movie producer put up, and more energy than I could have imagined."

I found out later the cow had been harpooned in the stomach, and unfortunately died the following morning while being moved into Namu's travel pen.

Ted was sad. "Killer whales are so special. The death of even one was an agonizing price to pay for being among the first to attempt capturing them alive, and not knowing the best way to proceed. It was little consolation, but I had read that in the early days of jungle animal capture as many as ten died for each one brought back alive, and they had experience."

When Ted transferred the calf from the traveling pen into Rich Cove, it stayed away from Namu until Namu came to the feeding dock for breakfast, and then it swam nearby, but ignored the salmon Ted threw its way. The following day, however, when Namu moved out into the lagoon, the calf grew braver and approached the dock.

Ted describes it this way: "The little whale surfaced at the feed platform; cautiously I slipped it a small chunk of salmon. The whale took the food and darted away, like a squirrel scurrying off to eat a nut in private. Several minutes later she was back. I held a fish above water; the young whale awkwardly reached for the morsel. The baby whale learned in only a few minutes that opening its jaw while upside down facilitated taking food held above water. Namu came over to investigate the commotion. This time the youngster held her ground, ignoring Namu's presence, and put away one hundred pounds of salmon by day's end."

With Namu in Rich Cove, attendance at the aquarium dropped, and Ted had to go back to the bank to keep the doors open.

Though he had retired the debt to bring Namu to Seattle, the expense of capturing the calf had gone substantially over budget. I suggested he sell the calf and clean up his debts. Reluctantly he agreed. Sea World, a recently opened oceanarium in San Diego, bought the calf.

Transferring the calf from Rich Cove to California was a classic "learn on the job" operation. After luring the calf to shallow water with salmon, Ted and a dozen of his diving friends manhandled the one-ton whale into a sling and then carried the sling, like a litter, to an open-bed truck, where they hung the sling from a cradle. The whale crossed the sound on the Vashon-Fauntleroy ferry, where she drew a huge crowd, and boarded a waiting Flying Tiger chartered swing-tail aircraft at the Seattle-Tacoma Airport. She flew to San Diego stretched out on sheepskin pads with a continuous flow of water to keep her wet to prevent overheating. Within minutes of entering her new pool, Shamu, as Sea World named her, quickly made friends with her dolphin pool mates and swam in formation with them.

With Shamu safely delivered to Sea World, Ted began preparations to bring Namu back from Rich Cove. Before making the transfer, I asked Ted if I could ride Namu.

"When my brother asked to ride Namu, I was not surprised but felt apprehensive and somewhat reluctant. I didn't want to share my companion, nor jeopardize the close relationship with the orca ... At times the big mammal could play rough. Hardened from years of skin-diving and strenuous physical activity, I had stamina, and rolled with the whale's punches, but what about Jim? I could have said no, yet if anyone was entitled to ride the killer whale, it was Jim ... Once I left the water, Namu took Jim for a long ride around the cove ... When Jim climbed back on the dock, I asked, 'Were you scared?'

"'No. Should I have been?'

"I wanted to see the expression on his face, but he turned away. On purpose?"

Me riding Namu (photo by Ted Griffin)

A few months after coming back to the aquarium, Namu became lethargic, and the abrasions that had begun to appear became more pronounced. Then late on a Saturday afternoon in July 1966, Ted got a call from the aquarium, saying Namu was swimming erratically. Ted got there at dusk, having raced across Elliott Bay from Bainbridge Island in the *Pegasus*. Shortly after he arrived, Namu died. According to the autopsy, Namu drowned. Bacteria in his digestive tract produced a toxin, which affected the nervous system and caused a delirium. During the autopsy, a tooth was cut and the rings were counted. Namu had lived seventeen years, approximately half his normal life expectancy.

Ted shares his grief. "I believed Namu could never be replaced, never equaled. At first I told myself he would come back, as I had believed my father would after he died. I had never faced the realty of death as a fact of life. It was a mystery which I had pushed away ... I wanted to see beyond my grief, to a time when I would feel good ... Now and then I lost a day somewhere, I couldn't even remember it passing ... I visualized killer whales, and tried to think what another one might be like. My imagination was blocked; I could get no sense of another whale's identity. All thoughts of starting over were blocked in pain."

When Namu died, a part of Ted died. I tried to involve him in a new business venture, but he showed no interest. It took more than a year for him to work through his depression. Eventually he reengaged, but not with the same enthusiasm or level of energy he had previously exhibited.

Nearly two years after Namu died, Ted and Don captured seventeen whales in Yukon Harbor near Seattle. They kept five. Two joined Shamu at Sea World, one went to the Vancouver Aquarium, and Ted kept two, Katy and Kandu. Over the following years, they captured a total of thirty whales. They sold them, with a guarantee of live delivery, in England, Japan, Australia, France, Germany, and throughout the United States. Eventually, Ted and Don were legislated out of business.

Sterling Kissing Kandu

Ted training Namu (photo from aquarium archives)

Ted recounts what happened this way: "In time the organized groups and some individuals brought about the enactment of state and national legislation protecting marine mammals. Ironically this legislation put an end to the live capture of a few killer whales, but did nothing to prevent other nations from annually harvesting many thousands of whales, including orca for their blubber ...

"In response to ... the changing political climate, I retired from the aquarium and the whale capturing business in 1972."

After Namu died, Ted's friend, Dr. Mark Keyes, DVM, a Fish and Wildlife Service and National Fisheries Services marine mammal research veterinarian wrote, "If anyone should ask what did Ted Griffin accomplished, I can answer with authority that by the single act of going into the water with Namu, Ted Griffin contributed more to the conservation and appreciation of killer whales by societies of the world than all the biologists and conservationists put together, from the dawn of time to that moment."

In July 1966, the motion picture *Namu the Killer Whale* premiered in Seattle and continues, more than forty years later, to appear on television. The title of the movie has changed to *Namu, My Best Friend* and is available on DVD under that title.

Jon Frederic Griffin, Jill Parks (Griffin) Sunberg, Jay Edward Griffin and Gaye Elizabeth (Griffin) Shumaker (Ted Griffin's children, 2009)

(7) Post Alpental: Of Lumber Mills, Banks, and Other Businesses

In 1964, I bought a sawmill. I'd been intrigued with the lumber business since listening as a ten-year-old to logging and sawmill stories told by Joe Irving, Mom's stepdad.

I knew nothing about operating a mill, so I sought out a knowledgeable lumberman looking for an opportunity to get started in business. John Brazier, who I knew socially, seemed to be on everyone's shortlist. John worked for his godfather, Fred Karlen. Thirty seconds after being announced at the Karlen-Davis Company, John shook my hand. *A good sign*, I thought. It showed confidence—no airs about making me wait to show his importance. We talked a few minutes about the University of Washington's Huskies football team—John had been a two-miler at UW and was an avid fan. Then I came right to the point.

"John, I'm interested in getting into the lumber business. Both my grandfather and my step-grandfather owned mills, and I grew up listening to their stories. I'd like to buy a mill, but I know nothing about the business."

"What do you have in mind?" John asked.

"You come highly recommended. If you're interested, I'll double your salary and finance a mill and lumber brokerage business. We'd be fifty-fifty partners."

A broad smile spread across John's face. "Of course I'm interested! How could I turn down an offer like that?" I put out my hand and John took it, consummating our arrangement. "How much do you want to invest?" John asked.

"Can we get something decent for a hundred grand?"

"Possibly! I'll know what's available in a few days. Mill owners are a close-knit group, and everybody knows what everybody else is doing."

A week didn't go by before John called. "Jim, we can buy the Coos River Lumber Company, in Coos Bay, Oregon, for sixty-five grand. The mill cuts 35,000 feet"—board feet of lumber—"a shift."

"Is that a good price?" I asked.

"You bet, assuming there's not a lot of deferred maintenance, and it won't take long to check out."

"Why so cheap?"

"Family problems. Three brothers, the Brunells, inherited the mill, and they don't get along."

"Do you know the mill?" I asked.

"Yes, I've purchased lumber from the Brunells. If I can arrange a meeting, are you available to fly down next week?"

"Sure."

"Okay, I'll set something up."

Wednesday we caught the early flight to Coos Bay, and one of the brothers picked us up. He drove faster than I cared for on a winding road paralleling the Coos River. A snag periodically broke the water's surface, which reminded me of hitting a deadhead when Wendy and I returned from a party in Wollochet Bay in our sixteen-foot Chris-Craft. We reached Day Island Marina seconds before sinking.

I saw smoke spiraling up from the mill's burner more than a mile before pulling into a dirt lot and parking next to a trailer. Brunell caught my questioning look at John.

"We office in a trailer so when the river comes up, we're on wheels."

"How often does that happen?" I asked.

"Every two or three years," Brunell said. "No problem with machinery, it's all above flood level."

"Let's start at the office," John said.

After half an hour with the book keepers, John said to Brunell, who had been listening to his questions, "We'd like to look around on our own, if it's okay with you."

"Go ahead," Brunell said, "but don't talk to machine operators unless they're on break. Too dangerous. I'll be in the trailer if you have any questions. When you're finished, we'll join my brothers for lunch."

John had picked a workday in order to assess the condition of the machinery, the operators' skill, and timber flow through the manufacturing process, to check for logjams. From a viewing platform, we watched logs conveyed out of the holding pond; cut into rectangular cants; resawn into various sizes, depending on customer orders; conveyed to the edger; pulled off the green chain and stacked according to size; and finally ferried by the lumber carrier to the dry kiln.

"What do you think?" I asked, after we left the platform. It had been impossible to communicate above the machinery noise.

"The equipment looks good. The boys' father was a real stickler for maintenance, and the operators are well trained. Let's take a look at the burner and then see if we can learn anything about the condition of the forklifts, lumber carrier [straddle bug] and grappler [backhoe with a claw shovel]." Two hours later, while looking at the mill's log raft, John said, "Everything looks in good shape."

"The decision is yours. You're the expert," I responded.

"Ok, let's go make a deal," he said.

Brunell met us on the office steps. "You guys seen enough?"

"Yes," John said.

"Okay, I'll phone my brothers and tell them to meet us at the restaurant."

When we arrived, the Brunell brothers were already seated. After introductions, John confirmed his latest mill orders, and then said, "Sixty-five grand, right?"

"Right," the oldest of the three answered.

"I'll tell you what," John said. "If one of you can take my partner in arm-wrestling"—John looked at me and winked; he knew the story of how I arm-wrestled my way into the Stanford Phi Delta Theta fraternity—"we'll pay you $70,000. If Jim wins, we get the mill for $60,000." *John you've lost your mind*, I thought. All three stood six feet plus and weighed over two hundred pounds; the biggest, with an overlapping gut, must have weighed 250.

"You've got to be kidding," the big guy said.

"I'm serious," John answered. Then he turned to me. "How about it?" *John, what are you up to?* I wondered. I couldn't believe he actually thought I could put any of them down. I had a strong arm from regularly lifting weights and years of tennis, but I hadn't competitively arm-wrestled since college.

"Okay," I said, "I'll give it a try." I thought, *He has nothing to lose. It's my money.* That's when I learned John never stopped looking for an opportunity. As I expected, the largest brother switched chairs and sat opposite me. We put our elbows on the table and clasped hands. At the last moment, I reached down and grabbed a table leg to increase my leverage and let my wrist unhinge, so my palm paralleled the table. After a few seconds of letting Brunell's arm tire, I reengaged my wrist and pulled his arm to the table. His brothers gasped in astonishment. Fortunately they didn't renege on our bet.

Coos River Lumber Company

John Brazier and me on Canadian mill trip

John and I made frequent unannounced trips to Coos Bay to check on operations, and when John wasn't at the mill, he bought and sold lumber through our brokerage company, Brazier Lumber, which shared an office with Alpental.

One day I stopped at a log-scaling depot near the mill. While watching the attendant measure each log on the truck to determine the cubic feet of lumber, I remembered Mr. Irving, telling me he was one of the founders of the Puget Sound Log Scaling & Grading Bureau in 1912, which protected both loggers and mill owners.

In December, I joined John on a trip to Canada to call on the mills that supplied us lumber. It had been cold and snowy, and north of Vancouver we didn't see the pavement again until we crossed the border back into Washington. We spent the first night in a Kamloops motel. As I got ready for bed, I noticed a small hole in the heel of a stocking, so I threw both stockings away.

"What are you doing?" John asked when he saw my socks sail into the wastebasket.

"Throwing them away," I said.

"Why?"

"Do you wear stockings two days in a row?" I asked.

"No! Jan washes them."

"Well, I don't ask Wendy to wash mine." John got off his bed, walked over to the wastebasket, retrieved the stockings, unzipped his duffel, and stuffed the stockings in his bag. I thought, *How can he believe I only wear stockings one time?*

The next day we drove up Highway 97, stopped at three mills, and then spent the night in Williams Lake. As I had done the previous night, I threw my perfectly good stockings into the wastebasket.

"Griffin, you're nuts," John said, when he saw another pair fly into the basket.

"Hey, they're yours if you want them." And he did. He took them out of the basket and put them in his duffel with my other pair. I had him hooked. I followed the same routine at Quenelle and Prince George. On the way home, I ran out of stockings and had to surreptitiously buy more.

A few days after returning home, John, with a smile that spread ear-to-ear, came into my office.

"You bastard!" *Somebody*, I thought, *Finally clued him in.* He and I shared many laughs over his believing that I only wore stockings one time.

Two years later, when lumber prices dropped and the mill began losing money; we sold it to Simpson Lumber Company, who as I remember, moved it to the Philippines to manufacture hard wood. With John now devoting full time to brokering, Brazier Lumber flourished. Next to my son Sterling, John was the best salesman I ever knew.

In the early 1970s, John bought me out of Brazier Lumber.

For many years the Griffins and Braziers alternated spending Christmas Eve at each others' home, and John and I took great delight in surprising one another with evermore outlandish presents. One year he gave me a pregnant rabbit, and the following year, I reciprocated with a chick that turned into a rooster and woke everyone in the neighborhood at dawn.

My most memorable gift was a pig I purchased at a farm while driving home from Snowline, a subdivision I was developing near Mount Baker. I couldn't resist the "piglets for sale" sign, and the farmer had no trouble convincing me that pigs were smart and could be housebroken, because I'd already made up my mind, thinking *Okay, Brazier, top this one.* For three months until Christmas, the piglet, who I named Wilbur, joined our home's menagerie: Sally the guinea pig, who squeaked, asking for lettuce whenever the refrigerator door opened; Scratchy the cat; Croak the very large toad; Max the German shepherd; Sprig the golden retriever; Him and Her, two scruffy pigeons, to train Sprig's puppies; Carmel, an eight-inch land turtle, who had to be retrieved by Sprig when he got lost on his daily walkabout; and an assortment of unnamed tropical fish, a present from my brother. We also had periodic nocturnal visits from a skunk and several less-than-friendly raccoons.

Sprig's twelve puppies born in our bedroom

Wilbur came home in a cardboard box in the passenger seat. I was not certain whether being bounced around in the box or the trauma of separation from his mother and siblings caused him to squeal nonstop until arriving home and adopting our children as surrogate parents. Wilbur slept in the house for one night only before being banned to the dog kennel—Wendy didn't believe the farmer's story about pigs being easily housebroken. Within days, Ashley had Wilbur leashed trained so he could stroll in the park with the best of dogs. Where she got the idea of dangling a corncob, attached to a long stick, in front of him is still a mystery.

Three months after ballooning to massive proportions from gorging on aging vegetables that Wendy picked up at local markets, Wilbur accompanied us to the Braziers' Christmas party. During the short drive, Wilbur, who now filled a large portion of the bed of the station wagon and probably still suffering from the trauma of his first road trip in a box, ate an ample portion of leather and foam off the back of the backseat, which we didn't discover until unloading him.

Then, after attaching a new rhinestone Christmas collar to his leash, Wilbur accompanied us into the house, not the least offended by John's and Jan's outbursts. Wilbur snorted a friendly greeting to the Braziers' black Lab whose hair on the back of its neck stood straight up and kept his distance rather than engage in the usual dog-sniffing ritual.

Jan, who looked like she had come down with some dreaded disease, said, "You've got to be kidding."

John's response was less accommodating. "No way, Griffin!"

The Brazier children couldn't have been more excited. They hugged Wilbur like they would a new puppy.

"Do we get to keep him, Dad?"

"What's his name?"

"I've always wanted a pig."

I looked over and saw John and Jan starring at each other in total disbelief, and thought, *I win this round.*

Unfortunately, Wilbur left the party with us. At dinner a few nights later, Wendy said, "Jim, the pig has to go." I thought, *She could have at least used his proper name.* After several dry runs, Pete Zimny, Snowline's sales manager, found an accommodating farmer who had a palatial mud hole and a herd of pigs for Wilbur to root with.

****

Banking: Getting Started

In the fall of 1965, before taking the family to Switzerland, Frank Cooper, my friend and fellow delegate to the 1964 Republican National Convention, called.

"Jim, would you be interested in going on our board?" Frank was president of the newly charted South Tacoma State Bank. "We're moving our main office to Tacoma and changing the name to Bank of Tacoma." I thought, *Frank knows I can raise money and assumes I'll also be able to bring in new accounts.*

"Is a Seattle bank behind the move?" I asked. State law prohibited banks from opening branches across county lines, so banks wishing to expand either acquired a bank in another county or surreptitiously arranged for a new bank to be organized and then bought it.

"Not at this point, but I can't say the subject hasn't been discussed." Then he said, "If it happens, our stockholders will do very well, and we have stock set aside for new directors."

"Yes, I'd like to join your board."

"Splendid! We have a directors meeting next Wednesday at 4:00. Come in at 3:30, and we'll talk about stock." As I'd predicted, a few years later Seattle First National (now Bank of America) bought Bank of Tacoma. We were well rewarded.

Then in 1968, Charlie Johnson, a Tacoma attorney who had served with me on the Bank of Tacoma board, suggested we buy a bank.

"I had lunch with Cooper yesterday," Charlie said. Governor Evans had recently appointed Frank Cooper as the State Supervisor of Banking. "He thinks Thurston County Bank could be available."

"Is the bank in trouble?" I asked.

"The owner, who is the bank's majority stock holder, put a branch at the county line in Olympia, hoping to annex into Olympia, before getting FDIC approval. The FDIC denied the branch because supervising agencies now limit bank organizers to owning no more than 5 percent of their bank's stock. The owner may have no option but to sell."

"How much?"

"Cooper thinks 350 grand," Charlie said. "The bank has $2,000,000 in deposits, but once we get FDIC approval for the branch and annex into Olympia, we'll double or triple the deposits by bringing Olympia's major business owners on the board."

"Where're we getting the $350,000?" I asked.

"Both Puget Sound National [now Key Bank] and Peoples Bank [now U.S. Bank] want branches in Olympia. Money won't be a problem."

Charlie, some former Bank of Tacoma board members, and I bought Thurston County Bank. As Charlie predicted, deposits doubled within a year of annexing into Olympia, and five years later, in 1973, deposits reached $16,000,000.

Serving on the board and the loan and executive committees gave me the opportunity to analyze many different businesses, and I quickly learned which companies would or would not profit from a loan.

Some years later, Puget Sound National bought Thurston County Bank. It couldn't have happened at a more opportune time because of an Alpental capital call.

****

Pursuing my Chosen Field: Real Estate Development

On December 8, 1967, Alpental opened, and my sixteen-hour, seven-days-a-week job ended.

After the Christmas holidays, I began a rezone and subdivision of property I'd purchased the previous summer after receiving a tip, while playing golf, from a Realtor buddy.

"Jim," Jack said, as we walked to the par three tee on the old course at the Tacoma Country and Golf Club, "I just listed a hundred acres near the Mount Baker ski area that has the potential to be another Alpental." *Jack,* I thought, *You must be high on something. Alpental is one of a kind.*

"How much?" I asked, trying to be polite.

"The same as Alpental, one thousand per acre." *Well,* I thought, *Why not?* I hadn't been to Mount Baker since a high school ski trip.

"Okay, I'll take a look."

Two days later, I went with Jack to Glacier, thirty miles east of Bellingham. As we walked the property, heavily treed with second growth fir, I became more and more excited. The land mirrored the Alpental valley, surrounded by National forest, adjoining a river and only an hour-and-a-half drive from a major metropolitan area, Vancouver, BC.

"Jack, do you have a purchase agreement with you?" I asked, when we returned to his car.

"Yes." I signed on the hood of his car at the listed price after inserting a thirty-day feasibility period to make certain the land drained, to allow septic tanks, and to check the availability of utilities. I wasn't going to chance losing the property by haggling price. "Pigs get fat and hogs get slaughtered," I could hear Jim March saying.

While waiting for Whatcom County to approve the plat, which I named Snowline, my partner, Walter Sterling Jr. (Wendy's brother), and I visited recreational subdivisions to find a Realtor to market the lots. Most Realtors charged 12 percent sales commission, but MacPherson wanted 30.

"Mr. MacPherson, why should I pay 30 percent?" I asked.

"Call me Bill," he said. "Because I can sell your plat in less than a year, but it'll cost me 20 to 25 percent. If time isn't a factor, bring in a 12-percent broker." We hired MacPherson.

Upon obtaining preliminary plat approval, MacPherson set up phone banks in Vancouver (BC), Bellingham, and Seattle. His company brought busloads of prospects to Snowline every weekend and provided them with a lunch, a gift of a radio, and a tour of the Mount Baker ski area. While children fished in a hastily constructed trout pond, MacPherson salesmen obtained $100 refundable deposits from their parents. Similar to Alpental, most lots had backup offers. Lots sold at an average price of $5,000 with 10 percent down and ten-year financing at 8 percent interest. The entire first phase, 171 lots, was reserved in six months. Like Alpental, we couldn't transfer title until final plat approval, which required the installation of roads and utilities.

Using lot reservations as collateral, the Bank of California (now Union Bank of California) loaned the money to install utilities and recreational facilities, which included a swimming pool and remodeling of the original homestead, where lot owners could stay while building their cabins. The one-hundred-lot second phase sold just as quickly. Two years later, in 1971, we built Snowline Inn condominiums.

Pete Zimny, MacPherson sales manager, and me
in front of remodeled homestead, 1968

Me, third from left, and Walt Sterling Jr., far right,
during construction of Snowline Inn

While developing Snowline, I bought twelve acres at 100th and Bridgeport Way, a major intersection in Lakewood. The Meyers, parents of a high school friend, owned nine acres and adjoining homeowners the other three. I'd spent hours looking for shopping center sites with Jim March, and I always thought this property would make a good center, but with Alpental and then Snowline, I'd been too busy to follow up. Then in 1968, Paul Meyer, my high school friend, and I happened to meet at a party. After a half-hour discussion of our lives since high school, I mentioned my interest in his parents' home.

"Paul, do you think your parents might consider selling their property?" I asked. "It's an ideal site for a shopping center."

"Why don't you call on them? They always liked you."

Taking Paul's advice, I periodically stopped and chatted with his parents. Eventually my tenacity paid off. After acquiring their property, along with two adjoining homes, I applied for a commercial rezone. Pierce County—prior to Lakewood becoming a city—indicated approval should be no problem with consent of the adjacent home owners.

Over several evenings, I called on the bordering property owners. As a lark, I brought my eight-year-old son Sterling. On the first call, he charmed the homeowners by playing with their cat, feeding goldfish, and sampling freshly baked cookies.

While the occupants were being entertained by Sterling, I reassured them that I would erect an eight-foot fence and landscape between our properties. I also emphasized that they would be within walking distance of all their needs: restaurants, doctors' offices, groceries, a gas station, and a post office. With Sterling's help, every neighbor signed a consent form.

****

Africa: "Con" 101

In September 1968, when Wendy and I were on safari in Africa, we dreamed about buying an African farm. A few days of picturesque savanna scenes rivaling the landscape paintings of Turner and nights viewing the Milky Way Galaxy as if we could reach out and touch the stars, had enchanted us.

"Why don't you talk to Chico and see what he thinks?" Wendy said. Chico was our "white hunter."

Over cocktails the following evening, I broached the subject. "Chico, Wendy and I are thinking about investing in Africa. Any ideas?"

Chico looked through the fire at me for a few seconds before responding. "How about going into the cattle business? Cattle can't be bred in northern Mozambique because tsetse flies kill the young calves. After the safari season, I plan to buy cattle in southern Mozambique and drive them north. I'd be happy to have a partner."

Over the next few days, Chico and I talked about the cost of cattle, helpers, permits and duration of a drive, and at night, while watching a never-ending array of shooting stars, Wendy and I discussed what I had learned.

"What a great opportunity if it's for real. We'll be able to come to Africa on a regular basis."

"Go for it," Wendy said. "We can afford to risk a few thousand dollars."

That evening, while celebrating bagging a leopard, I said, "Chico, about your offer, we'd like to be your partners. I'll write a check before we leave, and if the venture proves successful, we'll be back next year with more money."

Chico and Wendy discussing our business arrangement

Four months later, I received a letter from Chico explaining that most of our cattle had died from influenza. *Yeah*, I thought, *More likely you overhauled your jeep and made a down payment on a new bungalow.* I refer to that experience as "Con" 101.

****

Mining for Copper

After we returned from Africa, my friend and distant cousin John Hewitt, whose children, "JS," Eve, Maddie, Nicola, and Lisa, attended Charles Wright Academy with our children (your parents), asked me to help finance his geologist friend David Bissett. (Henry Hewitt Sr., the progenitor of our Hewitt line, was my great-great-grandfather and John's great-grandfather.) Bissett had taken a leave of absence from a mining company to investigate two promising prospects. *Leave of absence*, I thought; *More likely fired.* I sent John a check.

Over lunch six weeks later, Bissett gave his first report. After spending fifteen minutes listening to him explain why he'd put the prospect at the top of his list, I said, "Dave, just give us the bottom line."

"The ground contained silver ore, but not in the quantity or quality to be mined."

"Okay," I said. "We knew the risks. Now what?"

"I'm off to Nevada tomorrow to investigate the copper prospect." *Yeah*, I thought, *And spend the rest of my money.*

Bissett hadn't been gone a week when Hewitt phoned.

"Jim," Hewitt said. I could hear excitement in his voice. "Bissett called from Eureka. He says our copper prospect is going to make us rich. He wants us to fly down as soon as possible."

"John," I said, "you've got to know 'as soon as possible' is code for 'I need more money.'"

"Yeah, you're probably right," he said, "but we're in too far to back out now."

Friday morning, Hewitt and I flew to Reno, rented a car, and drove 250 miles to Eureka. Bissett met us at the town's single motel, which looked like it hadn't changed since the last stagecoach passed through. A wooden-wheeled ore wagon, with weeds growing from its rotting wood, sat at the entrance to the gravel parking lot. The car's headlights silhouetted Dave sitting in an armless wood chair propped against the door to his room. When I pulled in next to his porch, the front legs of his chair hit the raised deck, almost knocking over a bottle of Jack Daniel's.

"John, it looks like Dave started the celebration without us," I said.

"Yeah," John answered in a disgusted tone of voice.

"You guys want a drink?" Dave slurred, as we shook hands.

"Why not," John answered. Dave went into his room and brought out paper cups and handed one to each of us. He poured two inches of bourbon into each cup and then emptied the bottle into his glass.

"To the September Morn," he said. "That's what I've named our prospect." He swallowed his bourbon in one gulp. Then we walked to one of Eureka's two cafés, where we wound our way through a maze of slot machines and gaming tables before finding an empty table in the lounge. Smoke curled up from bar stools like Indian smoke signals. As I looked at my reflection in a gigantic mirror behind the bar, I wondered how many pistol slugs were embedded in the wall in back of the mirror.

As soon as we sat down, Dave started in again. "We're going to be rich!" he said over and over, only stopping to order a Jack Daniel's. John and I had agreed not to quiz him until morning because we wanted sober answers.

After breakfast, in the same café, Dave, suffering from a hangover, drove us in his jeep wagon to a vantage point overlooking the desert valley.

"It's government land," he said, "clear to the horizon." I looked out over the rock-scarred earth from the brow of a hill where Dave had parked and saw nothing but sparse grass, sagebrush, and an occasional thorny scrub bush. Dust funnels, like miniature tornadoes, moved intermittently above the vast waste. *How*, I thought, *Could settlers or Indians have survived here?*

Bissett analyzing rock fragments with John and me looking on

"I've sampled nearly a section [640 acres]," Dave said, "and found copper traces over the entire area. Once we file claims and get control of the property, I'll send a report to the major mining companies."

"What's that going to cost?" I asked.

"About fifteen grand," Dave said. "It would have been more if the sheriff hadn't given his prisoners the opportunity to make $10 a day, from which he probably takes a cut."

I turned to John and lifted my eyebrows, confirming my prognostication. Then I said, "Dave, my wife's godfather is the general counsel for Phelps Dodge." (Phelps Dodge was the largest copper producer in the US.) A broad grin spread across Dave's face. If his head still throbbed, he no longer felt it.

"Jim, you continue to surprise me," John said.

"God! What a break," Dave hooted. "We'll save months bypassing the management chain." On the way back to the motel, Dave regurgitated his previous evening's braggadocio, reminding me of what a Stanford geologist professor had said: "Geologists are dreamers and live for a major strike, which rarely happens."

John and I drove back to Reno that afternoon. A few weeks later, Bissett filed the September Morn's claims in the courthouse and then sent an assay report to Phelps Dodge and others. I'd previously alerted Wendy's godfather.

A month later, Dave called to tell us he'd received a contract offer from Phelps Dodge, and he was coming back to Tacoma to discuss it with us. We haggled with Phelps Dodge for weeks before signing. I'd learned from my brother's Namu movie to insist on a percentage of the gross profit, not net profit—Ted never received one dime.

Bissett was more optimistic. "Guys," he said, "the royalty on an open-pit mine could be a million dollars annually."

Dave returned to Eureka when Phelps Dodge moved onto the prospect. He wanted to witness electrodes being inserted into the ground and charged with electricity. Though the company's employees were sworn to secrecy, Dave got an engineer's assistant to talk after plying him with liquor.

"The circuit panels lit up like a pinball machine," whispered the Phelps Dodge employee, "but you didn't hear it from me." Bissett immediately called Hewitt, who called me. Supposedly an enormous anomaly that conducted electricity lay under the claims. Phelps Dodge immediately began drilling.

When Wendy and I heard about the possibility of a major strike, we talked the night through, fantasizing about how to spend the royalties. Though excited about "what if," I remembered my mother telling me Art Thompson, Norton Clapp, Booth Gardner's stepfather, and my father had had similar thoughts.

Unfortunately, their rich vein of Montana gold petered out long before they recovered their costs.

Phelps Dodge spent $250,000 drilling. Though most of the claims showed traces of copper, iron ore had caused the anomaly. Bissett never recovered and eventually died of alcoholism.

****

Not Your Regular Real Estate Deal

While still suffering from the mining disappointment, my Realtor friend Harold Allen called. Harold had sold Wendy and me our first two homes, and I'd told him if he ever needed an investment partner to call.

"Jim," Hal said. "An apartment across from Hyde Park is listed at a thousand a unit below market. Do you want to come in with me?"

"Why so cheap?" I asked.

"The listing agent thinks the seller needs capital for his business."

"Okay, tie it up and I'll take a look."

"I already have," Hal said, and then added, "I have a twenty-day feasibility period."

The next day, we walked through a few units; all appeared in good shape. Hall carpets were relatively new and clean; the central heating system was adequate; the roof had recently been replaced, as had the porch, porch railing, and stairs. Other than needing a coat of paint, the building looked in good condition. However, in the daylight we missed seeing the red glow of a single bulb filtering through the manager's sheer curtains. At the crack of dawn a few weeks after we'd closed the sale, Hal called.

"Jim, police just raided our apartment. They arrested our manager, who, it turns out, is a madam and hauled her and a number of 'Johns' to jail."

"Anything I can do?" I said, asking myself, *How could we be so naïve?*

"No. I'll have an ad for a manager in the paper tomorrow, and in the meantime one of my salespeople will be on site." Wendy and I laughed so hard we couldn't get back to sleep.

Over the years, Hal and I have shared many laughs over buying a house of prostitution.

****

Bank of Honolulu

"Why not start a bank?" Wendy asked, "The last two worked out well." It was January 1971. Wendy and I were in Hawaii on the Outrigger Canoe Club beach, pondering how we could spend more time in Hawaii.

"I have no idea if Hawaii needs another bank."

"Why don't you find out?" Wendy had never been shy about pushing me.

Why not? I thought.

Me and Wendy at Outrigger Canoe Club

Wendy and Jim March

"Okay. I'll see if I can get an appointment with the supervisor." I left Wendy on the beach and returned to Jim March's unit in the Colony Surf condominium adjoining the Outrigger that he had graciously loaned us. From his unit, I watched not-so-subtle surfers go out of their way to get a better look at Wendy. *How did I get so lucky?* I thought.

I got right through to the supervisor's office. His secretary, not recognizing my name, asked, "Why do you want to see the director?"

"I'm going to start a bank." I immediately had her attention. Fifteen seconds later, the director came on the line.

"How can I help you, Mr. Griffin?" he asked. After explaining my banking background, I reiterated what I had told his secretary.

"My afternoon is wide open; come on down." He sounded more defensive than curious.

After getting directions from his secretary, I showered off the salt and sunscreen, changed into slacks and an outrigger luau shirt, and returned to the beach. Wendy hadn't moved.

"I have an appointment with the director of banking." I said. "In Hawaii he's called a director, not a supervisor."

Wendy sat up and lifted her sunglasses to the top of her head. "That was quick," she said.

"My mentioning a new bank must have set off an alarm. I'll call as soon as I know something."

I got our rental car from the condo garage and headed into town, down Waikiki along the beach. When I reached the state capitol, I parked near a sculptured pool and let cool mist from water cascading over boulders refresh me. Once inside the massive structure, I had to ask directions twice before locating the director's office.

A couple of minutes after I gave the receptionist my name, the director appeared. He was a tall, lean Caucasian dressed in a dark suit, white shirt, and tie. We shook hands, and he ushered me into his office. His polished mahogany desk held nothing but a phone. I thought, *Either he's advertising his penchant for organization, or he doesn't have enough to do*—a typical government appointment. He sat in his cushioned swivel-chair and indicated for me to sit across from him. Two six-inch stacks of manila folders and a picture of his family were neatly arranged on a matching mahogany credenza behind his chair. *The folders must be part of the office décor,* I thought. With no paper ends or corners visible, they looked too neat for working files.

The director came right to the point. "Why does a Washington banker want to organize a bank in Hawaii?"

I wasn't prepared for his question and hesitated before answering. I couldn't tell him Wendy and I wanted a second home in the sun. "It appears banking hasn't kept up with population growth," I said, remembering today's headlines about skyrocketing condominium building permits.

"Hawaii has six state-chartered banks and is adequately served," he said. He spent a few minutes describing how branching existing banks fulfilled Hawaii's growth requirements, and then he rose from behind his desk. *Jim, you've been dismissed*, I thought. He came around the desk and shook my hand. As he walked me to the door, he said, "You might check with the comptroller's office." The comptroller of the currency regulated national banks. I thought, *The tone of his voice indicates he thinks he has dissuaded me; well; we'll see about that.*

At the door, I turned and said, "If I decide to proceed, who would you recommend for a feasibility study?" I knew the importance of an independent analysis from working with the Feds to obtain Alpental's Forest Service use permit.

"Ed Faison, Associate Director of Marketing at the University of Hawaii," he answered. "He's always looking for student projects."

From a lobby pay phone, I called the university to arrange an appointment with Faison. His secretary said his last class ended at 3:30 and gave directions. Then I called Wendy to tell her what had transpired. I arrived at Faison's office at 3:45. His secretary, an attractive multiracial Asian, said, "You must be Mr. Griffin."

"Yes," I said.

"May I tell Dr. Faison the nature of your call?" she asked. *Not only attractive*, I thought, *but a lovely smile.*

"Yes, I'm interested in contracting a marketing study."

"I'll let him know," she said. "Please have a seat." Then she left her desk, I assumed to brief Faison.

I began jotting down important aspects for a feasibility study. She returned a minute or two later. "Dr. Faison will see you now, Mr. Griffin," she said. *That's quick*, I thought, *He must need a project.* The first thing I noticed when I entered Faison's office were two windows on opposite walls that looked out over the campus. *A good sign*, I thought. I knew from banking and Stanford Oil Company meetings that a corner office with windows indicated the occupant could make decisions without obtaining committee approval.

Two armless cushioned chairs stood in front of a desk piled high with books and reports. In what little uncluttered space remained sat a telephone, two half-empty coffee cups, and a yellow tablet. *This is a busy man*, I thought. Faison rose from his chair when I entered and came around his desk. We shook hands. He stood about my height, five-foot-ten, had thinning light brown hair, and wore slacks and a multicolored Hawaiian shirt, far more casual than the state banking director's attire. I knew instantly that we would get along.

"Mr. Griffin, my secretary tells me you are interested in a market survey," he said, while directing me to a low-rise table ringed with four matching cushioned chairs.

"Please call me Jim," I said. I still flinched when I heard Mr. Griffin.

"Of course, and please call me Ed." We sat at opposite ends of the table. "How can I be of help?"

"I'm interested in obtaining a marketing study to verify the need for a new bank. I met with the state banking director earlier today, and he seemed adamant that Hawaii didn't need another state bank. He suggested I look into obtaining a federal charter. I'm certain he doesn't expect me to follow through."

"Do you have any experience in starting a bank?" he asked.

"Not in starting, but in branching," I said. "I've been a director of two Washington state banks and presently serve as a director and corporate officer in a recently acquired bank."

"The comptroller just might be interested in a new national bank," Faison said. "The Feds must still be smarting over First Hawaiian converting to a state bank two years ago."

"Yes," I said. I hadn't heard about the conversion, but not knowing the most compelling reason for a new national bank would not have helped my credibility with Faison. I later found out that First Hawaiian, Hawaii's oldest bank, had been formed in 1858.

"I assume you represent a group of Washington investors?" he said.

"Yes," I said again. I didn't want him to know I was flying solo.

"What are the compelling reasons for a new bank?" Ed pulled one of the three pens from his shirt pocket and reached for a yellow tablet on the table.

"Population and business growth, consumer satisfaction, a multiracial bank that caters to small businesses, and the need for downtown banking services," I said.

"Any location in mind?" he asked.

"A high-rise commercial building in the heart of the city," I said. "Business accounts are the quickest way to build deposits. We'll put a multiracial group of prominent CEOs on the board." We talked another half-hour about possible board members, timing, and cost of a marketing study, which would not exceed $5,000. He said he would have an outline for my review in two weeks.

When I got back to the Colony Surf, I told Wendy what had transpired and then called Charlie Johnson, my Thurston County Bank partner. I would need both Charlie's legal expertise in preparing an application and his Washington DC connections to get it quickly reviewed—Charlie was plugged into Washington State's Democratic machine. With the three-hour time difference, I caught him at home.

"Charlie, I'm still in Honolulu." Before he could respond, I said, "I've commissioned the University of Hawaii to do a feasibility study for a national bank charter. Do you want in?" I heard heavy breathing. Charlie weighed two hundred and fifty pounds and stood six-feet-four. He'd been a starting tackle at the University of Washington.

"Of course, but you might've considered mentioning it to me."

"Yah, yah," I said. I didn't tell him the idea was conceived five hours ago. "Can you get one of your DC buddies to send us an application?"

"Sure, but why a national bank?"

"A long story," I said. "Short version, I met with Hawaii's director of banking, and he basically said, no way will he approve another state bank at this time. However the Feds should be interested because one of their two banks, First Hawaiian, with 32 percent of the state's deposits, converted to a state bank two years ago. It's been ten years since a new bank came on line and Hawaii's population has grown 21 percent since 1960."

"What's the feasibility study going to cost?"

"Five grand max," I said.

"Have you talked to Frank?" Charlie asked. Frank Cooper, after serving as Washington State Supervisor of Banking for two years, was now a senior vice president at the Bank of Hawaii.

"No, but I'll get together with him before I leave."

"He'll be a good resource," Charlie said. "He's processed a shitload of new state bank and branch applications."

"I'll call as soon as I get back to Tacoma," I said. After disconnecting, I thought, *I can just imagine what Charlie will say to our banking partners Friday; we have a loose cannon among us.* We met every Friday at Honan's or Harbor Lights for lunch.

I called Frank the following morning and arranged to meet. Then Wendy and I drove around the island, periodically stopping at deserted beaches to cool off in the ocean.

Frank couldn't have been more surprised that I'd taken the initiative to commission a bank feasibility study. *He must be wondering why he hadn't come up with the idea.* I suppressed a smile at the thought. Frank occupied a corner office with two windows. His mahogany desk held only a phone and family picture, like Hawaii's director of banking, but the three stacks of manila folders on the credenza behind his cushioned, swivel chair were not décor. Frank listened, without commenting, until I finished.

"The Caucasians control the state's two largest banks, Bank of Hawaii and First Hawaiian, and cater to the 'Big Five,'" Frank said, referring to Hawaii's five major companies. "That will be your strongest argument." We talked another thirty minutes about location and possible directors before I left.

Faison's confirmation letter had arrived by the time I returned to Tacoma. "Per our conversation, the cost will not exceed $5,000 … We're off and running," Faison wrote.

Two weeks later, February 21, he wrote again: "We have gathered a lot of material, but it will be another week or ten days before we have the figures we need. The consumer study does not return from the field until then … We are making a study of possible sites for a downtown location, which will also be complete by then … Could you get me some estimates on the following …?" I called Frank and told him what Faison had requested. When Frank's letter, with three pages of account information, arrived I forwarded it to Faison after deleting both Cooper's and the Bank of Hawaii's names.

The next correspondence from Faison arrived March 3, my thirty-fourth birthday. Faison wrote, "The consumer research arrives March 6. The following week, I'll be putting all the pieces together … It looks as if we have a case for a new bank, but the more compelling reasons are qualitative and based upon new growth rather than any glaring holes in the services now being offered ..."

On March 18 Faison wrote, "All of the information is in. The entire study should be complete by March 20 and you can plan to come any time after that. Here are the highlights. We have a good case in terms of economic growth ... This is a better approach than an analysis of the weakness of the services of the present banks ... We can make a good case for a new downtown bank because new offices buildings and urban redevelopment will increase the population in the downtown area by fifty percent in the next two years ... I can suggest possibilities for a board of directors. The Japanese community should be included. I'm convinced that you should have a Filipino ... We have run down what happened to the application for a Filipino bank application. Informed sources indicate that a key state official turned down the application because of pressure from the two leading banks. That official is now on the payroll of one of them. It's estimated that the Filipino community has five million dollars deposited in those two banks."

On March 28, I sent a draft of Faison's report to Charlie and Frank asking for their comments before Charlie and I returned to Hawaii in April.

"We're going to need people to vouch for our banking credibility when we call on prospective board members," Charlie said at our Friday lunch.

I thought for a moment and then said, "I know three."

"Are they well known?" Charlie asked.

"Yes. Mark Allen, Chevron Oil's Regional Manager for Western Operations; Rick Fried, a young *haole* who just made partner in one of the prestigious Honolulu law firms; and Henry Shigekane, a Japanese attorney. Mark Allen was Chevron's district manager in Tacoma when I was in the fuel business. We had extensive dealings and become good friends. Rick Fried grew up with Wendy in Scottsdale, and we'd become tennis buddies. Henry Shigekane represented Jim March when he opened a soft ice cream chain in Honolulu."

"Great," Charlie said. "Set up meetings." Before we left for Honolulu, I reached all three. They were eager to get together and expressed interest in becoming involved.

On the flight, we talked about a bank CEO. "The president must be loyal to us so we don't lose control," Charlie said. "And we should have someone committed prior to talking to potential board members."

"What about Cooper?" I asked.

"He would be great."

The following morning, we stopped at Bank of Hawaii and talked to Frank before meeting with Faison.

"I've been thinking about capitalization," Frank said. "Two and a half million dollars will satisfy the Feds, and you should be able to return 7 percent annually once you're up and running. With the Tacoma group committed to one third of the stock, you'll have no problem raising the remainder. I'd be surprised if you're not substantially oversold."

"Okay, $2,500,000 it is," I said, looking at Charlie for confirmation. After reviewing Frank's list of potential directors, all energetic, multiracial achievers, I gave Charlie a nod.

"Frank, would you consider heading up the bank?" Charlie asked. Frank looked at Charlie and then at me. After a few moments, his frown turned to a smile.

"Yes!" he sputtered. I thought *He's not only surprised; he's thrilled.* "But I'd like to keep it confidential until submitting the application to the comptroller. I prefer resigning from First Hawaii to being fired."

"That won't be a problem," Charlie said. We left Frank in a state of euphoria and went to see Faison at the University of Hawaii. Faison's secretary greeted me with the same lovely smile.

"It's good to see you again, Mr. Griffin. I'll tell Dr. Faison you're here."

I introduced Charlie, and then Faison ushered us into his office. The clutter on Faison's desk had expanded to the floor. *A good sign*, I thought. Faison led us to the same low rising table and handed each of us a copy of the fifty-page marketing rough draft.

We took a quick look, and then Charlie said, "Ed, rather than take up your time, we'll get back to you after we've had a chance to digest the report." We asked for a third copy which we dropped off at Cooper's office, before returning to the Outrigger for some beach time while reading the report. Faison had covered all pertinent aspects, but some needed less emphasis and some more.

The following morning, we met with Cooper and got his thoughts. After making changes to the feasibility study, we dropped off a redlined copy at Faison's office. Then we met Mark Allen for lunch and reviewed his suggestions for board members.

"I'll be happy to set up a luncheon," Mark said. "Just let me know your availability."

"Wonderful," I said, and then added, "Would you like to be a director?"

Mark hesitated before responding. "Yes, but as Chevron does business with all Hawaiian banks, it wouldn't be appropriate."

Before leaving for home, we met with Rick Fried and Henry Shigekane. Both indicated interest, and like Mark Allen, gave permission to use their names as references.

On May 5, I received a letter from Faison stating the study had gone to the printers and declining Mark Allen's luncheon the following week. He wrote, "My credibility as a specialist would be diminished if I were cast in the role of a salesman.

Of course, I will always be available to answer questions about methods or conclusions."

Charlie and I returned to Hawaii on May 9 for our first presentation. Over the next few days, we met one-on-one with those who expressed interest in becoming stockholders. Other than one exception, Henry Shigekane, we didn't mention board positions. We needed a respected, well-known non-Caucasian to be our Hawaii spokesperson and to help put together a board. Henry readily accepted.

Shortly after returning to Tacoma, I received an article from the *Honolulu Adviser* dated May 13 from Cooper. "New Isle Bank Hinted. A number of leading local businessmen have been approached over the past three days regarding the formation of a new bank in Honolulu, the *Adviser* has learned. Two Tacoma, Washington, men have interviewed prospective members for a board of directors for the new venture ... If successful, in its formation, the institution would be Honolulu's eighth bank ... The principal figure in the venture is James Griffin, an investment banker from Tacoma who reportedly has some investments here now ... One informed source said that a feasibility study already has been completed on the establishment of the new bank. The recent move to recruit potential board members would seem to indicate that the study showed promising results ... A spokesman for the FDIC said that any application for a new bank would have to be filed in Washington, DC."

Charlie and I made four additional trips to Hawaii lining up potential bank directors and securing a location, prior to submitting our application to the comptroller, October 1, 1971. We named Frank Cooper as chief operating officer and listed those directors who had committed.

May 4, 1972, seven months later, an article appeared on the front page of the *Advertiser*. "The US Comptroller of the Currency has approved formation of what will be Hawaii's eighth bank ... The bank plans to sell $1.5 million of stock to the public as soon as the prospectus is cleared with the Comptroller, the chief regulator of national banks. That will be in addition to $1 million of stock to be purchased by the eleven organizers ...

A May 25 follow-up *Advertiser* article stated, "The Bank of Honolulu Names Chief Executive: The Bank of Honolulu, which three weeks ago was granted a national charter, yesterday named Frank Cooper as president and director. Cooper, 43, resigned as Bank of Hawaii's Senior Vice-President for Marketing, effective June 1 ... Cooper for months has been mentioned as a possible chief executive of the new bank. A native of Seattle, he is a longtime friend of the two Tacoma men, James S. Griffin and Charles R. Johnson, who initiated a feasibility study for the bank ..."

****

Reflections:

It's now the spring of 2010, thirty-five years after my resignation from the board of the Bank of Honolulu. I'm sitting at my laptop on the patio of our Palm Desert, California, condominium looking west over the tenth fairway at the Santa Rosa Mountains. Why, I wonder, did I become involved in a myriad of unrelated businesses? What drove me? Was it the challenge to make money that I learned from Mr. Irving? Grandmother Elsie saying I had big shoes to fill and could accomplish whatever I set my mind to? Jim March introducing me to the euphoria that comes from real estate development? Trying to prove my stepmother, Gail, wrong, when she humiliated me by implying that I didn't have the instincts to manage my own business? I don't know; probably some of each. But one thing I do know: I could not have lived through the successes and failures and the thrills and despairs of these endeavors without the support of my family, associates, and particularly my life-partner, Wendy.

(8) Nine Lives: Flying a Floatplane

As a teenager vacationing in the American San Juan Islands in the Strait of Juan de Fuca, I watched floatplanes flying north to fishing lodges and summer cabins and dreamed of becoming a pilot.

In 1962, my dream came true when my brother Ted and I bought a sixty-acre island, Long Island, with eight gravel beaches, ringed by rock cliffs and topped with windswept fir trees, where we'd camped as boys. To drive to Anacortes, take the ferry to Lopez Island, and then cross to Long Island by outboard, took all day. To fly there from American Lake, near my home in Lakewood, took just over one hour, so I got a seaplane license.

Long Island, San Juan Island in background

Wendy and I and our children camped on Long Island at every opportunity. We fished, crabbed, gathered oysters, dug clams, and searched for agates. We slept in a one-room tent cabin, snuggled in sleeping bags, on a bluff overlooking the cove where I docked my Cessna 172 floatplane. Some weekends we flew to Canada and visited friends on Salt Spring Island or Savary Island.

Ron Barr, Bob Smelick, Walt Sterling, Jim Kitchel, and me (Walt Sterling's bachelor party on Long Island)

Me, Lisa Kellogg, Tony Kellogg, Wendy, and Bob Kellogg at Salt Spring Island

We even flew to Vancouver, BC, to see Margot Fonteyn, regarded as one of the greatest classical ballet dancers of all time, and Rudolf Nureyev, who'd defected from Russia, on their final tour together. Wendy and I left Long Island Saturday afternoon with Scott and Sterling after flying from American Lake the day before. We cleared customs on the Fraser River in Vancouver near where it flows into the Strait of Georgia. Then we made the short flight to Vancouver Harbor and secured the plane at the Bay Shore Inn seaplane dock. While checking into the hotel, we ran into our neighbors, Goodwin and Mullie Chase. Goodwin was president of National Bank of Washington (now Wells Fargo Bank).

"What a surprise," Goodwin said.

"We flew up in the floatplane for the night," I responded. "We're camping on Long Island." Goodwin knew we owned an island.

"I'm hosting a cocktail party in our suite at six o'clock for the bank's executives," Goodwin said. "Mullie and I would love to have you join us." I'm certain he didn't expect us to take him up on the invitation, dressed as we were in Levi's, T-shirts, and tennis shoes, but Wendy and I had brought formal clothes for the ballet.

"Thanks, we'll see," I said. Two hours later when Wendy and I arrived at the Chases' suite dressed in a tux and evening gown, the looks on Goodwin and Mullie's faces were priceless.

Over nearly twelve years of flying, we had many wonderful family vacations. However, some of the trips nearly ended in disaster. Following are the most memorable of those calamitous flights.

****

Storm

The storm's full fury struck over Cattle Point at the southern tip of San Juan Island. The Cessna bounced like it was on a trampoline, one moment thrown skyward and the next slammed down. I held the yoke, which felt like a jackhammer, with both hands trying to keep the plane level and on course.

A cloudless sky and temperature in the high seventies greeted me when I arrived at American Lake Seaplane Base in July 1962 for my one-hundred-mile, solo cross-country flight to Friday Harbor on San Juan Island, my last requirement before receiving a floatplane license.

Me at American Lake Seaplane Base (1962)

Through the office window where I filed my flight plan, so aviation authorities would know where to search if I didn't return, I watched a forklift drop my red and white Cessna 172 in the lake. When I got to the dock, I made the usual preflight inspection, checking the pontoons for water, checking the oil and gas levels, and manipulating the controls, which operated the flaps, aileron, tail, and water rudders to verify they were operating correctly.

Once off the lake, I circled until I reached twenty-five hundred feet, so I would have enough elevation to glide to water if the engine quit. Then I turned west toward Puget Sound. As I skirted Steilacoom, Washington State's oldest city, I watched the open-decked McNeil Island prison ferry leave its terminal. Minutes later, I flew over the Tacoma Narrows Bridge; the original bridge—named "Galloping Gertie" because it rippled in the wind like the tail of a kite—collapsed in 1940. I continued north up the west side of Vashon Island, flew over Bainbridge Island, where Ted lived, across Elliott Bay from Seattle, and then crossed over the Kitsap Peninsula and Hood Canal.

I passed Port Ludlow over Admiralty Inlet on the east side of Whidbey Island and left the Washington coast at Port Townsend, where sun reflected off Mount Baker's snowcapped peak in a rainbow of colors. Halfway across the Strait of Juan de Fuca, I dropped down to look at the Smith Island sand spit, where Ted captured seals for his aquarium. I was surprised not to see any lounging on the hot sand.

When I reached Long Island, the sky began to grow dark, as clouds blotted out the sun. *How stupid,* I thought, *for disregarding a pilot's cardinal rule: check the weather forecast!*

I switched the radio band to the weather channel. "Sixty mile-an-hour gusts in the Strait of Juan de Fuca" blared over and over. The empty beach at Smith Island was no longer a mystery. The seals, sensing the falling barometer, had sought shelter.

I knew I must get out of the air before I lost control of the plane. But setting down in four-foot waves would be like landing in a field of stumps. Over Cattle Point, the plane felt like a bumper car at the Puyallup fair. I looked down for a grassy field at the south end of San Juan Island, but cattle and horses were everywhere. I would have to make Friday Harbor. Five minutes later, I dropped over the fir trees into the harbor. *Oh God!* I thought and I began to taste bile. Gigantic waves funneled into the harbor and crashed on every shore. I was out of options.

I turned into the wind, reduced power, set the flaps to twenty degrees, and let the plane settle. If a wing hooked a wave before the pontoons touched the water, the Cessna would cartwheel and I would surely die. I thought, *What will happen to Wendy and the children*?

The concussion of pontoons bouncing off a swell brought me back from my fearful thoughts. The Cessna momentarily went airborne and then dropped into a trough between waves. Whitecaps cascaded over the windshield, blotting out all visibility. I cinched my seat belt, grabbed a life preserver, dropped my head into my lap, and braced for the collision. It came with a shuddering impact, when the pontoons dove into a breaking wave.

I unfastened my seat belt and opened the cockpit door. If the struts that connected the fuselage to the pontoons collapsed, I didn't want to be trapped in a sinking plane. The Cessna bobbed like a log in a raging river, but the struts held. I engaged the water rudders, and then maneuvered the foot petals while simultaneously applying pressure on the steering yoke, which controlled the tail rudder. No response. The wind and tide held the plane in a death grip and drove it toward a reef. "Think, think!" I said aloud, trying to remember my instruction in power turns.

I felt barnacles grind under the pontoons. I jammed the throttle in. The surge of power tore the pontoons free, and the plane bulldozed its way forward. I felt like I was driving through an automatic car wash in the middle of an earthquake. The pontoons climbed the swells and fell into the valleys as wave after wave smashed over the cockpit, but the increased speed had given me direction control. I passed the ferry landing and then the seaplane dock before turning shoreward.

A Good Samaritan, seeing my predicament, ran down to the dock. When I got close, I opened the cockpit door and hollered, "Grab the wing." I stepped down onto the pontoon and reached for the rope to tie to the dock's cleat. A swell cresting above my waist nearly swept me into the fifty-degree water.

The Good Samaritan took hold of the wing. "I can't hang on," he shouted. I watched the wing slip from his grasp. Then a gust pushed the Cessna forward, like a sailboat on a spinnaker run. When I realized what was about to happen, I climbed into the cockpit and cut the engine, but not in time to keep the plane's propeller from imbedding itself into a ferry-terminal piling, like the blade of a chainsaw wedged in a log.

I began to hyperventilate, and my mind turned inward. I heard voices, but they didn't penetrate. When my focus returned, I climbed back out onto the pontoon and saw ferry-terminal employees struggling with a crowbar to dislodge the propeller. "Anacortes ferry!" one shouted, pointing out into the harbor.

Through foam and spray, I saw the ferry closing rapidly, less than one hundred yards away. I could feel my heart pound as I thought, *The ferry will crush the plane like a foot squashes a bug.*

I heard more shouting and looked up. The propeller was free, and the attendant was hurling a rope to me. "Tie it to the pontoon," he hollered.

While I fastened the line to the pontoon's cleat, the attendant, carrying the other end, dropped to the beach and sprinted to the seaplane dock. I heard the sound of accelerating engines and saw salt water churning. Though the captain had seen the plane and put the engines in reverse, momentum carried the ferry ever closer. I took a deep breath and prepared to jump into the icy water as passengers on the ferry's upper deck watched the impending disaster unfold.

Then the plane began to move. I saw the attendant and the good Samaritan pulling on the rope. I quickly slipped the buoy pole from its holder, and using all my strength, I pushed the pole against a piling, giving the plane enough clearance to be pulled around the pilings—but not enough to keep the wing from banging against the pilings. Minutes later, the Cessna was secured to the seaplane dock.

After thanking my rescuers, I called my flight instructor, Dick White, from the ferry landing pay phone so he could alert Search and Rescue not to come looking for me. By the time I reached Wendy, I was an emotional wreck. Two hours later, I was on a commuter flight to the South Tacoma airport.

The following morning Dick White, a mechanic as well as flight instructor, flew to Friday Harbor to check the plane's condition. He called that afternoon.

"Jim, with a new prop and half a dozen rolls of plastic tape you'll be able to fly it back. I've ordered the prop, and the factory has promised it by noon tomorrow. We can go up tomorrow afternoon in the 180"—the Cessna 180. "Okay?"

"Okay! Call me when you get the prop."

The following afternoon it took only minutes to change the prop, but a couple of hours to tape the holes in the wings and fuselage's aluminum skin. After we finished, Dick checked and double-checked the control cables. Then he said, "Let's go home," and I froze like a zombie, staring at my reflection in the mirror-like water.

"Griffin, get in the plane!" Dick shouted from the pontoon of the 180. He'd just cast off. His angry voice brought me out of my malaise. By habit, without thinking, I released the line from the dock cleat, pushed off, climbed into the cockpit, buckled up, put on my headphones, and started the engine.

Then I panicked. The plane began to drift with the tidal current. "Griffin, God damn it! Get with it!" Dick's piercing voice boomed through my headphones.

Reacting like a puppet manipulated by strings, I followed Dick's Cessna 180 into the air, mimicking its every change in direction and elevation, until arriving at American Lake Seaplane Base.

Dick told me a few days later he had expected my confidence to be shaken.

"Jim, I knew that if you didn't fly the plane home, you might never fly again. I saw it happen during the war [Dick had been a World War II bomber pilot]."

****

Flooded Pontoons

"Hang on. We're going to hit hard," I shouted, when the stall buzzer began blaring.

It was the summer of 1966, a month after we'd returned from Switzerland. I was flying the family home from Long Island after inaugurating a ramp Ted built so I could taxi the floatplane out of the water. Ted had fastened the ramp to the dock with a steel bar swivel. The other end of the ramp floated just beneath the water's surface. The dock was connected to the beach by a walkway supported by piles.

Long Island dock and ramp

Ashley, Wendy, Sterling, Scott, babysitter, and Whitney

A day earlier, I had tested the ramp—which worked perfectly—and then we scoured the beaches looking for agates and treasures that might have washed ashore during a storm. We picked up a bucket of oysters to roast over the campfire along with hamburgers and hot dogs. After dinner and a game of kick-the-can, Wendy, my half-brother Charlie, who'd come to live with us, and I put the boys to bed. We had left Ashley, our one-year-old, at home with Nancy, our Au Pair.

Later, when the wind came up and lightning streaked across the sky, followed by what sounded like the clash of a cymbal, I said, "Wendy, you'd better make a run for the cabin, the sky is about ready to open up." Ted and I had built a cabin with a canvas roof on the cliff above the cove. "Charlie and I will put out the fire." When I got to the cabin, I wrung out my clothes and toweled off before joining Wendy in our double sleeping bag.

"What's the forecast?" she asked, as I zipped up the bags.

"Fifteen to twenty knot winds tonight, but calm tomorrow," I said. "With the plane out of the water, there's nothing to worry about."

Twice during the night, fir branches rattling against the canvas roof woke me up, and I went out on the bluff to look down in the cove. Waves were breaking over the dock covering the plane in spray and foam, but it hadn't moved.

At sunrise, a dazzling kaleidoscope of colors reflected off the Cascade Mountains. Last night's whistling fir branches were now motionless. After a breakfast of scrambled eggs, toast, and bacon, we headed off on another scavenger hunt, to see what the storm might have deposited. Halfway across the island, near where we'd drilled our well, we spooked a four-point deer feeding in the meadow. The buck bounded, in gigantic leaps, to the edge of the water, turned for one last look at us, and leaped into the Sound. Twenty minutes later, we watched it come out of the water and scamper into the woods, on nearby Lopez Island.

"Dad, Mom, look," Scott shouted after we lost sight of the deer. He came running from the water's edge holding up a softball-size glass fishing net buoy, which for many years sat prominently on the den's fireplace mantel at our home on Gravelly Lake.

After peanut butter and jelly sandwiches, Wendy and I packed the plane while the boys, under Charlie's supervision, searched for starfish and sea anemones in piling pools under the ramp. Then Charlie, Wendy, and I—Scott and Sterling pretending to help—spun the plane around and, holding on to the pontoon lines, let gravity take it down the ramp into the water. I did a preflight and then started the engine, while Wendy strapped the boys in the backseat with Charlie—which was precarious as they held glass jars filled with a bonanza of rock-pool treasures.

Then I cast off, climbed into my seat, dropped the water rudders, maneuvered around kelp beds, and taxied into the channel separating Long Island and Lopez Island. I turned into the wind—to get airborne quicker—pulled up the water rudders, set the flaps at twenty degrees, and engaged the throttle. I immediately knew something was terribly amiss. "Now what?" I sputtered, under my breath.

Wendy picked up on my apprehension. "What's wrong?" she asked. Her voice and frown lines indicated concern.

"I can't get the pontoons out of the water," I said. "We must be dragging kelp. It should break away if I get enough speed to bounce off a wave." Seconds later the floatplane sprung off the top of a crest, like a snow skier springing off a bump. The stall warning buzzer immediately began blaring.

"What's happening?" Wendy yelled over the buzzer and engine noise. Before I could answer, the Cessna dropped back on the water with a tremendous jolt.

"Charlie, get the kids into life jackets!" I hollered.

I opened the cabin door and climbed down on the pontoon to check the struts. They looked okay, and I didn't see any trailing kelp. *What can it be?* I wondered, and then I knew. The pontoons rode barely above the water's surface, well below their normal height. *They had to be full of water*, I thought. I hadn't checked before leaving the island because the Cessna had sat on the dock during the storm.

I removed a pontoon cap. "Shit," I shouted in exasperation.

"What, what's wrong?" Wendy yelled out her door.

"The pontoons are full of water. Too much weight for the plane to fly."

"Didn't you check them during the preflight?" Wendy asked.

"I should have, but with the plane up on the dock, I didn't think it was necessary."

I got out the hand pump from the storage locker and began pumping. The wind and tide continually pushed the plane toward a reef, and every few minutes I had to restart the engine and move it back out into the channel. When I grew tired of pumping, Charlie took over. By the time we finished, we were soaked and freezing from water cascading over the pontoons.

Back in the air, nearly forty-five minutes later, Wendy leaned over and whispered, "What would have happened if the struts collapsed?"

"The cabin would have filled with water and the plane would have sunk. That's why I told Charlie to get the kids into life jackets."

****

Wing in the Water

Seconds after the pontoons touched water, a gust lifted the Cessna's left wing, causing the right wing to plunge into Puget Sound.

It was August 1968, shortly after Charlie Johnson and I purchased Thurston County Bank. I was flying my family to Ted's home on Bainbridge Island. He had called a few days before with an invitation to a Sunday beach picnic. "Come in the plane," he said. "You've been promising my kids a ride all summer."

"I don't know. After the pontoon incident, Wendy has been reluctant to let the kids fly with me. I'll ask and get back to you."

When I came home from work and opened the back door, our hamster and Mastiff-sized German shepherd immediately hit me up for treats. Sally squeaked until I gave her lettuce and

Max, paws resting on my chest and our eyes level, licked my face until he got a taste of whatever Wendy prepared for dinner.

"High, babes," I said. After extracting myself from Max, I put my arms around Wendy as she bent over the sink and kissed the back of her neck.

"Oh God! What's it this time?" she mumbled as she wiped Max's saliva off with her shirt sleeve. I thought, *Am I that transparent?* Before I could release my hands, Scott, Sterling, and Whitney were clinging to me, all speaking at the same time.

"Hey, guys," I said. "One at a time." Then Nancy, the au pair, came out of her room, adjoining the kitchen, with an armful of folded laundry. Three-year-old Ashley followed, pushing a buggy full of dolls and stuffed animals.

I said, "Ted called and invited us to join them for a picnic on Bainbridge Sunday. Do we have anything on?"

"No, we're clear."

"He wants us to come in the plane, so I can give his kids a ride. I've been promising them all summer."

"Okay, but I'll take the children in the car."

"No! We want to go with Dad," the boys shouted.

By the end of dinner, they had worn their mother down. "Okay, okay, we'll go in the plane," Wendy finally said.

Sunday morning, I phoned the weather line. The forecast called for clear skies, temperature in the high seventies and twenty-knot wind gusts. Ted lived at the end of a sheltered bay, so wind wouldn't be a problem. Then I called American Lake Seaplane Base and asked to have the Cessna ready to go at one o'clock.

"Wendy," I said, when we arrived at American Lake, "I'm going to the office and file a flight plan. Take the kids to the dock and get them in life jackets. I'll be right down."

"Okay. Come on, kids," Wendy said. "Let's go down to the plane." By the time I got to the lake, Wendy had the children strapped into the backseat. After completing the preflight, I started the engine, cast off, and threaded my way through water skiers and fishing boats to the southern end of the lake. A light northerly breeze filtered through the cabin vents, which helped offset the heat of six sweating bodies. Less than a minute after lifting off the water, we were over Tacoma Country and Golf Club, in sight of our house on Gravelly Lake.

Our house on Gravelly Lake

"Look. There's Max," Sterling shouted. Everyone looked out the window as I circled the house to gain altitude before crossing to Puget Sound. I looked down and saw Max curled up asleep on the hot asphalt driveway.

When I reached Puget Sound, I flew north, skirting the east side of Vashon Island, then northwest toward Bainbridge Island. Mount Baker's snowcapped peak loomed on the horizon.

Over Ted's house at end of the Bay, I saw my brother at the dock working on the *Pegasus*. Joan and the children were on the beach.

Ted, sons Jon and Jay, daughter Gaye,
and Joan holding daughter Jill

"Dad, dip your wings," Scott yelled, "they're waving."

"Okay," I said, and I dipped the wings.

The bay reflected the plane like a mirror, but outside the cove whitecaps broke on the beach. I circled again before dropping over the fir trees at the back of their house.

Oh God, I thought, as the Cessna touched the water. *I'll never be able to stop before reaching the Sound. Stupid, stupid! Why didn't I approach through the entrance to the bay, instead of showboating?* I touched down inside the bay, but momentum carried the plane out into the white caps. The vivid memory of landing at Friday Harbor in a storm flashed through my mind. Then a gust of wind caught the wing and lifted it like the end of a teeter-totter.

"Wendy, move this way," I said as I pulled her into my lap, and then hollered, "Kids, quick! Unbuckle your seat belts." The transfer of weight caused the plane to slowly right itself. Had the plane been moving faster when the wing dove into the water, it would have cart wheeled and quickly sunk. I took a deep breath and sighed. Wendy was speechless, deep in her own thoughts. The children had no idea of what nearly happened.

I turned north into the wind and regained control of the plane before taxiing into the cove. As we came alongside the dock, the ashen faces of Ted and Joan made me realize how much I had put at risk.

****

Flying Blind

"We're almost within gliding distance," I said, when I saw tears running down Wendy's cheeks. Minutes before, I'd left American Lake heading toward Puget Sound.

It was the fall of 1969, a few days after Harold Allen and I learned that the apartment house we bought was a house of prostitution. From the bedroom window, I couldn't see the lake. The barometer rose overnight, so I knew the fog would clear by midmorning. Two weeks of ocean storms had kept me out of the air, and I had a fetish about flying twice a week. I knew from flight training that pilots who flew only occasionally could lose their "touch" and not react instinctively in a crisis situation.

"Wendy, will you call me when the fog lifts?" I asked, before I left for the office.

"Sure," she said.

She called at 11:30. "The lake's clear."

"Great. I'll come right home. Do you want to join me? We won't be long. I'm just practicing touch and goes on the Sound. We'll be home before the kids get out of school." No response, but I could hear her breathing. I thought, *What did I expect? The terrifying landing at Bainbridge Island following numerous other pilot errors had taken its toll.*

"Yes," she finally said.

"Okay, I'll see you shortly," I said, feeling relieved that she was still willing to fly with me.

"There's no rush," Wendy said. "I don't have anything going."

I phoned the weather line. The forecast called for clear skies, temperature in the high seventies, and ten-knot winds in the lower Sound. *Ideal conditions*, I thought. Then I called American Lake Seaplane Base and asked to have the Cessna put in the lake. I picked Wendy up just after 12:00, and we arrived at the seaplane base ten minutes later. From the parking lot, I could see the plane tied to the dock.

"Aren't you going to file a flight plan?" Wendy asked on our way down to the dock.

"No. We're not leaving the lower Sound."

During the preflight, I noticed the oil level was low, and I got a quart from the Cessna's storage cabinet. I opened the cowling and as I began pouring oil into the intake pipe, Dick White shouted down from the office.

"Jim, your secretary is on the phone!"

"Okay, tell her I'll be right up," I yelled. I emptied the can and then ran up to the office, depositing the can in the trash barrel on the way. Five minutes later, I returned to the dock and dropped the cowling hood back in place. When I climbed into the cockpit and started the engine, Wendy asked, "Is everything okay?"

"Yes. Ruth called to let me know that my four o'clock meeting has been cancelled."

I completed the preflight and taxied out onto the lake. There wasn't a ripple on the water.

"Where are all the boats?" Wendy asked, as the plane lifted off the water.

"The fishermen are home napping, and the water skiers are back in school," I said.

"Yeah of course," Wendy said.

When I reached 2,500 feet and turned west toward the sound, Wendy asked, "What's that sheen on the windshield?"

"What sheen? Oh," I said noticing what looked like mist. "It's probably aviation fuel jettisoned from a McCord plane." (McCord Air Force Base was located two miles northeast of American Lake.) Two minutes later, the sheen had turned to film.

"Oh God, it looks like oil," I said. Whatever the substance, it had now totally obscured the windshield.

"It looks like oil is spraying out of the engine vents," Wendy said. I knew from working in an auto shop as a teenager that an engine quickly freezes up without oil. Then I thought, *At any moment, I'm going to hear grinding metal, like the sound of a fork caught in a garbage disposal.*

"What are you going to do?" Wendy asked.

"Keep going," I said. "The Sound is now closer than the lake. I'll be able to glide to the water in another minute or so."

When I turned the engine off, the Cessna dropped quickly. I had just enough altitude to clear the trees on the hill above the water. I looked north through Wendy's window to make certain that my glide path was clear. A tug was towing a gravel barge north, two pleasure cruisers were headed south, and the usual salmon fishermen, in outboards, were clustered between the southeast end of Fox Island and the Narrows Bridge. I couldn't see anything that would intersect my glide path.

"All clear!" I said. I turned north into the wind, set the flaps to twenty degrees, and began my approach. Having no visibility through the windshield, I focused on the instrument panel, as I had been taught to do in simulated landings while wearing blinders similar to those worn by New York's Central Park carriage horses to keep them from seeing cars. The altimeter dropped rapidly.

"A sailboat!" Wendy shouted. "It's crossing in front of us."

"I see it." I turned the engine on, and then quickly turned it off. The sailors looked up when they heard the engine noise. We were less than one hundred feet above them and could see their terrified expressions. They instantly came about, tacking easterly. Moments later, the Cessna settled on the water. The north wind and incoming tide quickly stopped the plane's momentum.

"That was close," I said. Wendy didn't respond. The look she gave me said it all.

I stepped out onto the pontoon and unfastened the engine cowling. "No!" I exclaimed. I couldn't believe my carelessness.

"What? What's wrong?" Wendy asked, sticking her head out the cabin door.

"I left the cap off the oil intake pipe when I fastened the cowling. Luckily it got wedged between the engine and cowling."

"Do you have more oil?"

"One quart." I poured the oil down the spout and then pulled out the dipstick. The stick was dry. I couldn't remember how much oil the engine held.

At that moment, it didn't matter. I had a more pressing problem. The wind and eight-knot current were rapidly sweeping the plane toward the rock retaining wall that supported the railroad tracks along the Sound's eastern shore.

I got a roll of toilet paper out of the storage cabinet, and Wendy and I reached out the doors and began wiping oil from the windshield. "I'm going to start the engine and move away from the rocks," I said. I taxied out 100 yards, and we went back to absorbing oil until the plane again drifted near the retaining wall. "Let's go," I hollered. We buckled up and seconds later were airborne.

We made the five-minute flight back to American Lake in a high state of anxiety, expecting at any moment to hear grinding metal.

Dick phoned the next morning before I left for the office.

"The engine is okay. You've avoided another one!" he said.

****

Holes in the Fuselage

The Cessna must look like a shot-up reconnaissance plane, from an epic war film, I thought, seeing the concerned looks of Wendy and the others when I taxied to the beach to pick up our luggage.

In July 1972, when I was still in a state of euphoria from receiving federal approval for the Bank of Honolulu, Wendy and I flew to Savary Island in British Columbia's Georgia Strait and spent a long weekend with the Shanamans. We cleared customs at Nanaimo, one hundred miles north of Victoria, BC, and then flew up the Strait of Georgia, on the east coast of Vancouver Island, before crossing to the mainland where Highway 101 ended. Savary Island, discovered and named by Captain George Vancouver in 1792, sat two miles off Lund.

I circled Savary until I spotted the Shanamans' cabin. Dick, his wife Betty, and Dick's parents, Marge and Fred Sr. were waiting on the beach when we arrived. After unloading our duffel bags, Marge said, "Dick, will you and Jim pick up the groceries in Lund? I needed a few things for lunch and called in an order."

Marge Shanaman, me, Wendy, Betty Shanaman (holding son Chris), Dick Shanaman, and Fred Shanaman

"Yeah, after we secure the plane to the buoy we'll head over to Lund," Dick answered. Dick and I towed the Cessna behind his boat to the buoy, which was anchored beyond extreme low tide. Minutes later, we were bouncing over whitecaps at thirty miles an hour. On the way back to Savary, after picking up the groceries, we stopped at the buoy to drop off the boat.

"Tie the plane to the back of my boat," Dick said, as he threw me the end of the water ski rope, which was fastened to the boat's transom. I secured the rope to both pontoons, in triangular configuration, so the plane would trail in the boat's wake.

"The current will keep them separated," Dick said. Then we rowed the dinghy to shore and carried it to the top of the beach. Later, as the tide came in, we saw the Cessna trailing well behind the boat.

The temperature remained in the eighties the next two days.

We water-skied, played touch football on the beach, tennis on a wood-planked court, and hit golf balls into the ocean, which we picked up at low tide.

Me playing tennis on Savary's wood court

Me water skiing

Our last night, I woke to the sound of hail bouncing off the roof and pine branches rattling against the windows. I jumped out of bed and grabbed my Levi's.

"What's wrong?" Wendy asked when she heard the door open.

"A storm," I said. I'm going to check on the plane." I went out on the deck. Through the mist and rain, I could just make out the Cessna's outline. It looked to be trailing behind the boat, so I quickly returned to the room.

"Is everything okay?" Wendy asked, as I rummaged through my duffel for a dry shirt and shorts.

"Yes."

The next morning, we sat on the porch, cradling coffee and tea mugs, enjoying an array of colors ricocheting off the snowcapped Coast Mountain peaks. When it was time to leave,

Dick rowed me out to the plane in the dinghy. Halfway to the buoy, I said, "Dick, we have a problem."

"What's wrong?"

"The Cessna's profile has changed."

As we drew nearer, Dick stammered, "*My God!*" and I began to hyperventilate—which seemed to be developing into a habit.

I saw gaping holes, some more than a foot long, in the aluminum skin of the fuselage and wings. A large piece of fabric clung to the boat's light pole, like a pennant from a ship's mast.

"Will you be able to fly?" Dick asked.

"I don't know. Maybe, if the control cables still function. The holes can be patched," I said, remembering my calamitous flight to Friday Harbor.

"The wind must have blown the plane into the back of the boat at slack tide," Dick said. "When there wasn't enough current to keep them separated."

Where can I get the plane repaired? I wondered. The nearest town, Powell River, was more than an hour's drive south, and I might have to go as far as Vancouver.

"Dick, why don't you take the dinghy to shore and tell the others what happened? If the controls check out, I'll follow you in." I examined each cable meticulously and then pumped out the pontoons. Forty-five minutes later, I started the engine. Everybody but Dick's mother watched me taxi to shore. When I climbed out of the cockpit onto the pontoon, nobody spoke.

Then Mr. Shanaman asked, "What's your speed?" I thought, He's an engineer, and might know the likelihood of losing more fabric.

"Just over a hundred," I said.

"Maybe," he said, "but it could be risky."

While I was trying to figure out what *risky* meant, Dick's mother came down the beach waving two rolls of four-inch duct tape, similar to the tape we used to patch the Cessna's punctures at Friday Harbor. "This ought to keep the fabric from tearing further," she said.

An hour later, after many hugs, Wendy and I climbed into the cockpit and I started the engine. "Will the tape hold?" Wendy asked, as we lifted off the water.

"Yes," I said, not wanting her to worry for the next four hours. The tape held. We made it back to American Lake without mishap. However, when we cleared customs at Roche Harbor on San Juan Island, the customs agent asked, "Who was shooting at you?"

"That's it," Wendy said, as she stepped onto the dock at American Lake Seaplane Base.

"What's it?" I asked.

"I'm not getting in the plane again, and if I have anything to say about it, neither will the children." True to her words, neither Wendy nor the kids ever flew with me again.

Flying without the family became a burden rather than a joy; and I finally had to accept the possibility that the next mishap could end my life. I quit.

(9) Off-Road Racing: The Baja 500

"Griffin!" Chris yelled, as a torrent of spray broke over the McKinsey River boat.

I laughed, watching the six-foot-four, curly-headed giant shake water from his hair, like Kavik, our German shepherd, when he came out of the lake.

"Hang on!" our guide shouted. "It's going to be a rough one." His biceps, beneath a T-shirt, looked like those of a weight lifter as he struggled to keep the boat from flipping. Thirty seconds later, we were through the rapids, out of the canyon, and back in the sun.

South Fork of the Salmon River (1972)

"What I started to say," Chris continued, "was next summer let's run the Baja 1000." The Baja 1000 is the world's most dangerous off-road race. It starts in Ensenada, Mexico, and finishes in La Paz, near the tip of the Baja Peninsula.

"I thought we're running with the bulls in Pamplona?"

"You guys are nuts!" hollered Chris's wife, Wendy. She and my wife's, Wendy, boat trailed just behind us.

"Okay," I said, trying to sound disappointed, "Baja next year, and Pamplona the following year."

Chris Reynolds and I met in the fall of 1969. He and his wife (who grew up in Phoenix with my wife) spent a night with us in Tacoma while on an auto trip from their Phoenix home to Canada. Chris and I talked until dawn. We had many things in common, in addition to marrying Wendys and graduating from Stanford, though he arrived after I left.

As we knew nothing about off-road racing, other than what we read in magazines and watched on TV, we agreed to meet in Las Vegas the following April, in 1973, for the Mint 400, the first race of the year. We talked on the phone regularly over the next eight months and sent off-road magazine articles to each other.

When April finally arrived, Wendy and I flew to Las Vegas a day before the race. On the way to the hotel from the airport, we passed dune buggies, Ford Broncos, jeeps, mini and full-size pickups, and motorcycles, including three-wheelers and those with sidecars.

The Reynolds were at the hotel when we arrived. After lunch, Chris and I went looking for someone to build us a car. When we returned, having had no success, our wives were all smiles.

"What's up?" I said. I knew they couldn't wait to be asked.

"We've been invited to the pre-race banquet," my Wendy said.

"By whom?" Chris asked.

"Stroppe team racers," Wendy Reynolds replied.

Chris and I were speechless. Bill Stroppe, the premier builder of off-road racing vehicles and under contract with Ford Motor Company, was famous for his winning Baja, Indy 500, and Pikes Peak cars, as well as Gold Cup hydroplanes.

"How did you pull that off?" I asked.

"How do you think?" Wendy Reynolds replied. Then I saw her wink at Wendy—as if to say, *You tell them.*

"Wendy and I went for a walk and stopped in the hotel parking lot to look at the off-road cars," my Wendy said. "When we passed a converted Ford pickup, two men wearing Stroppe team uniforms slid out from under the truck and asked what we were doing in Vegas. We told them we'd come to watch the race. They asked if we'd like to join them for the pre-race banquet tonight. We said sure, thinking it might give you guys an opportunity to meet someone who would build you a car. We told them there were four of us."

"Yeah," Wendy Reynolds said. "They obviously thought four women because they said, 'Bring them along and join us at the Stroppe table.'"

I thought, *There's no mystery here.* The drivers popped out from under their pickup to see if our wives looked as good from the waist up as they did from the waist down.

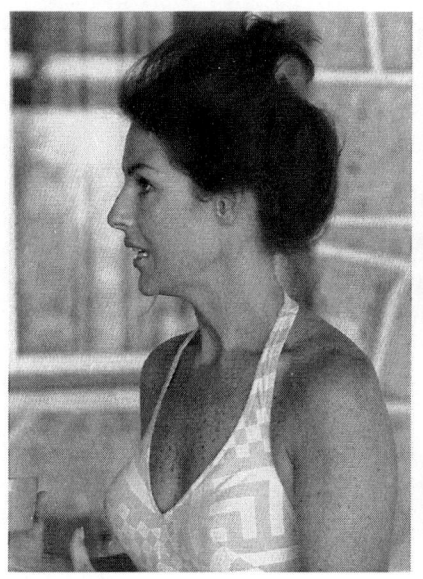

Wendy Reynolds   Wendy Griffin

When we arrived at the banquet, Chris and I immediately recognized Bill Stroppe from newspaper and magazine pictures. He stood nearly six feet tall, had a full head of graying hair, and looked like he spent time in the gym. His photos didn't reflect the sparkle in his eyes. He would have passed for a corporate executive if not for his stained and muscular hands, hardened from years of working with machinery and lubricants.

Introductions were awkward. Chris and I had to buy several pitchers of beer before the mechanic and driver forgave our wives for their chicanery. Eventually the drivers began reliving their past glories—our Wendys were a whole new audience—and we took the opportunity to ask Stroppe about a Baja car.

Chris said, "Mr. Stroppe."

"Call me Bill."

"Bill, would you build Jim and me a car? We'd like to race the Baja 1000." All conversation at the table immediately stopped. You could have heard a pin drop. Bill locked eyes with Chris and then with me, sizing us up—I didn't blink. Five seconds passed, then ten. You could feel tension around the table.

Finally Bill spoke, "I'll do it," he said. "I'll convert a Courier"—Ford's mini-pickup—"and you can join our team."

"Yes!" Chris and I shouted, as we slapped hands in a high-five. I glanced at Wendy. She raised her arms chest high, turned her palms toward the ceiling, and gave me a smug smile, indicating "What can I say?" Chris and I shook hands with Stroppe, who held my hand in a vise grip. I counted a half-dozen slaps on the back and heard "Welcome to the team."

"Do you have any suggestions for a race school?" I asked. We needed to acknowledge his offer, and I couldn't think of anything else to say, being so excited. An ear-to-ear smile spread across his face. Then I saw him wink at the drivers.

"There are no race schools for what we do," he laughed. "Run the Baja 500 with us in June, and you'll be ready for the 1000 in July."

I looked at Chris. He nodded. "Great!" I said.

"We're in!" Chris said at the same time. Then the conversation turned to race logistics and where and when Chris and I were to be at such-and-such a place, until the race chairman gave the usual—according to one of the drivers—safety speech.

"Chris, can you make any sense out of what just happened?" I asked, as the four of us walked back to the hotel.

Chris hesitated before replying. "Maybe he recognized in us those qualities he sees in his veteran drivers, a hard-core competitive spirit."

"Possibly, but one thing for certain, if it weren't for our wives, we would be watching the Baja on TV."

Wendy squeezed my hand three times, our signal for 'I love you.'

I'm certain that Stroppe's drivers, and later the entire race community, questioned Stroppe's judgment in allowing two novices to join his team. To this day, I'm not sure why he did. I would like to think Chris made the correct assessment.

Over the following weeks, we made several trips to Stroppe's Long Beach plant. To reduce weight, the mechanics discarded the side windows, dash board, interior fittings, and all nonessentials. Then they installed bucket seats with five-point harnesses and a roll bar with rubber padding, to protect our heads if the Courier flipped.

Other than the tachometer, which indicates how fast the engine is turning over, mechanics pulled out all dashboard instruments and reconnected them in front of the co-driver's seat. Then they bolted a two-gallon water cooler, with twin plastic tubes, to the cab behind the bucket seats and replaced the clutch, axle, shocks, springs, and every nut and bolt with alloyed materials capable of withstanding constant battering. The mechanics welded a quarter-inch steel plate over the oil pan to protect it from punctures; exchanged the fuel tank with a twenty-seven-gallon reinforced tank with an enlarged intake for rapid fueling, similar to that used by Indy 500 cars; replaced the tires with low pressure balloon tires to provide extra traction and shock absorption; and took out the muffler which reduced engines torque.

Then in late May, Chris and I joined the Stroppe team and pre-ran the Baja 500. With us were Indianapolis 500 drivers Parnelli Jones, Mickey Thompson, and Rick Mears. All three were Baja 500 and Baja 1000 winners. Also with us was seven-time Baja champion Walker Evans, who went on to win more off-road races than any other competitor; and motorcyclist Malcolm Smith, who was featured in the 1972 movie *On Any Sunday* and the 2005 movie *Dust to Glory*.

The final members of the team were Frank Vessals, owner of the Los Alamitos horse track (his horse, Time to Think Rich, had just won $1 million at Ruidoso Downs in New Mexico, the largest purse at that time); Vessals' son Scoop; Ron Price; and Stroppe's friend, musician Ray Coniff.

Me on pre-run studying the course

We followed the 612-mile course three days and two nights over hazardous terrain, driving a loaned Stroppe Bronco with worn-out shock absorbers. Every bounce felt like a chair being pulled out from under us. Though Chris's and my backsides were bruised and sore for days, the pre-run couldn't have been more fun—enhanced by tequila and Baja racing stories around campfires.

On June 6, 1973, when I was thirty-six, our team met Stroppe's low-boy truck and trailer at the Tijuana, Mexico, bull ring. We unloaded the cars and drove sixty miles south to a police-secured compound, safe from sabotage, in Ensenada. The drive gave us an opportunity to get a feel for the Courier's balloon tires.

Chris and me unloading Baja cars in Tijuana

We spent the remainder of the day assembling items to accompany us. We taped a canister to the roll bar so race officials could insert tags at the mandatory checkpoints—to verify that we had followed the prescribed course—and stowed a first-aid kit, sleeping bags, goggles, emergency food, compass, snake antivenin, pillows (for me to sit on because the bucket seats were designed for Chris's large frame), and a bottle of Jack Daniel's, in case the car broke down.

Before leaving, a Stroppe mechanic came by with a ten-foot antenna with an orange flag attached to one end.

"What's that for?" I asked.

"Without flags, someone might crash into you when you're crossing Diablo Dry Lake," he said. Once the ash and dirt, which washes down from the Sierra San Pedro mountains, gets churned up, visibility is virtually zero. After the mechanic bolted on the antenna, Chris and I left to join our wives, who were staying south of Ensenada near the town of Maneadero, at Chris's father's hunting club.

As we climbed into the pickup, Chris said, "Hold on. Stroppe is heading our way. He looks like he has something on his mind."

"Guys," he said, "I forgot to mention a couple of things. Until you get a feel for the road, follow another car, and for God's sake keep your eye on the tachometer. Rookies usually stress the engine in the lower gears."

His comment reminded me of my one race in an MG. "Yeah, I know all about that. I burned up an MG engine racing."

"Well, I won't worry then," Stroppe said. "The same principle applies when you use the gears to save the brakes descending the mountains. Don't under any circumstances stop on Diablo Dry Lake because some places the ash is like quicksand. And change drivers only when absolutely necessary. It takes precious minutes for a new driver to bring the car's speed back to where it was." This was one piece of advice Chris and I would ignore. We had agreed to change seats at every checkpoint.

"What about taking a pee?" I asked.

Stroppe laughed. "That's why you're wearing yellow racing suits," he said.

The race started early the next morning. With a car leaving every sixty seconds, it took nearly six hours for the 350 entries to get under way. Chris and I started 256, our car number. The sun was high in the sky when our turn came.

As we ran the Baja 500 and 1000 one month apart, nearly forty years ago, some of my recollections could apply to either race.

Ten minutes before starting, we zipped up fireproof Nomex suits (the kind designed for NASA astronauts), put on helmets, climbed into the Courier's bucket seats, attached restraining harnesses, started the engine—Chris won the coin toss and sat behind the wheel—and took our place in line. Our wives stuck their heads through the windowless doors and gave final hugs and an ill-timed lecture on safe driving—which we would ignore. By the time we reached the top of the starting ramp, I felt perspiration running down my back and chest and from under my arms.

"Are we crazy or what?" I hollered above the engine noise as the starter raised his flag. The flag dropped and Chris popped the clutch. "Hooo haaa!" he shouted as the Courier went airborne and then bounced off the pavement.

"Oh my God," I shouted, when I saw spectators blocking Ensenada's main boulevard. "Chris, slow down!"

We're off—road ahead blocked

"They'll move," he said and continued to accelerate. At the last moment, the crowd parted with inches to spare. *Christ! What a close call*, I thought, *and we're not even out of town.*

The route took us past La Grulla where our wives, Chris's parents, and their friends had set up a roadside picnic. As we passed, they cheered wildly and raised high their Bloody Marys.

Parnelli Jones overtook us just past Maneadero in his Olympia Beer Ford Bronco. As he shot past, Stroppe's head appeared out the Bronco's passenger window.

"Go get 'em, boys!" he shouted.

"My God!" I hollered. "Parnelli must be doing 150."

Minutes later, we left the pavement and turned west toward the Pacific Ocean into Santo Tomás Canyon, home of many fine vineyards. The Courier's 109.5 horsepower modified engine turned 7,000 revolutions per minute. In seconds, Chris could accelerate to one hundred miles per hour on the straightaways, but any bump in the road sent us airborne. Our copious notes from the pre-run were worthless at this speed, even assuming Chris could hear above the screaming engine.

Santo Tomás Canyon

A few minutes later, on a hairpin turn less than an hour from Ensenada; the Courier flew off the road and landed upside down. The sound of metal grinding against rock was ear piercing. When the pickup finally stopped skidding, Chris and I hung upside down, like monkeys hanging by their tails from a tree. Blood trickled down Chris's forehead and pooled on the cab ceiling. Chris still held the steering wheel, but it was no longer attached to the steering column.

"You all right?" I asked.

"Yeah, how about you?"

"I'm okay," I said, "but I hope the Jack Daniel's didn't break." My comment started a gut-wrenching fit of laughter, finally drowned out by an engine gearing down. Then a cloud of dust enveloped us. Seconds later, Walker Evans and Shelby Mongeon unhooked our harnesses and gently lowered us to the cab's ceiling. I'll never forget their looks of total disbelief when Chris crawled out clutching the steering wheel.

"Anything broken?" Walker asked.

"No. We're good to go if the engine starts," Chris said.

"It'll start," Walker said. "That's what you paid Stroppe for." As we took hold of the truck's frame, a Toyota pickup slowed and then accelerated again when Walker waved off the driver.

After righting the pickup, I saw Walker grimace as he scanned the cab's roof. "Diablo will be a tough crossing tonight without lights," he said. I followed his gaze. Spaghetti-like wire protruded from holes where the spotlights had been attached.

"Any suggestions?" I asked.

"Yeah, get on somebody's rear end and stay there," he chuckled as he and Shelby shared smiles. Then Walker said, "Reynolds, give me the wheel." Chris handed it to him. Walker wrenched open the pickup's door and inserted the wheel's shaft back into the steering column's sleeve. He tightened the locking nut with a crescent wrench which mysteriously appeared from his racing suit.

Then he turned to Shelby. "Let's get going," he said. I tossed my pillows on the driver's seat, jumped in, and hit the ignition switch as Chris climbed into the co-driver seat. The engine sputtered, belched smoke, and turned over.

The moment it began idling smoothly, Walker, who was already behind the wheel of his pickup, shouted, "You've got another sixteen hours. Are you sure you want to go on?"

"We'll make it!" Chris hollered and I added, "See you at the finish!" Within seconds, we were following their trail of dust.

"Chris," I said, "they don't think we have a snowball's chance in hell of finishing."

"Griffin, we'll finish if we have to push the Courier over the line," which elicited another high-five.

Fifteen miles later, before the town of La Bocana, we turned south onto a century-old wagon road that connected the coast settlements. We raced atop a bluff with magnificent views of ocean swells crashing into sheer cliffs, before descending and paralleling a series of uninhabited rock and gray sandy beaches. Then the course turned inland, circling the pueblos to keep from endangering residents and animals.

Mountain foothills   Ascending mountain

The first checkpoint was Camalu, 124 miles south of Ensenada. I stopped momentarily, so a race official could insert a tag into the roll-bar canister, before pulling into the adjoining Stroppe pit.

"You guys okay?" the pit boss asked, as he gawked at the Courier's dents and gouges. "Walker and Shelby said you flipped. They have some doubts about you finishing and asked me to alert Ensenada." A ham radio operator worked at every checkpoint to report injuries and breakdowns.

"We're okay," I said, as I leapt out of the driver's seat carrying my pillows and ran around to the passenger door while Chris jumped in behind the wheel. The pit crew filled the gas tank and checked the tire pressure, water, oil, and drinking water. We continually sucked on our hoses to replace the fluid sweating out of us. We were back on the road in less than two minutes and headed inland across the Baja Peninsula.

We had two mountain ranges to cross, Sierra de San Miguel and Sierra San Pedro, before reaching the desert of San Felipe and dreaded Diablo Dry Lake. Chris had no problem staying on course. When the road forked, he followed tire ruts.

We rarely overtook an "unlimited"; they were much faster. Dune buggies pulled over when Chris honked, but not the mini-pickups; they were our competition. He tried to pass on the straightaways, but if a mini driver wouldn't move over, Chris raced him into the corner and the person with the biggest *cojones*—usually Chris—led the way out, showering the other car with flying rocks and dirt.

Descending the mountain took precision timing to coordinate the gears and brakes. Chris quickly learned when to back off the accelerator and when and how much brake to apply. Too little brake swung the Courier to the opposite side of the road where the drop-offs could be severe. Too much brake put the Courier into a skid, causing the same result.

Back in the desert, Chris kept the pedal to the metal. Any deep rut or road indentation sent the pickup airborne. He passed cars on every straightaway. Whether they lacked our speed, or the drivers were being cautious, we didn't know or care.

Thirty minutes later, we went through the second checkpoint and changed seats in the Stroppe pit. "You're making good time," the mechanic said. "The latest report has you in the top third of your category."

I accelerated out of the pit in a cloud of dust. One hour later, we were in the San Pedro foothills looking up at 10,000-foot Cerro del Diablo. Then near the top of a steep incline, the engine stalled and died. We'd had no problem here on the pre-run, but then we'd been driving a four-wheel-drive Bronco.

"Take a run at it," Chris said.

I coasted backward to the bottom, made a wide turn, and hit the hill at forty miles an hour in third gear. Halfway up I shifted into second and two hundred feet from the summit into first. Before reaching the top, I had to disengage the clutch to keep from stalling. "How the hell are the two-wheelers doing it?" I shouted in exasperation. The screaming pitch of an accelerating engine drowned out my curse. And then the dune-buggy we passed a few minutes before clamored by us in reverse, backing up the hill. "Will you look at that?" I exclaimed. "Stroppe didn't tell us everything."

I coasted once again to the bottom, shifted into reverse, and backed the Courier to the top. After a quick high-five, I turned the pickup around and tore after the dune buggy, overtaking it minutes later.

We passed through ranch after ranch, each at a higher elevation. Race officials had arranged for the owners to leave their gates open. Periodically, a lone Saguaro cactus stood out like a sentinel, but the cattle had disappeared.

"Chris, what happened to the cattle? They were everywhere on the pre-run."

"Ranchers moved them to a safer environment. In this desert climate each skinny cow is worth a small fortune." Chris worked for a major farming corporation in Arizona.

We skirted Martir National Park and left the Sierra San Pedro foothills on the western edge of the desert of San Felipe. An hour later, checkpoint lights lit up the moonless night. We passed through and then changed seats in the pit, where we took on gas and more drinking water.

"Good going, guys," said the Stroppe pit boss, as he filled the gas and drinking water tanks. "The ham operator says you're only minutes behind the mini-pickup leaders."

"Thanks," I said, as Chris jammed his foot on the throttle and dragged away with dirt and sand flying out from behind the tires.

"Griffin," he shouted, "we're going to have a hell of a time holding our position on the lake." Most of our competitors had experienced Diablo's bottomless ash.

"Remember what Walker said: get behind someone who knows what he is doing and don't stop."

There was no mistaking our entry onto the infamous lake bed. It was like driving into a marsh. The further we progressed, the deeper the tires sank and the thicker the dust cloud grew. If we stopped, the race was over.

"Shit, I can't see a taillight or antenna flag." Chris's outburst brought memories of freaking out when I flew my plane into a fog bank. "What the hell should we do?"

"Over there!" I shouted, pointing off to the left. "It looks like a hill. Maybe we can get enough elevation to see over the dust." Chris took a run at the hill and stopped at the top with the Courier's back tires resting on the downward slope, to make certain gravity would get us going again. We weren't above the dust, but we were high enough to see through it.

"It looks like a tilted pinball machine out there," I exclaimed, watching cars go in every direction trying to find their way through the dust cloud.

"Get the compass out, and give me a northerly direction," Chris said. I located north and through the dust saw a long string of lights that looked like a train.

"Chris, look! Way out there. Those guys know where there're going." Chris accelerated off the hill before I finished the sentence, with me pointing the way. We crossed through the circle of confused drivers and five minutes later took our place in line behind a mini Toyota. Nobody passed. That would come soon enough. Half an hour later, the ground grew firmer, and all hell broke loose. Like the start of a horse race, where jockeys line up across the track and, at the sound of the gun, race for the rail, we raced for the road.

The big-engine vehicles surged ahead. Chris pulled in behind the Toyota, which had more horsepower than the Courier. But when the driver braked for a turn, Chris slipped in ahead.

We climbed back into the Sierra San Pedro foothills, onto a long-abandoned road that meandered from San Felipe on the

Sea of Cortez through the Valle de Trinidad, just north of Mike's Sky Ranch—elevation 6,000 feet—where we'd stopped for breakfast on the pre-run. Before the plateau town of Colonia Cardenas, we passed through the last checkpoint and made our final seat change.

"Less than one hundred miles to go, Griffin," Chris said. "Put the pedal to the medal!"

When we dropped out of the hills, I kept the accelerator pressed to the floor, breaking only on hairpin turns and when we circled pueblos. Spurts of smoke, like that from a coal-fired train engine, shot out of the exhaust when I shifted, and the engine begin knocking.

When Chris heard the knocking, he said, "Griffin, what do you think?"

"It will have to be rebuilt before the Baja 1000 so we might as well go for it," I said, and I did. We'd been on the road nearly sixteen hours. I was exhausted. If my eyes closed, Chris shook me and squirted water from his drinking tube down the back of my neck.

Finally, the predawn lights of Ensenada appeared on the horizon. When we reached the macadamized pavement, like a marathon runner getting his second wind, I pushed the Courier's 1,800-cubic-inch engine to its limit, pegging the tachometer in the danger zone. As we approached the finish, we could see our wives jumping and waving like high-school cheerleaders. We crossed the line as the sun peeked over the horizon and I geared to a stop—little brake pad remained—behind the recent finishers. Officials immediately cut away our token canister from the dented roll bar. Our wives reached through the windowless door panels and threw their arms around us, ignoring the overpowering smell of urine.

"Griffin, we did it!" Chris shouted, as he slapped my back. I didn't have the energy to lift my arm for a high-five. It took some doing to get extracted from the harnesses and out of the cab.

My back felt like a board and my knees like rusty hinges. After walking off the cramps, we drank a beer—which I immediately threw up—before taking the Courier to the secured impound area where our wives picked us up in the van and took us to the hunting club.

Though we were exhausted and caked with sweat-dried dust, food came before a bath—we'd had nothing to eat but a few energy bars. After a breakfast of eggs, bacon, hash browns, toast, and pancakes, we went to our rooms. When I shed my clothes, Wendy gasped. I turned to the mirror. Black-and-blue stripes crossed my shoulders and ran down my chest.

Wendy woke me when it was time for the awards banquet. As I struggled out of bed, still coughing up dust and blowing black mucus from my nose, I thought, *I feel like someone beat me with a baseball bat.*

At the banquet, the four of us joined our teammates at the Stroppe table. As Chris and I suspected, Parnelli Jones and Bill Stroppe won the "modified nonproduction four-wheel vehicles" category, and Walker Evans and Shelby Mongeon won the "two-wheel-drive utility vehicles" category. The table grew quiet when it came to the results of category 10. "In third place, car 256 driven by Jim Griffin and Chris Reynolds."

The table erupted in applause. Bill Stroppe threw his arms around us. "I've never heard of a higher novice finish," he said.

First place in category 10 went to veteran racer Jim Conner, owner of Conner Racing Enterprises. He'd driven a four-wheel-drive Datsun pickup, which had a distinct advantage over our Courier on hills and hairpin turns.

Chris Reynolds after race

Wendy and Chris Reynolds with trophy

Five months later, October 1973, a story and picture appeared in *Off Road Magazine* under the heading, "Here's Bill Stroppe's version of Ford's better idea from the East—a potent Courier pickup for off-road racing." The lead paragraph stated, "Category 10, which has become the fastest growing segment of off-road racing, is reserved for the small-sized but mighty mini-trucks. This Stroppe-prepared Courier, owned and driven by Chris Reynolds and Jim Griffin, made its debut in the recent Baja 500 and finished third in this highly contested class. It was the highest finishing Courier and, as such, bears some looking into."

Postscript:

In July, a month after finishing the Baja 500, Chris and I raced the Baja 1000. Sadly, our Courier's engine burned up one hundred miles from the La Paz finish, near the southern tip of the Baja Peninsula. When the engine quit, Chris and I were running in first place in category 10. Fortunately, we remembered to pack the Jack Daniel's Tennessee sour-mash whiskey. That year, for the first time, Mexico required all race participants to use Mexican Pemex gasoline. Unfortunately, Mexican gas didn't have the octane level required of a finely tuned Stroppe engine. Like us, many of the drivers who pushed their engines broke down.

Scott, Wendy, Sterling, me, Ashley, and Whitney, before start of the Baja 1000

(10) Real Estate Development: In Business with My Sons

While flying home from Hawaii after the first directors' meeting, following the Bank of Honolulu opening, my mind drifted back. Alpental had become an albatross requiring substantial annual capital contributions, and I had a large household to maintain in addition to four children and my brother Charlie in private school. Had I made the right decision in selling the fuel company? I thought, *If oil heat hadn't been on a downward trajectory, I would undoubtedly have stayed in the business, which would not have been my chosen profession.*

Ever since visiting construction sites and sitting in bank finance meetings as a teenager with Jim March, I'd wanted to be a developer and it was a propitious time to buy land, as the country was in the middle of a recession. Boeing had laid off forty thousand employees, which led to the highway billboard, "Would the last person who leaves Seattle please turn out the lights?" With the Bank of Honolulu opening soon, I now had the time to pursue real estate development.

That night, I told Wendy what I planned to do. "Where will you start?" she asked.

"I'm going to review county zoning at the courthouse tomorrow afternoon."

"What are you looking for?"

"Residential property designated to be rezoned commercial that is adjacent to an arterial with heavy traffic flows." I responded.

"Why not buy property already zoned commercial?" she asked.

"Residential property costs a fraction of what I'd have to pay for an equivalent commercial lot. Weather permitting, I'm flying over to Key Center in the morning. Thompson wants to show me his new trout pond and I need to practice some touch and goes on the Sound. It's been nearly three weeks since I've flown."

"You know, you might consider giving up flying. We can do without the expense, not to mention, your next mishap could make me a widow." She was right about the mishaps, but the way I figured it, when my time was up, it wouldn't matter if I was flying a plane or taking a walk in the park.

"If you'll remember," I said, "I got my pilot's license so we wouldn't have to spend all day getting to Long Island. You were all for it."

"Yes, but that's before I realized we could leave the children parentless."

"If it becomes a choice of keeping the kids in Charles Wright [Academy, their private school] or flying, I'll quit, but not because you think I might crash."

When I got back from the Thompsons' the following day, I went to the County-City building, which housed both the city and county courthouses, and reviewed their proposed land use and arterial plans. The next day, armed with pages of notes, I began looking for rural large-lot homes with for-sale signs. Acre parcels could accommodate multiple office buildings or a combination restaurant and gas station. After investigating Pierce County, I did the same thing in Thurston County.

Over the next few years I put a dozen partnerships together with friends who had expressed interest in investing in real estate. Periodically homeowners would fight the rezone to keep commercial zoning from encroaching into their neighborhood. One of my Denny's Restaurant rezones was particularly frustrating. Community activists, including a retired attorney who worked for free, appealed each of the four required approvals: environmental, land use, planning commission, and county commissioners. After losing every appeal, the homeowners filed a suit in Superior Court to overturn the rezone. It took nine months to get a court date, but the county's rezone held up. Then they turned to the state court of appeals which thankfully refused to hear their petition.

In 1973, while I was returning to my Lakewood office from one of the hearings, a very frightening incident occurred. As I braked for a yellow light during a typical Puget Sound cloudburst, I noticed a young African American propped against a telephone pole. He wore a rain-soaked, hooded sweatshirt, and his head bobbed like he was listening to music, but I couldn't see ear phones. I figured he must be high on drugs, but then thought, *If he's waiting for a bus, why isn't he inside the bus stop enclosure, and if he's intending to cross the street, why isn't he at the curb?* My sixth sense kicked in. *He's planning to hijack a car!* It was too late to change lanes. I hit the door-lock switch.

When the car came to a complete stop, he pushed away from the telephone pole, leaped off the curb and grabbed the door handle with his left hand. His right hand held a revolver pointed at me. Finding the door locked, he raised the gun barrel up and down motioning me to release the lock. Instinctually, I dropped my torso to the passenger seat, keeping my head below the angle of his gun and jammed the accelerator to the floor. The window didn't explode, I suspect because other cars were approaching the intersection. In one last act of defiance, he slammed the pistol against the car roof and then darted into the alley. I didn't follow; cell phones were still in the future. At dinner I told Wendy and the children what happened. The boys immediately ran out to look at the dent in the car's roof.

After the children had gone to bed, Wendy asked, "What do you think would have happened if the car doors hadn't been locked?"

"He would have forced me drive to a remote location, and since I could identify him, he probably would have shot me."

"And I thought flying was dangerous," Wendy said.

In 1974, I formed a partnership with John Wiegman, an Olympia contractor, to build professional offices, principally for doctors, on the partnerships' properties. Over the following years, we developed three restaurants, twenty-four suburban office buildings, two mini-retail centers, and a warehouse park. I still flew to Honolulu twice a month to attend board and executive committee meetings, but it had become a burden rather than a pleasure and took time away from developing. So in the fall of 1976 when Charlie Johnson called about an offer to sell our stock, I was receptive.

"Griffin! I just got a call from Hemmeter." Chris Hemmeter was a Hawaiian hotel developer and chairman of the Bank of Honolulu executive committee. "He and some of the other board members have made a substantial offer to buy us out."

"All of us?" I asked. Tacoma investors owned 22½ percent of the bank's stock.

"Yes."

"How about the rest of the group?" I asked.

"They won't stay without us," Charlie said.

"Go for it!"

"Okay! I'll call Chris back," Charlie said.

I'd expected the offer. Rick Fried told me he heard that Hemmeter and some of the other directors were embarrassed that "mainlanders" controlled the bank. The sale couldn't have come at a better time as I'd just received a significant Alpental capital call.

Every year around Thanksgiving, Harriett and Rick Kirk invited friends to cut Christmas trees from one of their tree plantations in Thurston County, south of Olympia. It had been a family tradition for many years. I remember as a young boy Dad going to parties at the senior Kirks and coming home with a tree.

We always went cutting on a Saturday morning; the Kirk Company worked seven days a week during the Christmas season. A Kirk company bus ferried us to a working site where we watched freshly cut tees conveyed through a giant funnel and come out rolled, like a rug, and bound in plastic mesh. The trees were loaded onto semis and hauled to market.

Between 12 o'clock and 1, depending on our arrival, we were served soup and sandwiches in the employee dining facility. Then Rick gave a short talk about the business and tree conditions. As each family was provided with a chain saw, Rick always ended his talk with a list of safety rules and what time the bus would depart.

After cutting our trees, they were labeled, by family name, and loaded in a truck which would follow us back to Lakewood. Usually, someone looking for a better tree over one more hill always delayed our departure. On the way home, we sang Christmas carols and drank hot buttered rum—hot chocolate for the children.

Rick and Harriett Kirk

Me cutting tree

In 1980, I formed a real estate business with Bill Riley, a Tacoma Realtor and longtime friend. In addition to real estate brokerage, the firm managed and leased my partnerships' office buildings. A November 24 Lakewood *Suburban Times* article stated, "Two longtime Lakewood residents, William M. Riley and James S. Griffin, announced today the formation of a new real estate firm to be known as The Riley-Griffin Company ... Tacoma landmark firm, Johnston-Sterling Co., owned by Linn E. Larson, will merge with Riley-Griffin ..." Wendy's brother, Walter Sterling, had sold his interest in the Johnston-Sterling Company in 1975 and moved his family to Arizona. "Griffin, a prominent land developer and real estate broker, is a grandson of the pioneer Tacoman, Fred Griffin, who settled in the area in the early 1880s ... He has been developing real estate since selling the family fuel-oil business fifteen years ago ... He has been active in community affairs, having served on the board of the Tacoma Art Museum, Tacoma Philharmonic, Fort Steilacoom Community College Foundation, Charles Wright Academy, Greater Lakes Mental Health Center, Pacific Northwest Lawn Tennis Association and Lakewood Community Center ..."

At dawn on a Friday morning before Christmas weekend the following year, I remember thinking, *How am I going to get out of this one?* The sun's rays peeked over the horizon as I pulled in front of the Riley-Griffin two-story, brick-veneer office in Lakewood. I stepped out of my car into a circle of light cast from spotlights inserted into the office's overhanging rain deck. Looking back, I figured he must have been hiding behind one of the brick columns supporting the deck. As I inserted my key in the lock of the glass door, I thought how nice it would have been to take the day off. Unfortunately, I had Christmas bonuses to distribute as well as a year-end real estate closing. I walked across the lobby and flipped on the lights. When I turned back to relock the door, my chest constricted, and my heart began to pound. A broad-shouldered, six-foot African American, dressed in desert fatigues, brown leather army boots, and a knitted olive-green face mask, stood inside the door pointing a .45 automatic pistol at me.

"Get on your belly!" he commanded.

The word "belly" triggered a mental alarm. A few days before, Tacoma had made national headlines with a story about robberies and execution-style killings. Witnesses reported seeing an African American dressed similarly to the man pointing the gun at me running from a mini-mart and from a gas station the following day.

Office personnel wouldn't arrive for another forty minutes, and Bill Riley, another early riser, was out of town for the holidays. I was on my own. Flashing through my mind was a picture of the mini-mart employee lying dead on his stomach. Somehow, I had to deflect his gun.

"I have money," I said. I withdrew my wallet from my suit jacket and stepped forward, hoping to get within reach of his gun. He immediately backed up, assuming the classic military position: gun held in both hands chest high and arms extended.

"I won't tell you again," he shouted. "On your belly now or I'll blow your f——ing head off!"

He's going to kill me! I thought as I dropped to one knee. My mind raced for a course of action.

"Toss the wallet over here!" he said pointing to the floor in front of him. The solution came like a bolt of lightning. I spun the wallet at his face, like a Frisbee. The moment his hands flew up to protect his eyes, I took two quick steps and dove behind the reception console in front of the corridor leading to the inner offices.

By the time he came around the counter, I had crawled into the hall. He didn't come after me. With no skylights, the corridor was dark, but I knew he would be listening for footsteps. If I ran, he would come into the hallway, turn on the lights and shoot me in the back before I could get out the fire exit. My heart pounded like a kettle drum. I thought, *How can he not hear it?* He stood there, outlined by the dawn light streaming through the front window, for what seemed an eternity. Finally, he backed up. I heard the door open and close, but I didn't move. It might be a ruse to get me to show myself. Then through the window, I saw him run across the lawn into the woods.

I raced down the hall and after a quick look out the door to make certain he was nowhere in sight, I sprinted through the landscaping to the adjoining apartment house. I woke the manager and while gasping for breath, I told him what happened. He let me in, bolted the door, and called the sheriff.

Two patrol cars, with sirens blaring, screeched to a halt in the parking lot minutes later—the precinct was only blocks away. The deputies came out of their cars with pistols drawn. After I explained what had happened, they released a dog. The shepherd immediately picked up the scent and bounded into the woods with the deputies in close pursuit. I followed. In the parking lot on the other side of the wooded area, the dog handler said, "He had a getaway car stashed. This was no random robbery. You were stalked. I imagine your assailant had previously seen you arrive alone at a dark office." They finished filling out their report and then suggested I check back with them in a few days.

Sleep didn't come easily that night, and when exhaustion finally overcame me, I dreamed I was out of my body looking down at my corpse with a bullet hole in the back of the head.

Following the deputies' recommendations, because the killer had my wallet and knew my address, I contracted for an automatic driveway gate and security fencing around the perimeter of the yard. Also, I now carried a 9mm pistol tucked into my pants, in the small of my back—I had a permit to carry a concealed weapon.

A week later, I stopped at the precinct and talked to the detective assigned to my case.

"We have no leads, nothing. We believe your assailant was a Fort Lewis soldier scheduled to be transferred. Robberies normally increase a few days prior to a unit going overseas. Without fingerprints or facial recognition, military personnel are virtually impossible to track down once they leave the area." Walking out of the precinct, I overheard the detective tell the duty officer, "That man is lucky to be alive."

Grandchildren, it is highly unusual to experience multiple life-threatening encounters. I just happened to be in the wrong place at the wrong time. If it should happen to you: assess the situation, wait for an opportunity, and act decisively. You have the genes for survival.

The following June, 1982, six months after my trauma, Scott (James Scott Griffin Jr.) returned from Colorado College, and I asked him if he wanted to come to work for me. I couldn't believe his response.

"No, but I'll come to work with you," he said, looking me in the eye and smiling. I knew then he'd become a man.

"When do you want to start?"

"A couple of years. I want to see the world. Once I start working and have a family, I'll be tied down."

"Is there something you haven't told me?" I asked.

Scott laughed. "No, Dad! There's no one on the horizon, but I do want to marry young and start a family so I can grow up with my kids, the way you did with us." That was a backhanded way of telling me how much he enjoyed his childhood playing two on two, basketball, football, pool, and later Ping-Pong, tennis, and pickle ball, with his brothers and me and later Ashley, who was a few years younger. I took out my handkerchief on the pretense of blowing my nose so he wouldn't see my tears as I thought, *They kept me from growing old.*

When I regained my composure, I asked, "Where're you getting the money?"

"I've got a few thousand stashed from commissions, and when I run out, I'll find a job." Scott had had a real estate license since turning eighteen—one of the youngest, if not the youngest to obtain a Washington real estate license. He'd worked for my friend Boyd Lundstrom's real estate firm the past two summers in the same building Riley and I bought from Lundstrom and where I'd been robbed.

Two weeks later, Wendy and I drove Scott to the airport. After checking in, we accompanied him to the British Airways terminal for his flight to Singapore. I carried his guitar and his mother his tennis paraphernalia—Scott won the state high school doubles tournament two years in a row.

Wendy always said Scott was drop-dead gorgeous, and it was never more obvious than today. As we entered the terminal, I couldn't help noticing every young woman, both vacationing American college students and Asians returning home for the summer, eying the young man with a pack on his back, hoping to be his seatmate.

Also in 1982, I published *How to Make Money in Commercial Land*. My Realtor friend, Victor Lyon, past president of Realtors National Marketing Institute, wrote the book's foreword (see Appendix).

My book became a text for Introduction to Commercial Land, an accredited course for Washington State real estate license requirements. And Booth Gardner, who was now dean of UPS Business School, invited me to the university as a guest lecturer in commercial real estate.

In July 1983, six months after it became available; I received a letter from Thomas E. Schillar, PhD, a professor at Fort Steilacoom Community College.

"Several of your book's chapters are especially notable in the area of fundamental investment principles," he wrote. "Two in particular are the effects of inflation on the investor and a description of leverage and how it works.

"Your book will become required reading for our Small Business Management program this fall ..."

In August 1983, less than two years after the office robbery, I experienced another trauma. It is natural for parents to protect their children in a dangerous situation. But what a profound experience, when the circumstances are reversed and a child becomes the protector. It happened a few days before my son Sterling (Edwin Sterling Griffin) left for preseason football practice at Colorado College—Sterling had been a Washington State National Football Foundation Hall of Fame high school scholar athlete.

Sterling followed me in my car to South Tacoma, where I took Wendy's 380 Mercedes to be detailed. When I arrived at the warehouse complex, there wasn't a vacant stall in front of the detailer's shop, so I parked in front of an adjoining business. I'd no sooner gotten out of the car when I heard, "You can't park there!"

I looked back and saw an enormous young man scowling at me from his doorway. He looked like he spent a lot of time in the gym. His bulging biceps and stomach muscles rippled beneath an undersized tank top.

"I'll only be a minute," I yelled. I continued toward the detailer's shop.

Seconds later, pounding footsteps echoed in my ear. I turned and watched in horror as Muscles, swinging a baseball bat in a threatening manner, came running after me. I was about to take off for the detailer's shop, when Sterling came sprinting up and stepped in front of me.

"You touch my dad and I'll kill you!" Sterling said without raising his voice.

Fortunately, Sterling had overheard the conversation, and when he saw Muscles grab a baseball bat and come after me, he came running.

Muscles must have seen Sterling's look of determination and lack of fear because he turned and walked away, causing me to think, *Another incidence of "more than luck."* Muscles didn't look back.

Ashley (Ashley Evenson Griffin) graduated from Charles Wright Academy in 1983 and entered Stanford in the fall. Over the summer, she'd ridden in various horse shows and qualified to compete in the Junior Jumper Zone Finals to be held in Harrisburg, PA in October, but that conflicted with college so she had to quit riding. She missed horses so much that by her junior year she discovered Stanford's polo team and though never having played, she made the team. When I asked her how she picked it up so quickly she said, "I already knew how to ride and how to hit a ball."

Ashley graduated in 1987, and after marrying (Neil Collins) spent nearly ten years in London before returning to Seattle. All three of Ashley and Neil's children were born in London.

Ashley (Griffin) Collins

Charlie Spaeth

After Sterling returned to Colorado College, Bill Riley, my brother Charlie, who after graduating from Stanford in 1973 spent ten years in New York, and I looked into syndicating apartments. Unlike my land syndications ten years before, apartment limited partnership units provided income as well as tax shelter and required the sales person to have a securities license. After we put up earnest money on an apartment, Bill decided not to participate because of the inherent liability associated with syndication, so Charlie and I formed Griffin-Spaeth Company.

We operated out of the Riley-Griffin office in Tacoma—Bill and I had closed and leased our Lakewood office—until moving to South Center, midway between Seattle and Tacoma, so we could be closer to the Seattle broker dealer selling our partnership units. Also Charlie now lived in Seattle.

Scott returned from his around-the-world adventure in December 1983 in time for our family Christmas celebration. After the holidays, he joined Charlie and me in the business. Then in June 1984, Sterling graduated from Colorado College and came to work with us. A few months later, Charlie sold his interest in the company to pursue real estate opportunities in Seattle.

In 1985, we relocated our business, renamed the James S. Griffin Company, to the new Washington Convention and Trade Center building at the Port of Tacoma I-5 freeway interchange. It was an advantageous move because I was one of the developers and owners of the building.

Shortly after getting settled in new quarters, Scott and I went to southern California to make a presentation on our current apartment limited partnership. An oil and gas syndicator, Energy Sources Group or ESG, also made a presentation. That evening, Scott and I had dinner with the ESG principals, and before parting we'd bought units in each other's partnership. Over the ensuing years, we invested in multiple East Texas and Louisiana oil and gas wells drilled by Marshal Exploration.

Grandchildren, there is nothing more exciting than watching a well come in. When a drill bit breaks through into an oil reservoir, like puncturing a pressurized canister, natural gas and oil spurt out like a whale spouting, only hundreds of feet higher. At that time, if the reservoir didn't have a pipeline to collect gas it burned off like a giant blowtorch. Today, because of energy conservation, the gas is rerouted back into the ground or into containers. In the fall of 1989 thirty-three ESG oil and gas limited partnerships—some with twenty or more wells—many of which we had invested in, were converted to stock in a publicly traded oil and gas company. Shortly thereafter, we sold our stock.

I'll never forget Scott's account of visiting the Carlile family—like us, a father and three sons—owners of Marshal Exploration which drilled ESG's Limited Partnerships' wells. Sterling and Whitney were in my office for our regular Monday morning meeting—we each reported on our particular area of responsibility—when Scott arrived wearing a grin from ear to ear.

"What a weekend," Scott said. "I watched a well come in and gained a lot of credibility with the Carlile brothers"—they were a few years older than Scott.

"How so," I asked. Scott had obviously talked to Sterling and Whitney because they were smiling.

"Saturday the Carliles had a barbeque at their ranch, which is not unlike the "J.R." Ewing ranch in the Dallas TV series. They asked if I wanted to shoot a round of skeet [twenty-five clay discs are sprung out, one at a time, from two opposing buildings at various angles]. I told them I'd shot trap, but never skeet. I broke twenty five in a row and neither of them broke twenty"—Scott began hunting with me at eight years of age.

I imagined that I would be getting a full report from Clinton, the boys' father.

In 1986, Governor Gardner appointed me to the Washington

State Convention and Trade Center Board. When he called—we talked frequently about our children's activities and his most recent Washington State problem—I couldn't have been more surprised by his request.

"Jim, I'd like to appoint you to the Convention and Trade Center Board. I'm sure you're aware of the controversy it's causing in the House and Senate."

"Yes, and controversy is an understatement."

"My antagonists would love to see me take a hit," Booth said. "I need someone with development experience to be my eyes and ears on the board. I don't want to be blindsided by a construction or budget glitch. Can I count on you?" I hesitated before answering, thinking.

"Are you there?"

"Yes, I'm here."

"Well?"

"I'll do it, but I'll have to confide in Jim Ellis." Ellis was chairman of the board. "I wouldn't want him to think I'm undermining him."

"That's no problem."

By the end of the 1987 legislative session, the fate of the convention center hung in the balance. The Senate approved temporary financing, but the House voted to adjourn without acting on the proposed legislation. The Democratic majority leader in the Senate, who had previously been an opponent of the convention center, marched onto the House floor and told the representatives that it took two houses to adjourn and they were going to be there until they worked out a financing solution. He was quoted as saying, "I'm not going to leave that project half-built over the freeway." The majority leader's intervention led to a meeting that same day with Jim Ellis, me, our attorney, and a member of Booth's staff on one side of the table and the Speaker of the House along with two other house members, one being Gary Locke who later became governor, then Secretary of Commerce in the Obama administration, and finally US Ambassador to China. Well past midnight, we agreed to a compromise bill authorizing temporary financing and creating a bipartisan committee to find a solution for permanent financing.

When the Convention Center opened a year and a half later, Jim Ellis stated, "We are open for business on schedule because this community is full of people who won't let good things fail. This is a great day for believers! For those who believe that visions can happen. That public processes can work. That patience and persistence can overcome misfortune and conflict ... Building a vision as productive and beautiful as this ought to be easy. In fact, it has encountered every obstacle that Murphy's Law could conjure up—four lawsuits, two successive bankruptcies, four life-or-death legislative sessions, bitterly contested public hearings, bidding problems, construction problems and an unceasing barrage of criticism, second guessing and negative publicity. The fact that the project has survived this onslaught of events is due primarily to its intrinsic merit."

Me making presentation at the Washington State Convention and Trade Center

I served on the Convention Center Board fourteen years for three governors, finishing my final term as vice-chairman of the board in 2000.

In 1986 Bill and I folded up the Riley-Griffin Company. Bill had offered to turn the business over to department managers, but they declined.

The Tax Reform Act known as TRA 86 became law in October 1986, and our business hit the wall leaving no skid marks. Real estate investments, which had been held more for their tax-advantaged status than their inherent profitability, collapsed like a freeway overpass in an earthquake, precipitating a savings and loan crisis. Seven hundred and forty seven financial institutions failed at an estimated cost to the US government—aka the US taxpayer—of $160 billion.

Beginning in 1983 and ending with the tax law changes in 1986, the James S. Griffin Company syndicated sixteen apartment units and four retirement homes, raising nearly $100 million. A large part of our success was due to three employees: Dave Cantu, our in-house attorney and partner; Marta Tegge, the company's controller; and Betty Stringham, who could do and did everything. Long after I retired, Marta and Betty remain an integral part of my sons' businesses. Though Dave Cantu is back in private practice, he continues to handle most Griffin family legal matters.

(Twenty-four years later, in the summer of 2010, I'm sitting on my deck on American Lake watching a Cessna floatplane make touch-and-goes and thinking that the devastation TRA 86 caused pales in comparison to the 2008 "Great Recession," brought on by a housing bubble and banking crisis, which precipitated nearly a 50 percent drop in the stock market and 30 percent drop in home value. As I write, the US government is on its way to spending more than $1 trillion, six times what it spent in 1986, to bail out the US economy. Government economists estimate that US debt to China, Japan, and others equates to $40,000 for every American. Hyperinflation, though I may not live to see it, is surely building and, like an ocean's perfect storm, one day will bring havoc to our shores. Grandchildren, this is a legacy that I'm not proud to leave you. Hopefully, your generation will be better stewards of our nation's economy.)

With the syndication business at a standstill, we had to quickly find a new source of revenue. The obvious solution was to manage our syndicated apartments with existing personnel rather than contract out the management. We formed Griffin Management Company. We also began syndicating land, similar to what I'd done fifteen years previously, and joined ESG as a general partner in one of their oil and gas syndications. The following year, we started Retirement Management Company to manage our syndicated retirement facilities, in addition to starting both a landscaping and credit report company.

While we were reorganizing our businesses, Booth called. "Jim, I've asked Greg to chair my reelection campaign. I'd like you to be his co-chair." (Greg was General Greg Barlow, Booth's appointee to head the Washington State National Guard.) "Greg's a political insider, and my adversaries will cut the legs out from under him trying to get at me. They can't touch you. You have no political enemies or skeletons in the closet."

"Hey! I'm trying to get a new business going, and the convention center is taking considerably more time than you said it would."

"I know, but you owe me." And I did. Alpental was on the brink of bankruptcy until Booth stepped in.

"Okay, what do you want me to do?"

"I want you to referee. My advisers aren't in sync. They have their own political agendas." By *advisers* Booth meant the members of his kitchen cabinet, which I had just joined.

"You know, you and Norm"—Representative Norm Dicks, Washington's legendary Congressman—"are the only Democrats I've every voted for."

"What a shame!" Booth said. I could just see the smile spreading across his face.

"Will you listen to me?" I asked.

"I'll listen, but I can't promise to take your advice."

"Fair enough," I said.

The kitchen cabinet met weekly. If Booth didn't have a conflicting meeting, he joined us. Interestingly he didn't set the agenda and normally went along with the majority opinion—I can't recall ever being with the majority. After a luncheon at my home prepared by Wendy, our house became the meeting place of choice for the remainder of the campaign.

Booth won reelection handily.

In 1993 President Clinton appointed Booth US Ambassador to the General Agreement on Tariffs and Trade (GATT) in Geneva. GATT, an international organization, worked to lower trade barriers and encourage trade. In 1995, the GATT name changed to the World Trade Organization, primarily due to Booth's lobbying.

A short time after Booth's appointment, Wendy and I visited him in Geneva. He met us at the airport in his private car—normally a state department limo chauffeured him—a few minutes after his doctor confirmed his Parkinson's disease. As he drove us to his home, which turned out to be a palatial US government house, he tearfully repeated what the doctor had reported.

Wendy and Booth on our tour of Geneva

Also in 1987, my son Whitney (Whitney Paine Griffin) graduated from Colorado College and joined Scott, Sterling, and me in the businesses. I'll never forget the story told to me by a friend who took the real estate licensing preparation course with Whitney. As best I remember, it went something like the following:

"If you buy a house for $X and pay $Y down, what will be the monthly payment over twenty years?" the teacher asked the class. "Speak up when you have the answer." My friend said everyone, including the teacher, began punching numbers into their calculators.

"Approximately $Z," Whitney said a few seconds later, then added, "within a few dollars one way or another."

Everyone continued punching in numbers until the instructor said, "That's pretty close. Now assume you buy the house for $A with a down payment of $B and make monthly payments of $C. How many years will it take to pay the house off?"

"Approximately D years give or take a few months," Whitney said before anyone else spoke up.

The teacher, still punching in numbers, asked, "What kind of a calculator do you have? I thought my Hewlett-Packard was the latest."

"I don't have a calculator!" My friend said he wished he'd had a camera to catch the looks of bewilderment. Whitney had a knack for mathematical calculations.

The following article appeared in the *Daily Journal of Commerce*, April 25, 1988. "James Griffin has been involved in about every phase of the real estate business, including broker. He put that knowledge to use when writing the respected real estate guide, *How to Make Money in Commercial Land*.

"Griffin, as befitting a member of a well-connected Tacoma family, has numerous civic obligations, including membership on the board of directors of the soon-to-be-completed Washington State Convention and Trade Center in downtown Seattle.

"The Griffin family first made its mark here with the founding in 1889 of Griffin Transfer & Ice Co. ...

"James's brother Ted, now a computer software consultant in Seattle, gained fame as the captor of Namu, the killer whale.

"The latest Griffin generation features Scott, 27, Sterling, 26, and Whitney, 24. All are part owners and vice presidents of the James S. Griffin Co. and Griffin Management Co. ...

"Being involved in a family business has its advantages and disadvantages. 'Things get emotional sometimes,' admits Sterling. And that can lead to difficulties when, according to a family rule, 100 percent agreement is needed before a project proceeds. 'The good side, in this family's opinion, is that you can trust your business partners.'"

Scott, me, Sterling, and Whitney at a real estate function dinner

The Griffin family, Sterling, Scott, Ashley, Wendy, me, and Whitney

We worked hard and played hard, and as in every family, there were disagreements, which I let my sons sort out. It was a learning experience for all of us. After a five-year apprenticeship, I gifted each son 5 percent of the companies' stock each year until we were equal partners. My nearly twenty years in business with my boys couldn't have been more enjoyable or rewarding.

March 18, 1989, Levi Edgecombe, a securities broker who sold our limited partnerships, wrote the following letter:

"Jim, I have been heavily involved for over twenty years working with young people and just wanted you to know I left your office with real joy when I witnessed the relationship you have with your sons. Mike [Levi's partner] and I both talked about this in the car on our way home ... I'm sure in your later years these relationships with your sons will be far more significant than any money raised/made in the real estate business."

Me, Sterling, Scott, and Whitney steelhead fishing on the Snake River

Whitney, me, Scott fishing in Canada

Me, Walter Sterling, and Whitney dove hunting in Columbia

Scott and me fly-fishing for tarpon in Florida

That same year, while returning from steelhead fishing on the Cowlitz River with Scott and Whitney, we passed a "Geese for Sale" sign. As I'd recently read that geese made good watch dogs and the memory of my office robbery lingered, I thought *Why not?*

"Scott," I said, "Turn around."

"Why?"

"I want to buy a goose. Did you see that sign we just passed?"

"Yea, but Mom will never go along with a goose." Whitney's response was even less enthusiastic, "Not a good idea." The car continued down the road.

"Damn it, I'm serious, turn around."

"Ok, ok!" Scott said.

Scott made an illegal U turn and pulled off the macadam onto a rutted dirt driveway which split an alfalfa field. Two dogs of mixed parentage raced out of the field and gave chase, sending ducks, geese and chickens fleeing in all directions.

As soon as we got out of the car, the dogs engaged in the usually crotch smelling until the farmer, who came out of the house with two teenage boys, called them off. The farmer's wife, a large bosomed, plumpish, women dressed in a plain, light brown, sack dress and red scarf over hair curlers followed them out. The farmer and his sons wore coveralls held up by straps and faded green John Deere baseball caps. As they approached, Whitney said, just loud enough for me to hear, "The farmer is zeroing in on the SUV and Mackenzie River boat. The price of geese just doubled." Scott obviously overheard because I saw him smirk.

After bargaining and agreeing on a price, the farmer, pointing to the largest, but not the prettiest, gander, said, "Boys get that one and grab a gunny sack from the barn."

Even though the gander's wings had been clipped, to keep him from flying, it took some effort for the teenagers and their dogs to corner and bag the goose, who had hold of one of the dogs ears causing a series of painful yelps. When they returned with the gyrating gunny sack, the farmer tied the open end with a piece of cord, that mysteriously appeared from his back pocket—causing me to think that we weren't the day's first customer.

Whitney opened the back of the SUV and the farm boys—it

took four hands—literally threw the honking gander into the cargo hold.

As we said our farewells, the farmer asked, "How about a piglet?" His comment elicited chuckles from Scott and Whitney.

"No thanks, maybe another time," I said.

The boys had not misjudged their Mother's reaction. As I held up the largest steelhead, trying to deflect Wendy's attention, she shouted, "No you don't. Put that thing right back in the bag and get it out of here."

Unfortunately, Wendy's outburst sent the goose fleeing—on foot of course—with Kavik, our German Shepard, in close pursuit. Our arrival, I thought, wasn't going as planned. The magazine article stated a large goose could honk down almost any critter—though I had to admit Kavik was intimidating; bare feet he could look into a car without jumping up.

Well, by the time we caught up with the goose, he'd found our swimming pool and considerable goose poop slowly drifted to the bottom, which I thought understandable considering his trauma.

Wendy took one look at the feces and said, "Let Sprig out."

Moments later Sprig, our Golden Retriever, who had been watching out the window, flew off the side of the pool—Sprig was not unaccustomed to geese, having retrieved many at our Nisqually duck club. The goose, after checking the location of Kavik, quickly paddled to the opposite side of the pool, hopped out and scurried down the bank towards the lake with both dogs in pursuit. Seeing the water must have had a calming effect because the pitch of the goose's honk seemed less stressful. The goose increased his land speed by flapping his wings and scooted into the lake gaining valuable yardage over Sprig who momentarily had given up the chase to rid his mouth of goose tail feathers.

"Well that takes care of that," Wendy said, watching from the top of the bank. Though she tried to look stern, wrinkles formed at the corners of her mouth.

Whitney in his normal dry sense of humor said, "I don't think we've seen the end of Honk—Whitney had named the goose Honk. As it turned out Whitney was right.

The following Saturday night at a friend's lakeside barbecue, I overheard, "What the hell is a barn-yard goose doing on our lake? That dam thing starts honking at four in the morning, then added; I'd like to get my hands on the son-of-a-bitch that brought him to the lake."

"Are you sure it's a goose? I thought geese were white, somebody chimed in." There was no doubt that Honk's lineage was suspect.

"It's a barnyard goose all right. We use to chase them at my grandfather's farm," the agitated guest responded.

Sunday, Wendy and I went to check on Honk in the Chris-Craft. We found him gorging on bread. In-between lobbing snacks to Honk, two lake residents flipped through a book whose cover looked very much like the cover of National Geographic *Complete Birds of the World*, which I often referred to. We traded pleasantries and continued on our way.

"Can you believe it?" Wendy asked, as we tied the boat to the dock. "They think Honk is some exotic species taking a break during migration. We laughed all the way up to the house.

That night at dinner, Wendy said, "You'd better do something about the goose. It's not a secret that will keep."

The following Saturday morning, when most lake residents were on their way to the Husky football game, Whitney and I set out to capture Honk. We went in the canoe rather than risk an environmentalist seeing us chasing a goose in the speedboat. We located him right away as he hung out near the bread line. His wing feathers had started to grow, but not sufficiently to enable him to fly. We paddled up close. He let us approach because I was pitching dog treats in his direction. Whitney made a gallant effort with the net, not unlike netting a steelhead, but Honk dove before he could get the net under him. He popped up a few seconds later twenty yards from the canoe. We chased Goose for half an hour before he tired and could remain under water for only a few seconds. When Whitney finally netted Honk, he tried to drop him into the gunny sack that I held open. Honk immediately recognized the gunny sack and wedged his bill and flippers into the net rather than succumb to a second sack experience.

"Damn, his strong," Whitney said. "I wouldn't want him to get ahold of one of my fingers." *Me neither*, I thought.

After getting the goose into the sack and rapping the opening with thick twine, we quickly paddled home, hoping no lake resident witnessed the capture. Once in the Car with the windows up, we breathed a sigh of relief. We took Honk to Wapato Lake—which I'd previously checked out.

A few days later, I visited Honk. I couldn't have been more surprised to find him "leader of the pact." I watched in amazement as another gander circled the harem and Honk chased his rival away, after pulling out a beak full of feathers.

In the spring of 1988, I got a call from the Reverend William Sullivan, president of Seattle University. We'd never met, but his reputation was legendary.

"Mr. Griffin, this is Bill Sullivan from Seattle University. I'm chairman of the Seattle Organizing Committee for the 1990 Goodwill Games. We'd like you to represent Tacoma and Pierce County on our board of directors." I'd known about Seattle's involvement because of the negative media publicity on financing, similar to that preceding the Seattle World's Fair, Seattle Center, and the Washington State Convention and Trade

Center. In addition, doomsayers couldn't believe Americans and Soviets could work together in such hostile times.

"Why me?" I asked.

"I called Norm Dicks to get his suggestion for someone from Tacoma, and he recommended you." I was totally overwhelmed. Sure, Norm and I were friends. We periodically played tennis—George Weyerhaeuser and I usually played Norm and Booth Gardner—and Norm had come off the House of Representatives floor to take a call from Wendy, during a critical time for funding of the National Endowment for the Arts. I couldn't say no.

"I'm honored to be considered. When and where do we meet?" He gave me the information. "Bob Walsh" [the originator and president of the Organizing Committee] "and I look forward to meeting you." His assignment accomplished, he said good-bye and hung up. He had a university to run.

A month later, I was appointed to the Goodwill Games executive committee; speaking to civic clubs to bring awareness to the community, solicit volunteers (we needed ten thousand) and fundraising—the budget was $100 million, not including venue security.

The games focused world attention on Washington State and the Puget Sound region. Twenty-three hundred athletes from fifty-four countries competed in a unique format. The best American, the best Russian, and the world's six best athletes, not including the American or Russian, were invited. There were no time trials; all events were finals.

In the early 1990s, because of increasingly stringent federal wetland regulations, my sons and I quit syndicating.

After I retired, Whitney took over the management company under a new name, Olympic Management. Scott became a contractor, principally building homes, and Sterling left the family businesses to pursue other opportunities.

Wendy and I spent more time at our second home in Sun Valley; skiing in the winter and golf, hiking, and fishing in the summer. For me, there was nothing more euphoric than following Neil, my son-in-law, who had been a Junior Olympic skier, down Sun Valley's Christmas ridge in two feet of fresh powder snow—which I can no longer do, because of a heart condition—and before my knees gave out, walking side-by-side through a sugar beet or cornfield with my son Scott, watching dogs "on point" before flushing a pheasant. Fortunately, I can still stand in the Big Horn River alongside my son Whitney, near where he has a lodge, and cast trico flies, into a trico hatch, at rising rainbow and brown trout. There is nothing more exhilarating than dropping a fly eighteen inches up river from a twenty inch, feeding, trout and then watching the fly drift downriver into the trout's open mouth.

Me on the Big Horn River in front of Whitney's lodge

Retirement proved more difficult than I'd imagined, so I undertook one last development, Griffin Ranch. I bought 250 acres five miles south of Haley, Idaho (a twenty-five minute drive from Sun Valley) on the Picabo–Gannet Road near the Silver Creek Nature Conservancy, a fly-fishing paradise, and developed sixty-six lots from one to ten acres, bordering large open spaces. Grandchildren, many of your names appear on the ranch's road signs (i.e., Wyatt Drive and Gibson Lane).

By 2000, I became officially retired.

The following year, the most catastrophic national disaster of my lifetime occurred. On September 11, 2001, Arab Al-Qaeda terrorists hijacked four commercial passenger airliners. Two of the planes were purposely crashed into New York City's Twin Towers, causing both buildings to collapse and killing thousands. The third plane struck the Pentagon and the fourth crashed on the way to the White House or Capitol buildings when passengers and the flight crew unsuccessfully tried to retake control of the plane.

In the early part of the "Cold War," starting after World War II, the Western world faced the possibility that Communism would take over the world. Now, sixty years later, the Western world faces a far more serious threat, a religious philosophy espoused by fanatic Muslims.

After thwarting Russia's attempt to conqueror Afghanistan, many mujahedeen (Muslim guerilla warriors engaged in a jihad "holy war") freedom fighters became followers of Osama bin Laden, a member of a prominent Saudi family, who espouses a holy war to kill anyone, Muslim or not, who doesn't believe in Allah and follow Allah's laws (interpreted by bin Laden) given to Muhammad in divine revelations. How ironic that we armed and trained the mujahedeen.

Grandchildren, hopefully, your generation will stop Al-Qaeda before they hijack some Muslim countries' nuclear arsenal and let fly at the US or Israel.

It is mid-December 2010. I just returned from my regular Friday morning tennis game with Rob Grenley—going on thirty years. Why Rob continues to play with an old man—he's twenty years younger—is somewhat of a mystery. I'd like to think I'm still a backboard, but I've accepted the fact that I'm a step slower and beginning to have balance problems. I can no longer run backward for an overhead without serious consequences. While stretching before play this morning, I read a message stapled to the wall by our club professional, Greg Smith, "Be at peace with yourself." The placard has been there for months or maybe years, but today was the first time it registered with me. Grandchildren, as you come to grips with the universal question, "What is *your* purpose in life?" take heed of Greg's message.

MY MOST RECENT ADVENTURE

"Dad, let's go sky diving," Scott said at a family dinner in July 2010.

I thought a moment and said, "Why not. Set it up," thinking *it will never happen.*

Scott called on a Tuesday evening a few weeks later. "Dad we're jumping Thursday morning, assuming clear weather. Okay?"

"I'm good," I said, wondering, *if I really was.*

Scott phoned the following morning. "Dad, I just got a call from the skydiving company. Somehow, they missed seeing your age on the form I submitted. No one over 65," I was 73, "can jump without their doctor's approval and they need it before closing today.'

"I'll see what I can do," I said, thinking *how am I going to get an appointment with my physician DR. WILSON, on such short notice? My heart doctor, Doctor Momah, would say no. I couldn't call him.* As soon as I hung up, I went to Dr. Wilson's office—a phone call would get me nowhere.

Fortunately I knew his receptionist—we had been seeing a great deal of Dr. Wilson because of Wendy's cancer. As I suspected, he was booked solid. I explained my dilemma.

"Is there any way you can get a note to him in-between appointments?" I asked.

"I'll see what I can do. Call me before noon; the office is closed between twelve and one."

I called at 11:30. "I have a permission slip," she said.

"You're a jewel, I owe you one." Dr. Wilson had written on his prescription pad, "James Griffin is fit to skydive"—nothing more—and it worked.

The following day as the converted Cessna 182 ascended to fourteen thousand feet, *I thought am I out of my mind—freefalling for sixty seconds, dropping ten thousand feet, the entire time in a state of panic wondering if the shoot will open?* I wondered *after surviving a helicopter crash and a number of floatplane mishaps, had my time come?*

When I had one foot out the door less opening planted on the strut and the other wedged in the plane, my instructor said, "Go." I froze. However, a nudge from him with a little help from Scott, and I was doing a three sixty, like a back flip off the side of a boat when scuba diving.

Scott touched down a few seconds after me. "Dad, wasn't that great? I'm going to arrange a trip for the boys. Do you want to join us?

"No!"

Me freefalling from 14,000 feet

My last and most important chapter, "One of a Kind," describes a fifty-two-year romance with your grandmother, who recognized her life's purpose at an early age.

(11) Wendy: One of a Kind

"Volunteering for the arts has been a satisfying experience for me," Wendy said in an interview while chairman of the board of the Pacific Northwest Ballet. "I've learned I can effect change. If you feel strongly enough, giving time and energy to a cause is easy and a joy."

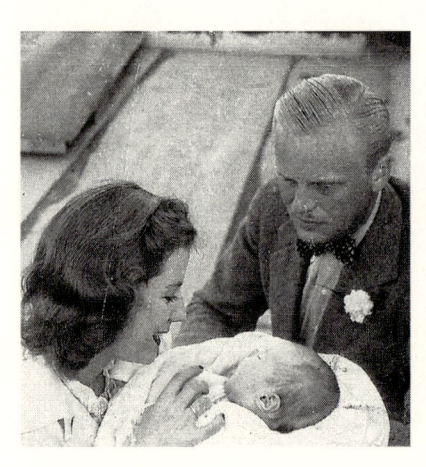

Dottie, Wendy and Walter Sterling   Wendy on pony (1943)

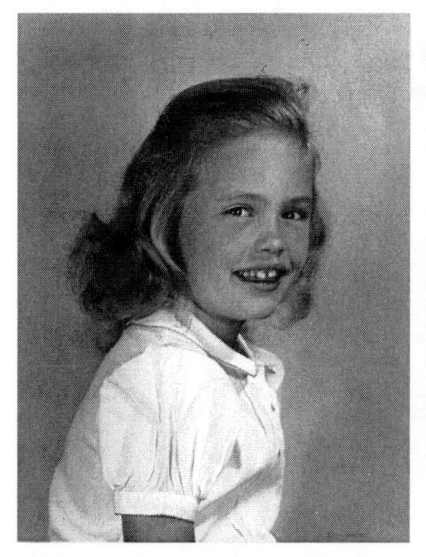

Wendy nine years old (1948)   Wendy at eighteen (1957)

In June 1960, our second year of marriage, Wendy and I experienced our first crisis. I arrived home from work a few minutes before six. We lived on Steilacoom Lake adjoining Ponce de Leon Creek. When I pulled into the driveway, I saw Wendy across the creek talking to our neighbor, Margaret Boscovich, who appeared to be pouring lighter fluid on her barbecue.

As I got out of the car, Wendy screamed. I looked over and saw her legs burning. Oh God, I thought, the barbecue exploded. I raced to the water, jumped in, took a half dozen strides—the water was less than two feet deep—climbed out the other side, picked up Wendy, and walked into the lake. Margaret somehow had avoided the flames. Dr. Ootkin, who lived up the creek across Brook Lane from the Boscovichs, had also just come home. Like me, he heard Wendy scream and came running.

"Bring her to my office," he said. "I'll leave the door open."

Ten minutes later, I carried Wendy into his office across from Lakewood Center. "Dr Ootkin," I hollered.

A moment later, the doctor, looking like a baker in his white coat and cap, stuck his head out of a doorway. "In here," he said. I carried Wendy who was crying incoherently into the room and laid her on the examination table. Rolls off tape, gauze patches and tubes of aloe covered the adjoining counter.

"What about the baby?" Wendy stammered. She was seven months pregnant with Scott.

"There's no way of knowing," Dr. Ootkin said, as he stuck a needle into Wendy's buttock. "For shock!" he said, seeing my inquisitive look. After he finished applying aloe and wrapping Wendy's legs, he said, "I'll stop by after work for the next few days and change the bandages. Keep her off her feet."

On the way home, Wendy said, "Margaret poured lighter fluid on the coals." *What an idiot*, I thought. "When the flames shot up," Wendy continued, "she dropped the can and fluid splashed on my legs."

Fortunately Wendy's legs healed quickly with little scaring and the trauma had no effect on Scott, born two months later. At the hospital, I remember squeezing Wendy's hand when she left her room on a gurney—I wasn't allowed to watch the birth—and wiping away her tears as she whispered, "I wish Mommy was here." Wendy's mother died when Wendy was 11.

The next day while sitting with Wendy as she nursed Scott, I asked about her mother.

"My mother always made an entrance. She lighted up the room. She was not conventional and embarrassed my father by doing things like taking off her shoes and walking barefoot down Fifth Avenue in New York City. At that time, well-brought-up ladies not only wore shoes when going out, but also hats and gloves. I heard her described as beautiful, exciting, outrageous, fiercely loyal, and according to Aunt Maud and Uncle Jordan [Dottie's siblings], she loved her children above all else. "I wish you could have known her," Wendy said. "You two would have gotten along fabulously."

"What about your father?"

"Daddy was loving, tender, conservative, and Hollywood handsome. In fact, he went looking for the Lost Dutchman Gold Mine in Arizona's Superstition Mountains with his friends Clark Gable and Jimmy Stewart." Gable and Stewart were leading movie actors of that era. (The Lost Dutchman was the name given to a cache of gold ore supposedly found by a German miner that had been hidden by Spanish explorers who were killed by Apache Indians.)

"Daddy was an artist. He loved to draw a horse playing a piano to entertain friends and young children. While he was serving on a destroyer during World War II, a Japanese Kamikaze suicide plane crashed into his ship intending to sink it. The bomb did not explode, and he carved a Japanese soldier from the plane's aluminum nose [propeller] cone."

"My parents were a glamorous couple and wonderful dancers. Whenever they walked onto a dance floor, the others quickly left to watch from the sides. Weekends were spent in fierce tennis matches with their friends while I and my friends played dress-up in long-forgotten ball gowns and the boys did whatever boys do."

Dottie and Walter Sterling (1942)

"My mother liked to act in the Phoenix amateur theater and I remember hearing that somebody wrote a play for her. After her death, a new wing in the Phoenix Memorial Hospital was dedicated in her memory," (see Appendix, Dottie Paine Sterling Stories).

When Scott was old enough to leave with a babysitter, Wendy began working one-half day each week with the Junior League, an organization that mentors women in becoming community activists. Through the League she worked in hospitals, taught high school parenting classes, volunteered at Pacific Lutheran University's KPEC Public Television station—later becoming a member of its board of directors—and helped organize a children's museum for the Tacoma Art Museum.

Between 1960 and 1965, Wendy gave birth to four children, and in 1961, my half brother Charlie Spaeth came to live with us.

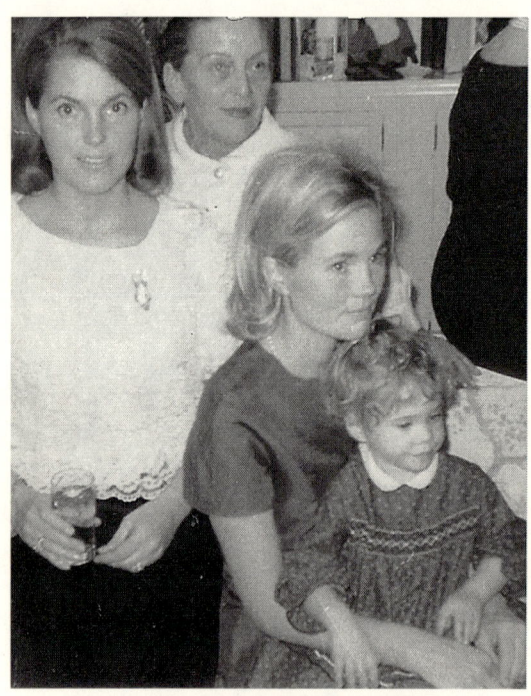

Wendy holding Ashley

Wendy, Ashley, Whitney, Scott, and Sterling

In celebration of our fifth wedding anniversary, Wendy and I returned to Honolulu. We stayed at the Holiday Inn across from the Diamond Head Park tennis courts, less than a block from the Outrigger Canoe Club. We called it the Pink Palace because the entire building was painted an iridescent pink.

One morning on our way to the tennis courts, we met Jerry Zeitman, a Hollywood movie producer, and his wife who were also on their way to the courts. We joined them and had such a good time that mixed doubles became a regular morning activity. Before leaving Honolulu, we exchanged phone numbers and agreed to stay in touch.

Jerry called six months later.

"Jim, we'd like you and Wendy to join us next weekend and meet some of our friends, and play tennis of course."

"We'd like that. I'll check with Wendy and get back to you."

The following Friday, Wendy and I flew to southern California. Saturday evening, after a day of tennis and swimming at the Zeitmans' home in the Hollywood hills, we joined a lively cocktail party. As we entered the room, I saw Steve McQueen talking to Charles Bronson, two of my favorite cowboy actors. Then, the booming voice of James Backus, who portrayed the near-sighted cartoon character Magoo, drew me like the legendary siren. I joined Backus who was talking to James Coburn, another leading actor. They showed no interest in my arrival. A moment later, the Zeitmans and Wendy passed on their way to greet the Lowes, our dinner companions. Wendy caught Coburn's eye and he stopped talking in midsentence.

"Who's that?" he exclaimed.

"My wife!" He looked at me, and I thought, *I finally got your attention.*

"Who are you?"

"James Griffin." Without another word, Coburn left Backus and me and followed after Wendy and the Zeitmans.

At dinner when the entrees arrived, Mrs. Lowe took a thermos out of her handbag. Seeing my questioning look, she said, "My work requires a special diet."

"What do you do?" I asked. Wendy kicked me under the table and you could have heard a pin drop.

"I'm Carol Channing," she said. When she realized the name didn't mean anything to me, she said, "Have you seen *Hello Dolly?*"

"No!"

"Have you heard of it?"

"Yes! Isn't it a musical?"

That's when Wendy came to my rescue. "Jim is developing a ski area and works long hours. We haven't been to the theater or seen a movie in ages. And frankly musicals aren't his thing; he's a sports fanatic."

After getting over the shock of meeting an educated American adult that hadn't heard of Carol Channing, she and I got along fabulously because she was in the presence of someone not in awe of her.

In September 1966, my half sister, Nancy Spaeth, came to live with us. She had entered the University of Arizona in the fall of 1965; however, by the following February she had become too sick to stay in school—Nancy had been diagnosed with kidney disease in the seventh grade. After a lengthy interview process, by what became known as the Life and Death Committee, Nancy was accepted at the Seattle Artificial Kidney Center, which could only accommodate twenty-four patients. Those not accepted, in the thousands, died.

"My sister-in-law [Wendy] reminded me that I might not be chosen, but I was eighteen and the implication of death never really occurred to me." Shortly thereafter, Nancy moved to Seattle to be closer to the dialysis center and entered Seattle University (see Appendix).

In 1970 when Ashley started school, Wendy began to become more involved in community activities. She had helped establish a residency for the Joffrey Ballet at Pacific Lutheran University, which led to her becoming one of the founding members of Seattle's Pacific Northwest Ballet, a world-class ballet company today. At a ballet fundraiser, I remember hearing Wendy say, "A thriving community must have a strong cultural basis in addition to providing a helping hand for those in need."

Wendy worked tirelessly for Building a Scholastic Heritage "BASH," an annual auction to benefit Tacoma's private schools. One of her first solicitations was always Nordstrom, a major northwest department chain. At that time, Jack McMillan, who owned a unit near us in the Alpental condominium, was president of the company. "It must be that time of year again," Jack said when Wendy entered his office. "Bash, right?"

"Yes," Wendy answered. "Jack, do you have any idea the

amount of money Tacoma women spend at Nordstrom's?" At that time, Tacoma didn't have a Nordstrom store.

"Well?" she said.

"Go down to the fur department." Jack said with a chuckle. "I'll let them know you're on your way." They spent a few minutes talking about children and by the time Wendy reached the fur department, three coats were laid out. Wendy's dealings with Nordstrom's, led to her being asked to model, which she did for the next few years.

Wendy modeling   Wendy modeling

Every fall, beginning shortly after our marriage, Wendy and I attended a pre UW "Husky" football brunch at my aunt and uncle's, Fred and Bea Griffin, Lake Washington home. Then we joined them in their seats on the fifty-yard line for the football game (see Appendix).

After Alpental opened in 1967, we spent nearly every winter weekend in our mountain condominium adjoining the Gardners' unit. Their children, Doug and Gail, and ours took ski lessons, built snow forts, and rained snowballs from our condominiums on cars and busses entering the parking lot.

Family games of Battleship, Monopoly, spoons, and chess went late into the night. Summers, when the children were older, Booth and I escorted our boys to tennis tournaments and basketball camps, while Jean and Wendy accompanied Gail and Ashley to horse shows.

We also visited my stepmother Sarah and my sister Beth at Sarah's summer home on Coeur d'Alene Lake in Idaho, where we water skied, picnicked, and searched for Indian arrowheads. Ever since Sarah had offered to adopt me, after divorcing Dad, we had been close and she was now Ashley's godmother.

I'll never forget the night at Coeur d'Alene Lake when we sent Scott and Sterling out with gunny sacks and flashlights to capture the mythological snipe. They eventually figured out it was a prank, but not before they assured us they had let their captured snipe go free.

After the children went to bed, Wendy and I sat on the porch overlooking the lake to watch shooting stars and reminisce.

"What comes to mind when you think about the children?" I asked. Wendy momentarily closed her eyes and then began to smile.

"Holding Scott (our first born) when the nurse put him in my arms immediately following his birth."

"And Sterling?" Wendy began to laugh.

"Sterling following me up the hill from the beach carrying his towel and saying, 'I'm too tired, I'm too little, it's too heavy.' And Whitney, flying off the stair landing with his batman cape spread like the wings of an eagle."

"How about Ashley?"

Wendy thought a moment and then said, "The look on her face when she saw her Christmas gift - a pony. Remember we brought it to the house Christmas morning."

"I remember. What about Whitney picking your prize dahlias and having Ashley, with her Charles Wright sweatshirt turned inside out, sell them on Gravelly Lake Drive while he orchestrated from the bushes?" We were now both laughing.

All our children and Charlie were now attending Charles Wright Academy and Wendy rarely missed a recital, teacher's conference, or sporting event.

From the mid-1970s through the 1980s, in addition to her work for Pacific Northwest Ballet, Wendy volunteered with both the Tacoma Philharmonic and Tacoma Actors Guild and served as a member of their boards and executive committees. She was also appointed to the Tacoma Cultural Council, a committee selected from community leaders to act as a catalyst for cultural development.

Starting in the early 1970s, Wendy, Gwen Carlson, Mary Jane "Squeak" Allen, Wendy Weyerhaeuser, and Charlotte Chalker—until Charlotte entered law school—had a regular doubles game at the Lakewood Racquet Club, and once a year we took a tennis vacation. Whenever we are together, we reminisce and laugh about incidences that occurred on those trips, i.e. when our wives after shopping all day in San Francisco, predominately looking for a hat for Squeak, returned to their hotel in a cab. When they arrived, the cab driver was wearing Squeak's new hat and Wendy Weyerhaeuser the cab driver's hat. However, I think the funniest incident occurred in Hawaii when George Weyerhaeuser and I were challenged to a tennis match by an acquaintance and very competitive tennis player who was also staying at the resort. George and I had played him before and always prevailed, even though he progressively teamed up with better partners. On this occasion, unbeknownst to us, he had lined up the head pro, a recent member of the Stanford tennis team, to be his partner. The following morning, with Allen and Carlson and the four wives cheerleading, we won in a third set tiebreaker thanks to George's superb net play. We always wondered how much he had paid the pro to be his partner.

Front row: Gwen Carlson, Squeak Allen, Wendy, and
Wendy Weyerhaeuser; back row: Stan Carlson, me,
George Weyerhaeuser, and Harold Allen

In 1976, a few days after Wendy returned from visiting her father in Phoenix, who was recovering from surgery in the hospital, she woke up in the middle of the night crying.

"What's wrong?" I asked.

"Daddy just died."

"Hey, come on you've just had a bad dream. Your father is fine," I responded.

"No! He's dead." She said.

"How do you know?"

"Don't ask," she said. "Walt [her brother] is dialing our phone number right now." A few moments later the phone rang. It was Walt.

Summers our sons' Charles Wright classmates congregated at our home after work and on weekends for basketball, water skiing, and pickle ball. One Saturday morning, I remember Sally Hokanson, our next-door neighbor, calling Wendy to ask if she would talk to the boys about not using their colorful language on the pickle ball court Sunday because her elderly mother was coming for tea—our court and the Hokanson's lakeside patio sat adjacent, separated only by thirty feet of landscaping.

At the end of the 1987–88 ballet season, Arthur Jacobus, Pacific Northwest Ballet chief executive officer, stated, "On June 30, 1988, a very special individual will end an unprecedented three years as chairman of the board. Wendy Griffin has overseen the near doubling of the ballet's balanced budget, the production of a major new full-length ballet, the national release of a feature-length movie, a triumphant Kennedy Center debut [which Wendy and I attended], the successful matching of a National Endowment for the Arts Challenge Grant, the establishment of a cash reserve fund, and many other accomplishments too numerous to mention. The total integrity, absolute dedication and impeccable style Wendy brought to the job will leave an indelible mark on the organization. She has set a standard of leadership excellence, which will be an inspiration to her successors."

A few months later, Kent Stowell (Kent and his wife Francia Russell were co-artistic directors of Pacific Northwest Ballet) sent Wendy a note.

"Francia and I are aware of all your efforts and there is no way that we can adequately express our appreciation. You are very much admired, and I only hope to live up to all the expectations."

For over thirty years, Wendy remained active with the ballet; she now serves as a board member emeritus.

Gail Smelick (Wendy's sister), Peter Paine (Wendy's cousin), Wendy, me, Bob Smelick, and Patty Paine at Wendy's fiftieth birthday party in Sun Valley

Jean Gardner, wife of Washington Governor Booth Gardner, and Wendy in Kobe, Japan, for the dedication and opening of a Washington State-affiliated college, which included a Washington State Arts Commission exhibition

Then in 1988, Governor Booth Gardner appointed Wendy to the Washington State Arts Commission; two years later, she was chairman.

In 1991, Wendy served on the National Endowment for the Arts, Dance on Tour Panel.

In 1992, she participated in the American Leadership Forum (ALF), a year-long training program to help community leaders enhance their communication and leadership skills. ALF training included an Outward Bound wilderness experience in Colorado. Wendy still talks about getting into her sleeping bag fully dressed in a coeducational cabin, having to climb over a twenty-foot wall, rappelling down a rock cliff, and being helped down the mountain by the head of the Longshoremen's Union—shortly thereafter, Wendy had both her knees replaced. Wendy served as vice chairman and then chairman of the Tacoma chapter of the American Leadership Forum.

Also in 1992, Wendy was selected to participate in Leadership America, a national program of the Foundation for Women's Resources (for women with impressive accomplishments who represented a broad range of leaders throughout the United States). That same year, she helped incorporate the City of Lakewood, as a member of the Steering Committee, and she became involved with the local YMCA, serving on its board of directors.

In 1994, Wendy joined the board of Greater Lakes Mental Health Center. In 1998, she became vice chairman of the board, and the following year chairman. In addition, she worked with Greater Lakes' capital campaign, raising money for a new center. Every Thanksgiving if Wendy and I are in town, we work at Greater Lakes—in the building Wendy helped make possible—serving turkey dinners to street families.

Also in 1994, Wendy was appointed to the Governor's Mansion Foundation, a nonprofit statewide organization that maintains the public rooms of the governor's mansion; two years later, she served as the foundation's Tacoma/Pierce County chairman and from 1996 through 1998 as president.

In 1995, the Aloha Club, a Tacoma woman's study group, invited Wendy to become a member. She was elected president in 2000.

In 1996, she helped found Forward Together, a group formed to determine how, through innovative public and private funding of capital projects, the quality of life in Tacoma and Pierce County could be sustained, improved, and expanded.

In 1988, Wendy was appointed to the board of the Tacoma Art Museum and served on their exhibitions, development, finance, nominating, and executive committees. From 1993 to 1997, she served as president and chairman of the board. From 1999 to 2002, Wendy and I served as co-chairmen of the capital campaign for a new museum. Wendy continues to serve as a board member emeritus.

Wendy at Tacoma Art Museum with Dale Chihuly, one of the premier glass artists of the world

Me, Wendy, and Congressman Norm Dicks at the Tacoma Art Museum ribbon cutting (May 3, 2003)

With the arrival of grandchildren—Nicholas, our first, Sterling and Karrie's son, came in 1988 and thirteen more, eight boys and five girls, followed over the next twenty-one years, ending with Sterling and Trina's (Sterling had remarried) twins born in 2009—Wendy took up knitting again and a blanket awaited the birth of each grandchild. Whitney and Gretchen adopted our twelfth grandchild, Gaby.

When Gaby was seven months old, I went to Guatemala with Whitney to pick her up. After the transfer, we spent the night in Guatemala City before flying home. The hotel furnished a crib, but Gaby wouldn't cooperate. She cried until Whitney let her snuggle up next to him in bed. I awoke in the middle of the night to a scene as magnificent as any Rembrandt painting. Moonlight filtered through window curtains spotlighting a sleeping Gaby in Whitney's arms.

The following evening when we arrived at SeaTac airport, I had a similar emotional rush watching eleven grandchildren, who were waiting behind the rope barrier, leading out from the exiting corridor, stampede like cattle through and around security personnel—who gave up trying to corral them. Screaming, they swarmed, like bees, around Whitney and the baby, trying to get a look.

It wasn't long before Wendy and I were back attending recitals and sporting events. The apple doesn't drop far from the tree, and our sons and daughter seldom miss a child's activity. Scott and Kristine's three sons, Jamie, Malcolm and Gus, played Select Soccer, A Division, as well as high school soccer. Sterling coached his and Karrie's sons', Nicholas and Tyler, little league football team, as well as their ninth grade high school team and he and Karrie watched their daughter, Natalie, win her first national kayak championship—as did Wendy and I. Whitney coached his and Gretchen's sons', Wyatt and Cooper, little league baseball, soccer, and basketball teams and Gaby's soccer team. Ashley and her husband Neil coached soccer for their son, Gibson, and daughters, Wendy and Maude. Like her mother, Ashley travels the horse show circuit with her daughters—until Maude turned to tennis. Ashley also rides. Wendy is an accomplished rider and winner of many show championships. We love and cherish all of our grandchildren and when in town we join their parents at grandchildren events.

Larry and Natalie Humphrey, Dede Winters, Wendy Griffin, John Winters, and me, staying at the Winters' condominium in Sun River, Oregon

Bill and Bobby Street, me, and Wendy kayaking Rogue River

From 2005 through 2007, Wendy worked tirelessly to bring a $10 million Hope Center to the city of Lakewood. This center, a partnership between Clover Park School District and the Boys and Girls Club of South Puget Sound (BGCSPS), became a reality in 2008. Wendy's passion and dedication were directly related to a commitment she gave to a dying friend, Carol Milgard. According to Judy Hosea, VP for Development, BGCSPS, "Wendy helped recruit the right people to the committee, set up tours and meetings with individuals that could help and closed many of our significant gifts. Wendy did this first in support of her friend as Wendy values her friendships above all. Wendy also did this for the children and families in the community that would benefit for years to come."

Wendy's many years of volunteerism led to the following awards: Evergreen State Society Award in 1991, a statewide recognition program to strengthen public appreciation for the value of Washington's cultural recreational resources; Tacoma Arts Commission Excellence in the Arts Award in 1992, presented to individuals who have made outstanding contributions to the arts in the city of Tacoma; Junior League Sustainer of the Year Award in 1993, for community improvement through effective action and leadership of trained volunteers; and the Murray Medal in 1994, awarded by the Tacoma Art Museum as special recognition to those who have served with exceptional loyalty and dedication.

At the presentation of the Evergreen State Society Award, Jane Williams, chairman of the Seattle Foundation, quoted John Firman, executive director of the Washington State Arts Commission: "Wendy has managed to bring to the table both the concerns and interests of the citizens of Tacoma, and all the citizens of the state. Wendy exemplifies the definition of leadership through volunteerism, and is an invaluable asset to the commission and its constituents. Wendy has the capacity and ability to lead in the most difficult of times, as demonstrated by the changes she has wrought at the organizations on whose boards she serves. She has a tremendous understanding of how to balance the complex relationships between pragmatism, philosophy, and politics. Her skill in negotiating problematic issues and moderating divergent opinions among her colleagues on the board is superb. Wendy's vision and imagination will be a valuable contribution to the state as it enters the twenty-first century."

Wendy, me, and Charlotte Chalker, 2007, at the Chalkers' cabin on Copalis Beach

Wendy before flight in Ray Chalkers' Stearman

In 2007, our grandson Nicholas (Sterling and Karrie's son) entered Whitman College, and the following year, their son Tyler entered the University of Oregon. Both boys helped their colleges win national debate championships. In 2011, Nicholas and his debate partner placed in the top ten in the national debate championship. Also in 2008, Jamie (Scott and Kristine's son) entered Redlands College where he plays varsity soccer. In 2010, Jamie was the league's leading scorer. In 2009, Malcolm (Scott and Kristine's second son) entered Denver University, where he is majoring in construction management and intends to go into business with his father. In 2011, Gibson (Ashley and Neil's son) will graduate from high school and spend a year doing volunteer work, six months in Africa then six months in India, before entering a yet to be named college—he has been accepted at numerous colleges. Gibson writes poetry, plays the guitar and piano, and sings and acts. He will undoubtedly pursue an artistic career. Gus (Scott and Kristine's third son) will enter college in 2012 and Natalie (Sterling and Karrie's daughter) and Wendy (Ashley and Neil's daughter) in 2013. Wendy is hopeful of obtaining a riding scholarship and Natalie a kayaking scholarship. Our other grandchildren, Maude, Wyatt, Cooper, Gabriela, and twins Sterling and Hope, are some years away from college.

And then there's Wyatt (Whitney and Gretchen's son), the gutsiest kid I've ever known. Wyatt's every step is an effort, but you never hear him complain. Wyatt was run over at three and a half and suffered severe spinal cord trauma.

Wyatt spent one week in ICU, two weeks in Mary Bridge Hospital and two months in Seattle's Children's Orthopedic Hospital, where Whitney stayed with him, sleeping in a reclining chair in Wyatt's room.

Wyatt was determined to walk again, and after a month of therapy he began taking steps while clinging to a walker. His positive attitude and strength of character amazed his doctors and extended family, which included his eleven cousins who visited him often.

By first grade, Wyatt was participating in "Little League" soccer, basketball and baseball, which his father coached. Whenever he was asked, "What's wrong with your legs," he responded, "I was run over," end of conversation. Though slower than his teammates, he makes up for it in aggressiveness and a huge heart.

I watched Wyatt make his first soccer goal, hit his first home run—over the fence otherwise he wouldn't have been able to run the bases—and score his first basket. Today, 2010, Wyatt plays on Charles Wright Academy's eight grade J V soccer and basketball teams. He also plays ultimate Frisbee and summer recreational lacrosse.

Grandchildren, Nana and I couldn't be more proud of you and your accomplishments, whether athletic, artistic, scholastic or just loving and nurturing.

Me and Wendy with our children and grandchildren at the home of Whitney, our son, on Fox Island, Gig Harbor (fall of 2006)

Margarete Heiny, in her eighties, climbing Mt. Eisenhower near Palm Desert. Margarete came to work for us nearly forty years ago. She helped raise our children and is now another grandmother to our children's children.

The cliché, "behind every successful man is a good woman," has never been truer than with Wendy. Whenever I was faced with what appeared to be an overwhelming challenge, Wendy quickly pushed or pulled me out of my malaise. She supported all my endeavors whether she was in agreement or not—other than when I used up eight of my proverbial nine "cat lives" during my floatplane piloting years. No husband could have a more loving and supportive wife. I am grateful every day for my good fortune to have found Wendy.

When I retired we sold our home on Gravelly Lake and bought a duplex condominium on American Lake in the Tacoma Country and Golf Club. We split our winters between Puerto Vallarta, Mexico, where we've owned a beach condominium for thirty years, and Palm Desert, California, where in 2004 we bought a condominium in the Ironwood Country Club.

In 2006, Wendy was diagnosed with liver cancer. Fortunately, the tumor originated in the liver rather than migrating to the liver and the surgeon was able to remove the cancer before it metastasized. Two years later, she developed breast cancer. The tumor, which had invaded the lymph nodes, was removed and she underwent chemotherapy and radiation. According to her doctors, the cancers weren't related—just bad luck. They are optimistic she is now cancer free.

On July 2, 2006, when Wendy was fighting for her life, I received the following e-mail: "Jim, I love Wendy Griffin ... Almost everyone says that when they mention her name. She is one of a kind, unique ... so many qualities, she knows people through and through. You two have produced wonderful kids and grandchildren and have led exemplary lives. Not perfect ... exemplary. You're blessed ... we are blessed to have a Wendy in our life. I really do love Wendy Griffin ... and I say I am a real friend of hers. John" (John Braseth, owner of Woodside-Braseth Gallery)

Wendy and me at collection of rocks in the form of hearts celebrating cancer survivors that I found on the trail to a ten foot high cross, visible at night for many miles in and around Palm Desert.

Wendy, Prince William "Willy," and me on a hike in Palm Desert, California (2009)

Appendix

(1) Abraham Griffin (my great grandfather)

(2) Six Degrees of Separation

(3) Photos from the Paine One-Hundred-Year Reunion

(4) *Île de France*

(5) Dorothy "Dottie" (Paine) Sterling Stories

(6) Maud Eustis (Paine) Evenson and Alvah Jordan Paine (Dottie's siblings)

(7) Edwin "Ed" Lewis Griffin (my father)

(8) Gino Hollander

(9) Nancy (Mathewson) Spaeth (my sister)

(10) Elizabeth "Beth" (Griffin) Ferris (my sister)

(11) Bea and Fred Griffin (my aunt and uncle)

(12) *How to Make Money in Commercial Land*

(1) Abraham Griffin:

The following is paraphrased from *Griffin Families Marry*, written and published, June 1987, by John R Griffin, Library of Congress, Catalog card number 9089.

Abraham came to America in 1846, at age thirteen, with his parents, John and Mary Griffin, along with brother Isaac and sisters Rachel and Harriet, John Jr., age five, died aboard ship and was buried at sea. Abraham spent his teenage years working on the family farm in Waukegan, Illinois, a small town on Lake Michigan. The land was much like that of their home in Lincolnshire, England, other than corn (maize) wasn't grown in England.

In 1851, a cholera epidemic killed Abraham's mother and two sisters, Rachel and Harriet. They were buried on 3 successive Sundays. A year later, at age nineteen, Abraham left home. He married Henrietta La Grange in 1854 and farmed near Waukegan, Illinois' until 1861, when the family moved by ox-cart to a 120-acre Carr Valley farm near Ironton, Sauk County, Wisconsin.

At the outbreak of the Civil War, Abraham enlisted as a private in Company "K" 35th Wisconsin Volunteer Infantry at Milwaukee, Wisconsin. His Union Army "Muster-in-Roll" stated that he was a thirty-one-year-old farmer, born in Lincolnshire, England, had blue eyes, dark hair and fair complexion and was 5' 9" tall. His regiment took part in a dozen Civil War engagements, mostly in Arkansas, Louisiana, and Alabama ... Abraham was discharged at Brownsville, Texas ... and like many other soldiers, he paid the army $6 for his Springfield rifled musket and took it home to be rebored as a shotgun."

After the war, Abraham became a successful farmer. The first school in the valley was established on the Griffin farm, and Abraham served as the school district clerk, as well as a county tax assessor. He and Henrietta raised eight children, my grandfather Fredrick, the sixth, was born after Abraham returned from the war.

As Abraham grew older, he suffered from scurvy and myopia, caused by inadequate rations during the Civil War. The obituary in the Ironton newspaper stated, "Abraham Griffin had been called upon to fill a number of public offices and exerted considerable influence in local public affairs." Henrietta lived another eleven years. She died February 17, 1919, at age eighty-three, in Armstrong, Emmet County, Iowa.

Abraham Griffin, my great grandfather

A number of Abraham's letters appear in *Descendants of John Griffin*, published 1983, Library of Congress, catalogue card number 83-81522. Following is a paragraph from his letter of January 20, 1890, to his brother in Kansas. "We sold 800 tons of limestone to the Iron Company at 62 ½ cents a ton and took in 400 ton in 6 weeks and the rest we take after the next harvest. Two teams will commence hauling logs for the company tomorrow at 2 dollars a thousand feet, 4 mile haul. Everything is very low here wheat 85, (cents a bushel) corn 30, oats 15, buckwheat 20, potatoes 20-25 depends on the kind they are, hay $2 a ton, cows 10 to 15 dollars each. I sent 10 good steers and heifers to Chicago last September and brought me $145 clear of expense. The expense was $25. I had kept them 1 winter and 2 summers and all they made more than I paid for them before that time was $45. So you can see I did not make much out of them."

****

(2) Six Degrees of Separation:

Augustus Gibson Paine, the progenitor of the Paine line (Wendy's great-great-grandfather), born in Maine in 1839, descended from Thomas Paine II, who arrived at Plymouth in 1637. Augustus and his wife, Charlotte Bedwell, had three children: Augustus Gibson Paine Jr. "A.G." (Wendy's great grandfather), born in New York in 1866, and two daughters who died of typhoid in childhood.

After prospering in the dry goods business in Portland, Maine, Augustus moved to Boston and imported textiles from England. In 1885, he foreclosed on a pulp mill on Lake Champlain in Willsboro, New York. He'd sold the mill a Yaran evaporator, which recovered chemicals from cooked pulp and made manufacturing paper from wood chips economically viable. The evaporator was invented in Germany, and Augustus bought the US patent rights. As he knew nothing about operating a paper mill, he sent for his eighteen-year-old son, A.G. Jr., who worked with his (Augustus's) textile associates. Shortly after arriving in Willsboro, A.G. talked his cousin Alvah Jordan, a Yale forestry graduate, into coming to Willsboro to help him with the mill.

A.G. and Alvah perfected the soda process for making pulp, and the Willsboro mill flourished and became the foundation for the family's involvement in the paper business.

Augustus became a successful New York banker and was instrumental in founding the Great Northern Paper Company, which became one of the leading pulp and paper companies in the country.

Henry Hewitt (my grandfather Ted Mathewson's uncle) was born in 1840 at Yorkshire, England, one year after Augustus Paine. The following year, in 1841, his family immigrated to America.

At sixteen, Henry drove a team of horses and wagon twelve hours a day for his father's logging company. Two years later, he began cruising timber. Before turning twenty, he had contracted to build a dam at Portage, Wisconsin, and take his pay in a land grant, which provided the capital for his financial successes.

In the late 1880s, when Wisconsin and the upper Mississippi Valley had been stripped of forests, Henry, now a very wealthy man, went west. He eventually located in Tacoma, near abundant timber and close to the Northern Pacific Railroad terminus. Henry and an eastern acquaintance, Chauncey Griggs, built the St. Paul & Tacoma Lumber Company, which became the country's largest producing sawmill. When the mill became profitable, Henry began looking for other opportunities. He investigated most of Western Washington on foot and horseback, finally picking the mouth of the Snohomish River for a mill and log storage site.

While Hewitt explored northern Puget Sound, partners of John D. Rockefeller came west looking for a terminus for a railroad and location for a port. Hewitt convinced Rockefeller's associates to locate at Port Gardner Bay, at the mouth of the Snohomish River. Shortly thereafter, a Rockefeller syndicate (which included Augustus Paine) entrusted Hewitt with money to acquire land and build a shipyard, nail factory, smelter, and paper mill.

According to excerpts from *Whitfield's History of Snohomish County, Washington*, Volume II (Pioneer Historical Publishing Company, 1926), "Almost overnight, a city of six thousand with factories, churches, schools and six hotels was born."

"Everett was named in a most unusual manner. At a dinner party in the home of Charles Colby, Hewitt's eye caught the host's son, Everett, who wanted more dessert. 'That's it!' Hewitt chuckled; 'We should name our city Everett. This boy wants only the best, and so do we.'" (*Mill Town, a Social History of Everett, Washington, from its Earliest Beginnings,* by Norman H. Clark [University of Washington Press, 1982])

When my grandfather Ted Mathewson attended the University of Notre Dame, his uncle Henry convinced him to leave college and come to Everett and make his fortune in the timber business. Upon arriving in Everett, he filed for a homestead. With the profit from selling his homestead's timber and land, he bought homesteads from others and repeated the process. Eventually Grandfather went into the sawmill and logging business with Joe Irving. Grandfather died in 1911, at forty, when his chauffeur-driven car's tires bounced out of snow ruts while touring Mount Rainier and dropped over a cliff, landing upside down. Years later, my grandmother Elsie married Joe Irving.

In an interview at the Everett library on June 9, 1977 (describing the Paine family connection to Everett), Anson Moody, William Howarth's son-in-law (Howarth was Alvah Jordan's partner in the Everett pulp mill they bought from Rockefeller), stated, "The Paine family owned the New York and Pennsylvania Paper Company ... Eventually it made all the paper for the *Saturday Evening Post* and *Ladies Home Journal*, and that was a good many carloads of paper a day ... And Mr. Jordan's mother was related to the Paines in some way [Alvah's mother and A.G.'s mother were sisters] ... I think he [Alvah Jordan] must have borrowed a little money from his relatives."

In another "six degrees of separation" coincidence, my mother played bridge regularly with Alvah's longtime companion, though Mother at that time knew nothing of the family connection.

August Gibson Paine "A.G."   Alvah Jordan

In July 1985, Wendy, our children and I attended the hundred-year reunion of the Paine family in Willsboro, New York.

Through the generations the Boquet River mill site had been expanded to one thousand contiguous acres including three miles of Lake Champlain shoreline and two miles of the Boquet River, which had been a summer hunting and war party stopover for Algonquin and Mohawk Indians.

The following stories about the Paines' Willsboro property came from a college research paper written by Alex Paine, son of Peter (Wendy's cousin) and Patty Paine:

During the Revolutionary War, British General John Burgoyne camped on what became the Paine property shortly before being defeated by General George Washington's Continental Army at Saratoga, preventing the British from separating New England from the southern colonies.

Thirty-seven years later, in the War of 1812, a young boy happened to see British ships enter the Boquet River on their way to capture supplies at a grist mill (where grain is ground into flour), which later became the paper mill site, and sounded the alarm. The boy's father went out to greet the British and invited their officers to a meal, which gave the Willsboro militia time to gather on the banks above the river. In the ensuing shoot-out, thirty British soldiers were killed and one hundred wounded. There were no American casualities.

****

(3) Photos from the Paine One-Hundred-Year Reunion:

Back row from left: Sis Paine, wife of Peter Paine Sr.; Peter Paine Sr. (Wendy's great-uncle and brother of Wendy's grandfather Augustus "Gibson" Gibson Paine III); Lea Paine, daughter of Peter and Patty Paine; Patty Paine, wife of Peter Paine Jr.; Peter Paine Jr. Front row from left: Alex Paine and Peter Paine lll, sons of Peter and Patty Paine

Wendy and her cousin Peter Paine Jr. woodcock hunting in Willsboro

Photo of the descendents of Dorothy (Quimby) and Augustus Gibson Paine III "Gibson," Wendy (Sterling) Griffin's grandparents, who came to Phoenix in 1935. Back row from left: Kim Sterling, wife of Walter "Walt" Hubbard Sterling Jr.; Brooke Sterling, daughter of Kim and Walt Sterling Jr.; Walter "Walt" Hubbard Sterling Jr., son of Walter Hubbard and "Dottie" (Paine) Sterling, grandson of Dorothy and Gibson Paine; Whitney Griffin, son Jim and Wendy Griffin; James "Jim" Scott Griffin, husband of Wendy Griffin; John Ogilvy Houlton, husband of Christine Houlton; Christine (Evenson) Houlton, daughter of Marvin P. "Chick" and Maud Evenson, granddaughter of Dorothy and Gibson Paine; Michael John Evenson, son of Marvin P. "Chick" and Maud Evenson Second row from left: Ashley Evenson Griffin (Collins), daughter of Wendy and Jim Griffin; Jacques Marc Edward Evenson, son of Marvin P. "Chick" and Maud Evenson; Theresa Evenson, daughter of Mark and Vicky Evenson; Wendy (Sterling) Griffin, daughter of Dottie Paine and Walter Hubbard Sterling Jr., granddaughter of Dorothy and Gibson Paine; Theresa Vicky (Reich) Evenson, wife of Marc Evenson; Gail (Sterling) Smelick, daughter of Dottie and Walter Hubbard Sterling Jr., granddaughter of Dorothy and Gibson Paine; Robert "Bob" Malcolm Smelick, husband of Gail Smelick; Maud Eustis (Paine) Evenson, daughter of Dorothy and Gibson Paine; Maj-Britt (Dohlie) Evenson, wife of Mike Evenson First row from left: Walter "Bard" Hubbard Sterling III, son of Kim and Walt Sterling Jr.; Edward "Sterling" Griffin, son of Wendy and Jim Griffin; John David Houlton, son of John and Christine Houlton; Leeling Houlton, daughter of John and

Christine Houlton; Thomas Dohlie Evenson, son of Maj-Britt and Mike Evenson; James "Scott" Scott Griffin Jr., son of Wendy and Jim Griffin; Kristina Dohlie Evenson, daughter of Maj-Britt and Mike Evenson; Martha Louise Evenson, daughter of Mark and Vicky Evenson; and Jordan Sterling, son of Kim and Walt Sterling Jr. Doris Thompson and Alvah "Jordan" Jordan Paine, brother of Maud Paine and son of Dottie and Gibson Paine and their daughters Dorothy "Dotty" Quimby and Claudia Paine (Johnson) and Michael Tyler Eric Evenson, son of Marvin P. and Maud Evenson, and family did not attend reunion.

****

(4) Île de France:

The following story comes from the book, *Île de France*, by Don Stanford, Appleton-Century-Crofts, Inc., Library of Congress, Catalog card number: 60-9810:

In March 1932, four years prior to Dorothy and Walter marrying, the headlines of the Society page of a New York paper read, "So the French Aviator Followed His Sub-Deb Dream Girl through Air and Water to Romance. He Flew Out to Her Ship to Say Good-bye; Then, Splash—the Unexpected Sequel." The story:

The morning of March 15, 1932, was clear but blustery; a brisk wind whipped the sea into a heavy chop as the Île de France sailed from Le Havre. Among her passengers was the Gibson Paine family of New York, and as the ship reached open water and her parents went below to their cabin to unpack, pretty Dorothy Paine remained on deck, flushed with the March wind—and with anticipation. In Paris Dorothy had had a gay, attentive, and amusing escort in Pierre Van Laer, the son of a wealthy French cotton broker; last night Pierre had confessed humorously that seeing Paris with Dorothy had left him stony broke, and that he would have to take his little Blackburn Bluebird biplane and fly home to Normandy this morning to get his exchequer [bank account] pumped up and, he added, if she would be on deck to wave to him, he would buzz over the Île de France en route to bid her a last farewell.

The shores of France were already out of sight when a black speck appeared in the sky behind the ship, and rapidly grew into a small airplane. It circled the ship and swooped low, so low that Dorothy could see Pierre grinning and waving to her from the cockpit as he waggled his wings and climbed a little to dip low and go around again. Ecstatically she waved her scarf and blew him kisses, dancing up and down with pleasure, not at all unaware of the envious glances of other girls among the passengers who had been drawn out on deck by the snarl of the Bluebird's engine.

Captain Blancart was on his bridge, observing with satisfaction that everything was going smoothly and estimating that he would reach Plymouth exactly on schedule, when a junior officer appeared, somewhat out of breath, to announce, "Captain Blancart, an airplane has just crashed into the water behind us!"

"Reverse engines, full speed astern!" Blancart snapped, and spun on the junior officer to demand, "How far behind?"

"Estimate four miles," the junior officer answered, and continued, "It's a small plane. The pilot was stunting over the ship for the benefit of some girl on board; he turned back toward shore and flew three or four miles and his engine failed. You could hear it. He came down and—"

Blancart was making a series of swift computations. The forty-three thousand tons of the *Île de France* was moving at twenty-four knots; with full reverse power it would take three and a half miles to stop the ship, at least two miles to slow her enough to make the tight turnaround he had in mind. If the crashed airplane floated, it might be easy enough to locate and rescue the pilot—provided he hadn't either been killed in the crash or died of exposure in the icy water. But if the airplane had sunk, it would be almost impossible to spot the tiny black speck of a human head bobbing in the choppy waters of the Channel; there would be only one possible way to get back to the area of open water where the plane had vanished, and that would be to follow the only track there was—the *Île*'s own wake. It would be necessary to reach the crash area as rapidly as possible, yet the *Île de France* must be traveling at dead slow speed when the pilot was sighted, if he was sighted, in order to get a boat launched to pick him up before the ship had overshot him by a mile or two. Therefore he must turn around and retrace his own wake at full speed for two or three miles, then reduce to half-speed.

Blancart slowed the *Île de France* as he neared what the officer who had witnessed the crash estimated to be the immediate vicinity of the point where the little plane had gone down. There was no sign of anything that looked like an airplane or part of an airplane floating on the choppy water—actually the little biplane had sunk immediately, probably before the *Île* got turned around—and Blancart's heart sank: there was little chance of finding the pilot before he died of exposure in the March seas.

But at that moment the signal came through to the bridge that the pilot had been sighted. Blancart rang for full speed astern, the *Île*'s screws thrashed the water, and in less than four minutes the ship lay motionless in the water while a lifeboat pulled briskly away from her side.

Pierre Van Laer was brought aboard wrapped in blankets, soaking wet and blue with cold, but quite conscious and capable of a grin and debonair wave for Dorothy Paine as he was hurried to the ship's hospital to be treated for exposure ... and to radio his mother that he found himself unexpectedly aboard the *Île de France*, and without funds.

Blancart had got the *Île* under way again as soon as the lifeboat was hoisted aboard, turned around and headed once more for Plymouth. He could not quite make up the time lost; still, he would not be very late into Plymouth, and the embarking of Plymouth-to-New York passengers could be carried off on schedule unless the British Immigration authorities demurred at taking off the rescued pilot, who doubtless had no documents of any kind, and returning him to France.

At this point Dorothy Paine, who had already visited Van Laer in the hospital, appeared on the bridge, starry-eyed and breathless with gratitude and praise for the Captain, which Blancart found acutely embarrassing. She also had an idea to propose:

"Don't put him off at Plymouth, Captain Blancart, please don't! Can't you take him on to New York? He's such fun, and it would make the crossing just wonderful, and—"

"Certainly not," Blancart answered firmly. In the first place, the young man's passage hadn't been paid, and no doubt he had no way of paying it, and the French Line did not carry passengers for charity. In the second place, the United States Immigration authorities wouldn't permit him to land without a passport anyway, and what would be the point in carrying him all the way across the ocean only to bring him back again without having set foot on land? In the third place, Van Laer's irresponsible stunt had already delayed the ship and there would be paperwork and formalities enough involved in getting rid of him as it was, and the rules were clear enough: he would be put off at Plymouth, period.

"But he's suffering from exposure!" Dorothy mourned. "He's in the hospital right now! If you make him get up and get dressed and go ashore at Plymouth he'll get pneumonia or something and die, and it'll be your fault!"

Adamant, Blancart ordered the girl off the bridge again—but he was not surprised when she reappeared a few minutes later accompanied by the ship's doctor, who wore a distinctly sheepish look and did not seem to be able to meet the Captain's accusing eye as he mumbled that of course the young man seemed fit enough and could be put off at Plymouth, all right, but in cases of exposure it—ah—sometimes did no harm to have an extra day in bed, and ah.

Blancart was touched and amused, but unmoved—until the Chief Purser appeared and crisply reported, in line of duty, that the ship's passenger list had officially been augmented by one. Pierre Van Laer's round-trip passage to New York in First Class had been paid by cable, and there was a further thousand dollars in cash credited to him in the Purser's office.

Defeated, the Captain gave in, not ungraciously; and when Pierre Van Laer left the ship's hospital and later appeared in the dining room, at the Paine family's table, he was wearing the Captain's spare dinner jacket, which Dorothy had persuaded the Captain to lend him. And someone (probably Dorothy Paine) somehow (neither Captain Blancart nor Pierre Van Laer ever saw fit to inquire how) managed to persuade the United States Immigration Service to permit Van Laer to land and spend thirty days in the United States, passport or no.

"So," says Van Laer, "I invested my mother's thousand dollars in a glorious three weeks at the Waldorf-Astoria. I never had such a good time in my life … Dorothy? Dorothy was a wonderful girl, and a wonderful person. She never had any interest in me, except as a date or somebody to brighten a dull sea crossing; she was already engaged to a very nice guy, and she married him, and we all kept in touch for more than twenty years."

According to Peter Paine Jr. (Wendy's cousin), "A.G." (Dorothy's grandfather), called somebody in a high place and made arrangements for Van Laer to enter and remain in the United States for one month.

During World War II, Pierre Van Laer worked in the French resistance, helping the Allies. When Dorothy died in 1950, he came to her funeral in Phoenix.

Picture of article about Dottie and *Île de France*
(from unknown newspaper story)

****

(5) Dorothy "Dottie" Paine Sterling stories:

(contributed by Wendy's cousin Claudia Paine, as told by her father, Jordan Paine, about his sister Dottie)

Dorothy "Dottie" (Paine) Sterling, Wendy's mother

Stolen Car

"There was a time in Phoenix, when you would not have to lock your car and you could leave your key in the ignition without much concern. My dad [Jordan] told me of a time when he went downtown to the old Goldwater's department store—family of Senator Goldwater who ran for President in 1964—and there in the parking lot was his sister Dottie's car. Dad parked his car, not far from hers, and went about whatever he was there to do. When he returned to his car, it was gone. However, Aunt Dottie's car was still there, with a flat tire. Dad knew very well his sister had come out to find her car with a flat and taken his car leaving him to fix the flat and bring the car home.

"He did just that ... sort of. Dad fixed the flat and drove the car home, but parked it around the back and hurried into the house to report to his sister that his car had been stolen! He was really upset! All for show of course. She quickly told him she took his car, how her car had a flat tire and she was sure he wouldn't mind, and she was very sorry. Aunt Dottie asked if they could go back to Goldwater's to get her car and would he mind very much changing the flat tire. He said sure, he was happy to help.

"When they got to the parking lot, of course Aunt Dottie's car was not there. As Dad tells it, 'Aunt Dottie really was even more upset to find that her car had been stolen.' I don't know how long he let her go on, but eventually he told her that the car was back at her house."

No Bugs in My House

"With his love of flying, one of the jobs my dad had while living in Phoenix as a young man was flying crop dusters. It was during this time that his sister Dottie happened to mention there were many bugs in and around her house. I don't know whose idea it was (they were both nuts enough to come up with it), Dad wouldn't say. One day Aunt Dottie opened all the windows and all the doors in the house and as Dad tells it, 'someone flew over the house and dusted it.'

"The house, inside and outside was covered with about fifty lbs of white dust. It was everywhere ... over all the furniture, tables, floors, books, clothes, shelves, cabinets, absolutely everywhere. There were, however, no more bugs."

Men and Trucks

"Aunt Dottie had a very good friend, Nay Kitchel. As the stories unfold about the two, it is clear they really were quite a pair. Both had children about the same age, both were young, energetic, attractive gals who had fun in life. They spent a lot of time together and as the old saying goes, 'what one didn't think of, the other did.'

"During the war women stepped up to do many jobs once thought to be only in the man's arena. For some reason, Aunt

Dottie and Nay decided to take the driving test to drive semi tractors. Apparently, when these two 'gals' arrived, the men who were there also for the test had a good laugh and really, really razzed them. Aunt Dottie and Nay each hopped up into a cab and under very watchful and critical eyes took their test. The razzing stopped soon enough when the two of them scored higher than any of the men. As I remember hearing the story, I believe they actually did, for a time, work as delivery drivers."

Sticks and Dirt

"My father arrived at his sister Dottie's house and found his niece Wendy and nephew Walter, maybe age seven and five, playing in the back yard of their rented house—it was during the construction of their home in north central Phoenix which later became known as "Sterling's Folly," which is an altogether different story. The two were giggling and talking and having a grand time. Dad noticed that they were very busy poking around in the dirt, each with a stick. Upon closer examination, Dad saw that in amongst the roots they were poking at a snake ... a rattle snake. When I asked Dad what he did, he said 'I moved the kids, got a gun, and shot the snake.' Apparently, Wendy and Walter barely skipped a beat and soon were back in the dirt with their sticks."

****

(6) Maud Eustis (Paine) Evenson and Alvah Jordan Paine:

When Wendy's mother died in 1950, Wendy was eleven, her brother Walter, nine, and her sister Gail, three. Though Wendy's father promptly remarried, giving his siblings a stepmother, Wendy's Aunt Maud and Uncle Jordan and their spouses, Uncle Chick, Admiral Marvin "Chick" Evenson, and Doris Paine, took the three siblings under their collective wings.

I met the Evensons shortly after meeting Wendy. They lived in Atherton near the Stanford campus where I was attending college. I have many wonderful memories of visiting them over the years in Atherton and at their country house in the Santa Rosa hills in Sonoma County, California. Aunt Maud and Uncle Chick were only able to have one child, a daughter, Christine. They adopted three sons, an English boy and two French boys during Chick's European World War II naval postings.

Aunt Maud was a wonderful cook, an excellent tennis player, a pilot, and a fine portrait artist. Hanging in our home in Tacoma are Maud's portraits of Wendy's mother, Wendy, our daughter Ashley, and me.

After Maud's death in 2000, Jordan, a World War II flight instructor, told Wendy and me he remembered sitting in the copilot's seat and asking Maud (his sister) why she was flying her plane at a noticeable angle. Maud told him she didn't want the sun shining in the face of her dog, Robespierre, who was asleep in the backseat.

Uncle Chick, Maud's husband, graduated from Annapolis in 1926. He was commander of the first squadron of PBY sea planes stationed at Pearl Harbor—he made over eight hundred carrier landings—decorated for making a seaplane rescue of a downed pilot in the South Pacific, base commander of Munda Island Airbase in the Philippines during World War II, served on the aircraft carrier *Wasp*, commanded the aircraft carriers

Hogatt Bay and Cabot, and retired a Rear Admiral. He passed away in 1982.

Me and Uncle Chick

Wendy and Aunt Maud

I will never forget Uncle Chick telling me the harrowing tale of his days on Munda. Unfortunately, I did not have a tape recorder and am writing from memory.

"At the height of the war in the South Pacific, the allied forces needed strategic airbases from which their planes could harass the Japanese navy. The island of Munda in the Solomon Islands was one of those strategic locations, and I was assigned to build a base and command a squadron of fighters and bombers." According to Uncle Chick's son Mike, the famous Baa Baa Black Sheep Marine Corps fighter squadron under command of Major Pappy Boyington was stationed at Munda at that time.

"As soon as we started construction, the Japanese realized they had to protect their ships from our air attacks and they began building a fighter base just a few miles away on the other end of the island. The bases were separated by an almost impregnable dense jungle. On a daily basis, for a number of months, we strafed and bombed each other's airfields, destroying much of the previous day's work. We had a spotter positioned near their base who radioed us when the Japanese planes took off so we could get our planes in the air to keep them from being destroyed by Japanese fighters and vice versa."

Mike also told me that a visiting officer was killed by a Japanese sniper as he stood alongside his father. The visiting officer, of a lower rank than Chick, had worn his rank insignia and Uncle Chick had not.

Mike's biological mother died in childbirth and his father, a fighter pilot, died in the Battle over Britain.

Wendy's Uncle Jordan Paine led a very colorful life. He soloed in Willsboro at sixteen, flew crop dusters in Arizona at nineteen, was a navigator for Consolidated Airlines at twenty-one, flew a cargo plane to Hawaii eight days after Japan attacked Pearl Harbor in 1941, and served as a naval navigation and flight instructor during World War II. Jordan signed up to be a fighter pilot, but the navy found him more important as an instructor.

Jordan was an accomplished horseman and an excellent skeet shooter—he had a personal best breaking three hundred without a miss—and bird shot, having been taught by his father

(A.G.) as a boy in Willsboro, New York. Jordan was asked to participate in the equestrian Olympic tryouts in 1948 but did not, because of his impending marriage to Doris.

Jordan and Doris Paine

In 1951, Jordan and Doris moved to a ranch in Oregon where Wendy and her brother Walt spent the summer. In 1954, Jordan returned to Phoenix and bought a utility steel pole manufacturing and distribution company which he operated until retiring.

After Doris died in 1979, Jordan never remarried. He continued to sculpt, scuba dive throughout the world, and play tennis into his eighties. I had the good fortune to be with him on a number of hunting and fishing trips at my son Whitney's lodge on the Big Horn River in Montana. Jordan died in 2007.

Jordan (center) on his eightieth birthday

****

(7) Edwin "Ed" Lewis Griffin

My parents met, while attending the University of Washington. Dad had come to the Mathewson house to help my mother's brothers, Mark and Edward, make "bathtub" gin—it was during prohibition when it was illegal to buy or sell alcohol.

After Grandfather died in 1931, Dad returned from Harvard Business School and took over management of the Griffin Fuel Co. He had the foresight to realize the growing importance of Petroleum as a fuel for domestic heating and immediately began the transition from wood and sawdust to oil. Dad pioneered the oil treatment of stoker coal where jets of oil were mixed with low-grade coal to produce and inexpensive industrial fuel. He also expanded the business to include bunker fuel oil for industrial furnaces and inaugurated the "degree-day" oil delivery system where oil was delivered, without an order, according to a formula based on the size of the storage tank and the daily temperature.

There is no better description of Ed Griffin than that written by Charlie Mann, editor of the *Lakewood Log*. Excerpts from Mann's newspaper article, dated 12/30/49, under the heading ED GRIFFIN CONTINUES TO WIN NATIONAL PUBLICITY FOR HIS P. T. BARNUM TACTICS (Barnum was a circus promoter who became famous for his unusual stunts). "Ed Griffin's Griffin Fuel Co. is one of those Tacoma Institutions, like the City Council, the School Board or the Friendly Little Game at Lane's Cigar Store that goes on and on, forever, never dull, and always with some Weird and Wonderful Angle. Ed has used every trick in the book on merchandising coal, wood, oil and special fuels for big and little customers; is Tacoma's biggest fuel advertiser and as his competitors say of Ed, 'There is no Fuel like a Young Fuel,' or something more unprintable. The firm operates a huge private truck rebuilding plant, paint shop and service organization, which handles the 60 big trucks in the fleet, and houses Ed's private collection of ancient automobiles. In between spells and furious bursts of energy, he lives happily with his 2nd family of kids in the Lakes District, and worries over taxes, politics, Coca-Cola and black coffee, having been on the wagon for the past several years, as everybody knows. Ed's good-humored self-kidding about being abstemious has amazingly turned into one of his best Public Relations stunts."

Dad driving a 1929 J roadster Duisenberg

Dad driving a 1926 Pierce Arrow, my stepmother Sarah in back seat

****

(8) Gino Hollander:

Gino, an award-winning producer and director of documentary films, began painting in 1961 in Greenwich Village, New York. He was among the first artists to work with acrylic paint. Gino and Barb moved to the Costa del Sol in southern Spain in 1962, where we met them in the spring of 1966. Between 1963 and 1990, Gino had numerous one-man shows throughout Europe.

In 1982, Gino and Barbara established the Museo Hollander at their home, Cortijo de las Yeguas, in the hills above Malaga, near the village of Pizarra, to exhibit their collection of Spanish antiquities and artifacts spanning twenty thousand years.

Town & Country, May 1988, Europe's Finest Private Art Collections, Museo Hollander, Pizarra, Malaga, Spain:

"This museum was created by a former New Yorker, Gino Hollander, and his wife, Barbara, who have lived in Spain for twenty-five years. The house itself is a museum piece. It was built of bricks and tiles from a fifteenth-century palace which was being demolished in Cordoba and was fashioned in the style of a seventeenth-century Spanish *cortijo*...

"The museum contains many hundreds of artifacts from the Stone Age, through the centuries."

The museum gained worldwide recognition and was awarded the bronze medal on the HRH Juan Carlos honors list for its major contribution to Spanish tourism.

Our son Sterling, at age eleven, spent a summer at Cortijo de las Yeguas near Pizarra, and the Hollanders' son Scott spent the following summer with us in Tacoma. Prior to Sterling's arrival, award-winning author James Michener visited the Hollanders while doing research for his novel *The Drifters*. Today Scott Hollander lives in Aspen where he owns a "grip" (cameraman) company, which shoots on Hollywood stages or on location.

Wendy and I returned to Spain in the fall of 1972 and spent a wonderful few days on horseback, looking for Roman artifacts—I'd brought a metal detector—and playing tennis on Gino's new clay court. Most mornings, Wendy and I rode into the hills with the Hollanders' thirteen-year-old daughter, Siri, to watch the sunrise. Today Siri lives on a farm outside Taos, New Mexico, where she translates her lifelong love of horses into award-winning sculptures—we are collectors of her sculptures, as well as Gino's paintings.

A few years later, our son Scott (see below), spent a summer at Cortijo de las Yeguas, riding through the hills on horseback, learning to paint, and playing tennis. Scott told me he beat the son of Lew Hoad, the world-famous Australian tennis player, in a tournament in Malaga—Scott was a Washington State high school doubles tennis champion—and played tennis with Morley Safer (a principal of *60 Minutes*, CBS's TV newsmagazine), who was also visiting the Hollanders.

Scott's love for cross-country riding led him to enter and win the 2007 version of the eight-hundred-mile mile Santa Fe Trail race won by Francis Aubry in 1848. "In *True Tales of Old-Time Kansas,* author David Dary quotes Aubry, 'I'll kill every horse on the Santa Fe Trail before I'd lose that $1,000 bet, but it's not about the money I care about, I'm riding to prove that I can get more out of a horse and last longer than any other man in the West.'" (Erik Lacitis, October 7, 2007, *Seattle Times*). "I like opportunities where you have to dig deep and see what you're made of," Griffin said ...

At the race banquet, Kansas Governor Sebelius, now Health Secretary in the Obama administration, presented Scott with the winner's trophy, a commemorative belt buckle—Wendy and I joined Scott on stage for the presentation.

Scott Griffin crossing the finish line (picture by Jim Griffin)

When the Hollanders came to Tacoma in the midseventies, I arranged for Gordon Woodside, our art gallery friend, to hold a one-man show. As I remember, all of Hollander's paintings sold at the show opening.

The Hollanders returned to the United States in 1990. Gino spent the next twenty years in Aspen, Colorado painting and snowmobiling with his 180-pound Irish Wolfhound, Madigan—who rode on a sled behind the snowmobile—in the Rockies near where he trained with the US Army Ski Troops, 10th Mountain Division. During World War II, he spent six months on the front line in Italy, and as he says, "Under fire most of the time."

For health reasons, in 2009, the Hollanders left the mountains for Ojai, California, where Gino at eighty six continues to paint and Barbara to write.

****

(9) Nancy Spaeth:

My half sister Nancy Hewitt Spaeth was born October 16, 1947, in Everett, Washington. She is the daughter of Willard Henry Spaeth and Nancy Urline Mathewson.

Nancy attended public school in Everett, graduated from Roosevelt High School in Seattle, and went to the University of Arizona in 1965. "By February 1966, I had become too sick to stay in school. Vomiting in the planter boxes outside of my physics class became old after a while." Nancy returned home and lived with her mother while receiving kidney dialysis from the Seattle Artificial Kidney Center and continuing college at the University of Washington, and then transferring to Seattle University, where she received a Bachelor of Education degree in English.

Nancy was one of the early kidney failure patients to be accepted by what became known as the "Life and Death Committee" for chronic dialysis. The Seattle Artificial Kidney Center was the first out-of-hospital dialysis center in the world, and it only had two dozen dialysis beds. Today, in 2010, Nancy is one of the longest-surviving kidney patients in the world.

After receiving a kidney from our brother Charlie Spaeth in 1975, she married and gave birth to two children, Joshua "Josh" James Pitts and Sarah Hewitt Pitts. She went back to school and obtained a nursing degree from Bellevue Community College, graduating first in her class in 1982, and then worked at various Seattle hospitals and clinics before transferring to the Virginia Mason Clinic. She finished her career working for Washington State, helping injured workers get back to work.

In 1981, Nancy received a cadaveric transplant—her brother's kidney gave out after six years—from a young woman who fell from a ladder on a fishing barge in Alaska. In 1989, she received her third transplant, again a cadaveric kidney, this time due to a motorcycle accident. In June 2000, she had a fourth transplant, a kidney her doctor said had necrosed—a portion had died after the surgery—but is working well in 2010.

Currently, in addition to her work, Nancy teaches classes on "The

History of Dialysis and Rehabilitation" as well as "Living Long and Living Well with Kidney Disease"—the importance of self-management of chronic illness, for doctors, nurses, technicians, and social workers associated with renal disease.

Nancy loves family history, travel, and playing with her grandchild and her grand-dog.

Josh Pitts, Nancy's son, Karen (Marek) Pitts, Josh's wife (holding son Eli), Nancy, and Sarah Pitts, Nancy's daughter

My brother Charlie Spaeth, his son Shaffer and daughter Audrey and wife Becky (2009)

(10) Elizabeth Ann "Beth" (Griffin) Ferris:

My half sister Beth was born January 27, 1950, in Tacoma, Washington. She is the daughter of Edwin L. Griffin and Sarah Ferris Cowles. She graduated from the University of Montana with honors in English literature and at fifty received a Master of Fine Arts degree in creative writing from Warren Wilson College in North Carolina.

She writes: "I spent my early twenties in the Montana wilderness living up the Middle Fork of the Flathead River studying Mountain Goats with my ex-husband. We spent four winters eighty miles from any 'civilization.' It was the best thing I could have done, literally chopping wood and carrying water, skiing miles to watch the goats, living in a ten-by-twelve-foot wall tent. It was my job to climb the mountains and determine what the goats ate—and thus became a plant taxonomist and botanist, going to school in these fields at the University of Montana."

In 1979, Beth wrote and coproduced *Heartland*, a feature-length drama based on the life of pioneer homesteader Elinore Pruitt Stewart, with major funding from the National Endowment for the Humanities (NEH). The film was distributed theatrically throughout the United States and Europe from 1979 to 1982. Vincent Canby, *NY Times* critic, called the film "uncommonly beautiful."

Heartland awards:

Berlin International Film Festival, Golden Bear; Sundance Film Festival; Western Heritage; American Playhouse series; Neil Simon, award for the best screenplay, 1983-1984; *Esquire Magazine:* "The Best of The New Generation, Men and Women under Forty Who Are Changing America," 1984; Cowboy Hall of Fame.

Beth continued to write and produce documentaries:

Hearts and Hands, a social history of the nineteenth century as seen through the medium of quilt making, with major funding by NEH. *Hearts and Hands* won the Golden Plaque, Chicago International Film Festival, and received special commendation for "creative quality of the script," 1986–88.

New Year Country, 1982, WNET Nonfiction Series finalist, American Film Festival.

Kicking the Loose Gravel Home, the life story of nationally known poet Richard Hugo, with major funding from NEA, won the New Year Country, 1982, WNET nonfiction series.

Year of the Mountain Goat, a children's film distributed by Churchill Films, Inc., 2002, with major funding from NEA, was an American Film Festival finalist and selected by the New York Public Library for their permanent collection.

Beth wrote and codirected *Contrary Warriors*, the story of Robert Yellowtail and the Crow Tribe's struggle for survival. Excerpts from the December 1985 Billings *Gazette* (Roger Clawson) state, "The historic story line includes young Yellowtail's mission to Washington, D.C. Sent into battle against Sen. Thomas Walsh by Plenty Coups, the last great chief, Yellowtail used his wit and gift of oratory to crush Walsh on the Senate Floor. It's a war story as fine as any told around a campfire." *Contrary Warriors* won both the U.S. Film Festival's best picture award and the American Indian Film Festival "Golden Plaque."

At thirty-seven, Beth became ill with a serious retroviral infection, dubbed chronic fatigue syndrome, and no longer could walk miles, ski, or ride horses. While suffering with the virus, she began writing poetry. In 1992, she won first place in the prestigious Iowa's Women's Poetry contest with *Planting Onions* which appeared in the June 1992 issue of the magazine Iowa Woman. *Republic of Glass* won the semifinalist award from the *Crab Orchard Review* in August 2010.

In the 1990s, principally because of her chronic fatigue syndrome, she became interested in the process of mind and body healing through the use of creative arts as an alternate to medicine. She and a small cadre of kindred souls founded "Living Art of Montana," a charitable organization founded on the premise of using the expressive arts as a path through illness and produced a video documentary, *A Door in the Dark*, which plunges the viewer directly into the emotional world of cancer patients.

Today, 2010, Beth and cofounder of "Living Art," Youpa Stein, are writing a book. *You Can Write Your Way Out of This*, a story of healing and poetry, collects seventeen years of Living Art Poetry, and uses it as a guide to group facilitation. In Beth's own words, "This book is not about being a 'good writer,' but about how poetry brings us to believe in ourselves and the truth that is scrolled Inside us."

Beth continues to live in Missoula, Montana.

My sister Beth

(11) Fred and Bea Griffin:

My Uncle Fred (my father's brother) swam, wrestled, and boxed at Stadium High School and the University of Washington. According to my grandmother Adock, who religiously clipped newspaper articles of her son's prowess, Uncle Fred never lost a race or match until Johnny Weissmuller beat him at the 1928 Olympic Games swimming tryouts. Weissmuller went on to win an Olympic gold medal and play Tarzan in the movies.

After graduating from Harvard Business School, which my father also attended, Uncle Fred went into banking. When my father branched the fuel business into Seattle, they divided the company, with Fred owning and operating the Seattle branch and my father the Tacoma branch. Uncle Fred remained active in the business until his death in the early 1990s.

Aunt Bea, Uncle Fred, Wendy, and me at the Griffin home in Seattle. The paintings of Fred Griffin Jr., a well-known Seattle artist, hang on the walls behind us

Aunt Bea was a real character. Not only was she a tigress, she

once stood back to back with Fred in a bar fight slashing with a broken beer bottle at assailants attacking Fred from behind.

Bea's hobby was collecting tortoises and crickets for her solarium. Though she was normally law-abiding, she had no problem smuggling tortoises from around the world into the US in a very large traveling purse.

Still today, when Wendy and I catch crickets in the house, now mostly in Palm Desert, California, we release them in the garden instead of…

****

(12) *How to Make Money in Commercial Land:*

Foreword by Victor Lyon, past president of Realtors National Marketing Institute

"During thirty-five years of experience in real estate brokerage, appraisal and development, I have concluded that there is no investment that is more misunderstood or more mysterious, than speculative land. Also there is no investment that has had less literature written concerning it or less research published about it than vacant land.

"Jim Griffin's *How to Make Money in Commercial Land* explains in easy-to-understand language, many of the basics of land; zoning and its influence on value and the structure and importance of proper legal descriptions and real estate documents.

"Secondly, it can broaden the base of knowledge for those who invest in other fields and for the professional real estate salesperson who presently specializes in residential brokerage.

"Finally by carefully studying Jim Griffin's accounting of his own experiences, and by following the prescribed step-by-step procedure and suggested methodology for the duplication of successes, the reader can save years of painful experience in developing the skills and the savvy necessary to compete in the risky but potentially profitable field of commercial land investment."

Chronology

Grandchildren, listening to bedtime stories about kin who came west to the Washington Territory in the late nineteenth century to homestead and become lumber barons, mayors, judges, legislators, and entrepreneurs helped shape my character and the direction my life would take. Through my veins, and yours, runs Danish, English, French, Irish, and Scottish blood.

Joseph Matteson—the name was later changed to Mathewson—my paternal grandfather's (Edward "Ted" Mathewson) ancestor, was the first to immigrate to America. He left Denmark around 1658.[1]

Henry Hewitt Sr., my maternal grandfather's (Edward "Ted" Mathewson) grandfather, emigrated from Lancashire, England, in 1841 and settled in Wisconsin. Henry became one of the original contractors on the Illinois and Mississippi canal. His largest enterprise was the Menasha, Wisconsin, government lock. According to the 1909 Tacoma Ledger profile, "He" (Henry, Sr.) "was identified with the largest construction enterprises of those two decades."[2]

Richard Headlee, a tanner and currier, left Manchester, England, prior to 1665. He is thought to be my maternal grandmother's (Elsie Headlee Mathewson) first paternal ancestor to immigrate.[3] Headlees have been traced back to the beginning of English

Peerage created about AD 1230. The title "Baron of Headley" was bestowed at various times.[4] Richard Headlee, born in the colonies in 1690, is the progenitor of our family's Headlee line.

George Humes, born in 1698 at Wedderbun Castle, Berwickshire, Scotland, was my grandmother's (Elsie Headlee Mathewson) first maternal ancestor to arrive in America. Humes was deported to Virginia in 1715 after the British defeated the Scots in the Jacobean Wars. He later became a surveyor.[5]

John Griffin, a farmer, born circa 1804 in England, is the earliest known Griffin ancestor. Nothing is known of John's parents or exactly where and when he was born. The 1841 Census of Quadring Parish in Lincolnshire, England, shows John and his family, but John was not listed as a native of Quadring. John immigrated to America in 1845 and settled in Waukegan, Illinois.[6]

Henry La Grange, my grandfather's (Fred Griffin) maternal grandfather, emigrated from French Canada at the beginning of the 1800s. I was not able to find any information about his parents. Henry La Grange's daughter, Henrietta Elizabeth La Grange, married my grandfather's (Fred Griffin) father Abraham.[7]

William Parks, my grandmother's (Adock Parks Griffin) grandfather, emigrated from Glandermott Parish, Londonderry, Ireland, to New Brunswick, Canada, sometime before 1823. His son, Joseph Parks (Adock's father) was a blacksmith. In 1885, Joseph left Red Bank, New Brunswick and brought his family to Tacoma.[8]

Mary Jane (Bartlett) Parks, my grandmother's (Adock Parks Griffin) mother, was born in Maine in 1856. She descends from one of a number of Bartlett families that emigrated from the Sussex area of England starting in 1634. My distant cousin, Colby Parks—we share the same great grandparents—remembers his grandmother Eliza Parks (my great aunt) telling him she was related to Josiah Bartlett, the first signer of the Declaration of Independence and first governor of New Hampshire. The Bartletts came to England with William the Conqueror in 1066.[9]

Tom Humes, my grandmother's (Elsie Headlee Mathewson) maternal uncle, was the first member of her family to come to the Washington Territory. Humes, a member of the Kansas Legislature, arrived in Seattle in 1882 and opened a law office. In 1890 he became a Superior Court Judge, and in 1897 he was elected mayor of Seattle.

Henry Hewitt, my grandfather's (Edward "Ted" Mathewson) paternal uncle, arrived in Tacoma in 1888 and founded St. Paul and Tacoma Lumber Company, which became the country's largest producing sawmill. In 1890, with money from an eastern syndicate, Hewitt lay out and built the city of Everett.

Ted Mathewson, my maternal grandfather, at the urging of his Uncle Henry Hewitt, dropped out of Notre Dame and came to Everett in the early 1890s. After homesteading and selling his timber, grandfather went into the logging business with Joe Irving—who later became my step grandfather. In 1911, a self-made millionaire and commissioner of the Everett Board of Public Works, Grandfather Ted died in a tragic automobile accident on Mount Rainier.

Elsie (Headlee) Mathewson, my maternal grandmother, came west from Iowa in a wagon train in 1889, before completion of the Great Northern rail line. Her family, the Headlees, homesteaded in Snohomish County. Elsie's brother, Tom Headlee, was elected mayor of Everett in 1903 and served simultaneously with his Uncle Tom Humes, mayor of Seattle.

Frederic Griffin, my paternal grandfather, left his family's farm at Ironton, Wisconsin, in 1888. He hopped on a freight train and "rode the rails" to Tacoma, the terminus of the Northern Pacific Railroad. His first job, laying track for a trolley line with Chinese migrants, paid one dollar for a twelve-hour day. By the early 1900s, he'd built the largest freight and fuel delivery business in the city.

1. *Mattesons in the US,* www.matteson.us/joseph.shtml

2. Norman H. Clark, *Mill Town: A Social History of Everett, Washington, from Its Earliest Beginnings* (Seattle: University of Washington Press, 1982).

3. Ray L. Headlee, *A History of the Headlee and Headley Families* (New Jersey: printed by author, 1905); reprinted 1971.

4. Alvah John W. Headlee, PhD, *Headlee Migrations*, (Waynesburg College, West Virginia University, Morgantown, printed in New Jersey, 1905).

5. *Descendants of George Hume* http://homepages.rootsweb.ancestry.com/~hume, researched by my sister, Nancy Hewitt Spaeth.

6. John R. Griffin, *Griffin Families Marry* (published 1987, Library of Congress, Catalog Card Number 87-90891)

7. John E. Griffin, *Descendants of John Griffin* (published 1983, Library of Congress, Catalog Card Number 83-81522)

8. John R. Griffin, *Griffin Families Marry* printed by John R. Griffin, 1987, Library of Congress, Catalog Card Number 87-90891.

9. Bartlett genealogy www.selectsurnames.combartlett.html

10. Augustus Gibson Paine line of descendants, from the August 1985 Paine Family Reunion notes by Patty and Peter Paine Jr. and Frisky and David Irwin.

Griffin/Mathewson Family Tree

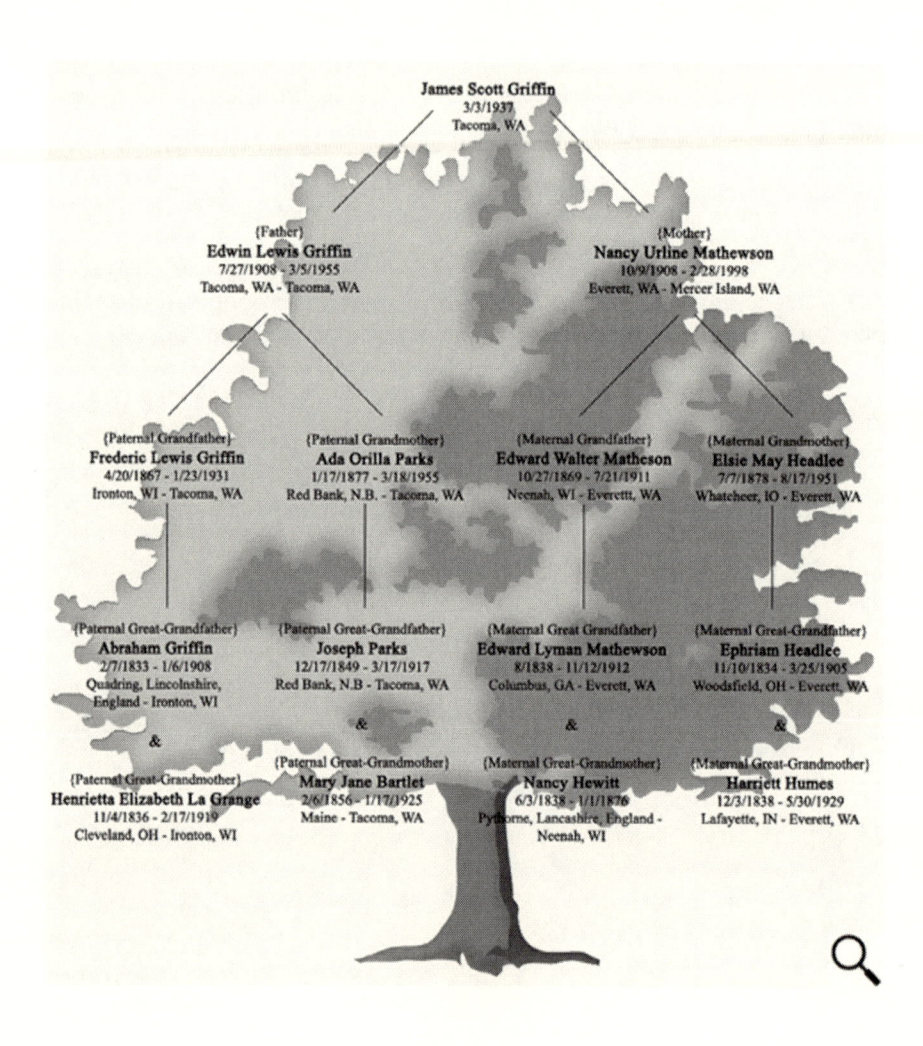

James Scott Griffin
3/3/1937
Tacoma, WA

{Father}
Edwin Lewis Griffin
7/27/1908 - 3/5/1955
Tacoma, WA - Tacoma, WA

{Mother}
Nancy Urline Mathewson
10/9/1908 - 2/28/1998
Everett, WA - Mercer Island, WA

{Paternal Grandfather}
Frederic Lewis Griffin
4/20/1867 - 1/23/1931
Ironton, WI - Tacoma, WA

{Paternal Grandmother}
Ada Orilla Parks
1/17/1877 - 3/18/1955
Red Bank, N.B. - Tacoma, WA

{Maternal Grandfather}
Edward Walter Matheson
10/27/1869 - 7/21/1911
Neenah, WI - Everettt, WA

{Maternal Grandmother}
Elsie May Headlee
7/7/1878 - 8/17/1951
Whatcheer, IO - Everett, WA

{Paternal Great-Grandfather}
Abraham Griffin
2/7/1833 - 1/6/1908
Quadring, Lincolnshire, England - Ironton, WI

&

{Paternal Great-Grandmother}
Henrietta Elizabeth La Grange
11/4/1836 - 2/17/1919
Cleveland, OH - Ironton, WI

{Paternal Great-Grandfather}
Joseph Parks
12/17/1849 - 3/17/1917
Red Bank, N.B. - Tacoma, WA

&

{Paternal Great-Grandmother}
Mary Jane Bartlet
2/6/1856 - 1/17/1925
Maine - Tacoma, WA

{Maternal Great Grandfather}
Edward Lyman Mathewson
8/1838 - 11/12/1912
Columbus, GA - Everett, WA

&

{Maternal Great-Grandmother}
Nancy Hewitt
6/3/1838 - 1/1/1876
Pythorne, Lancashire, England - Neenah, WI

{Maternal Great-Grandfather}
Ephriam Headlee
11/10/1834 - 3/25/1905
Woodsfield, OH - Everett, WA

&

{Maternal Great-Grandmother}
Harriett Humes
12/3/1838 - 5/30/1929
Lafayette, IN - Everett, WA

Paine/Sterling Family Tree

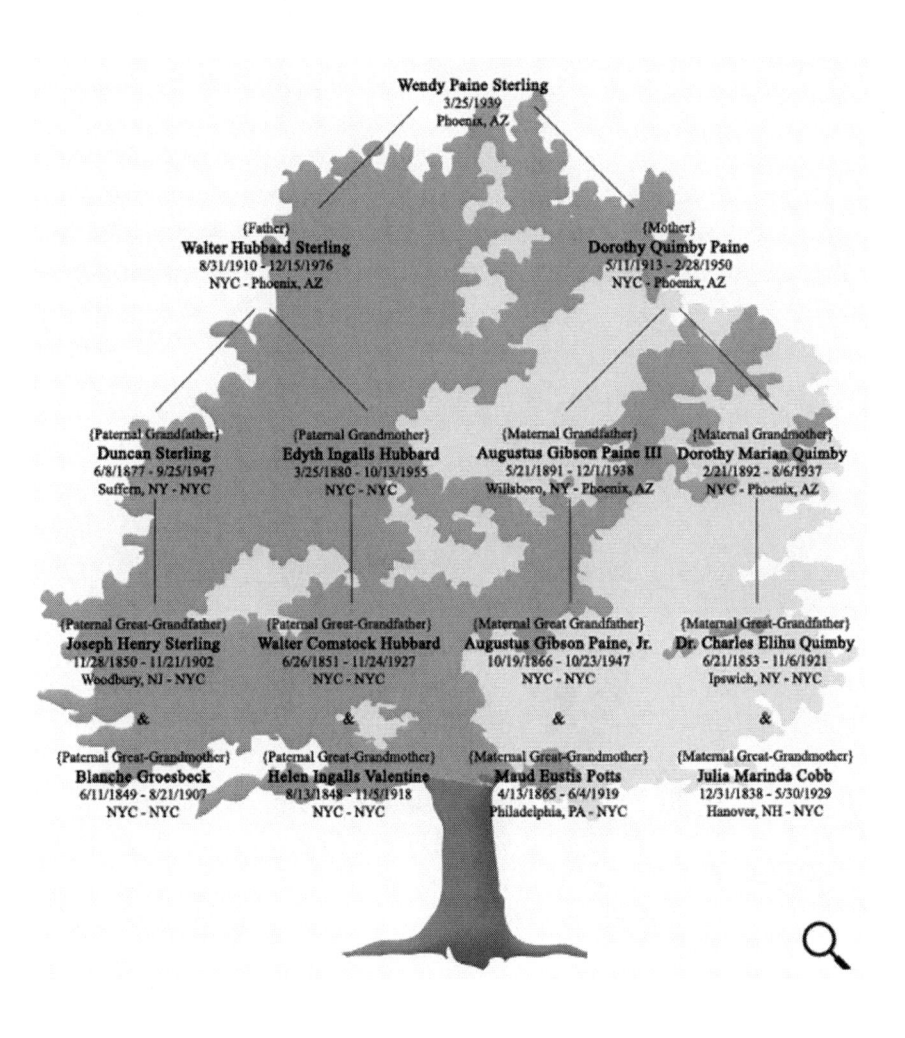

Wendy Paine Sterling
3/25/1939
Phoenix, AZ

{Father}
Walter Hubbard Sterling
8/31/1910 - 12/15/1976
NYC - Phoenix, AZ

{Mother}
Dorothy Quimby Paine
5/11/1913 - 2/28/1950
NYC - Phoenix, AZ

{Paternal Grandfather}
Duncan Sterling
6/8/1877 - 9/25/1947
Suffern, NY - NYC

{Paternal Grandmother}
Edyth Ingalls Hubbard
3/25/1880 - 10/13/1955
NYC - NYC

{Maternal Grandfather}
Augustus Gibson Paine III
5/21/1891 - 12/1/1938
Willsboro, NY - Phoenix, AZ

{Maternal Grandmother}
Dorothy Marian Quimby
2/21/1892 - 8/6/1937
NYC - Phoenix, AZ

{Paternal Great-Grandfather}
Joseph Henry Sterling
11/28/1850 - 11/21/1902
Woodbury, NJ - NYC

{Paternal Great-Grandfather}
Walter Comstock Hubbard
6/26/1851 - 11/24/1927
NYC - NYC

{Maternal Great Grandfather}
Augustus Gibson Paine, Jr.
10/19/1866 - 10/23/1947
NYC - NYC

{Maternal Great-Grandfather}
Dr. Charles Elihu Quimby
6/21/1853 - 11/6/1921
Ipswich, NY - NYC

&

&

&

&

{Paternal Great-Grandmother}
Blanche Groesbeck
6/11/1849 - 8/21/1907
NYC - NYC

{Paternal Great-Grandmother}
Helen Ingalls Valentine
8/13/1848 - 11/5/1918
NYC - NYC

{Maternal Great-Grandmother}
Maud Eustis Potts
4/13/1865 - 6/4/1919
Philadelphia, PA - NYC

{Maternal Great-Grandmother}
Julia Marinda Cobb
12/31/1838 - 5/30/1929
Hanover, NH - NYC

Travel Pictures

Through the years, Nana and I have had the good fortune to travel and visit some of the most beautiful and exotic places in the world. Following are pictures from our most memorable trips.

Roger and my cousin Joan O'Neil (my mother's brother Mark Mathewson's daughter) and Wendy and me in Rome, 1986, where we toured Emperor Nero's (AD 15 – AD 68) temple, "Golden House," over which Emperor Hadrian built public baths. The remnants of the temple, rediscovered in the 15th century, had never been open to the public, in order to preserve the wall frescos. Roger, who was President of Mobil Oil's Italian refinery, was able to arrange a tour.

According to the archeologist who accompanied us, when Michelangelo was repainting the Sistine Chapel's ceiling, he went down a rope into the undamaged lower level of the palace. After seeing the frescos, he painted a portion of the Sistine Chapel in the same style.

We also visited Pompeii, which had been rediscovered in 1599 after being covered in twelve to eighteen feet of ash and pumice in 79 AD. Again, Roger arranged a tour of a steam bath not open to the public. I can still picture the three hundred perfectly preserved skeletons, in sitting position, lining the walls of bath. Death came slowly from volcanic gas seeping through the bath's vents or suffocation from being covered in ash.

Me, 1990, in front of the Great Pyramid of Giza, tomb of Pharaoh Cheops, one of the Seven Wonders of the World. Built in 2560 BC, over a period of twenty years, by slaves moving rocks from a quarry, it remained for 3,800 years the tallest man-made structure in the world.

Wendy and me, 1990, at Victoria Falls on Zambezi River

Zambezi River, which separates Zambia and Zimbabwe
(one of the Seven Wonders of the World)

Me, 1990, at the Olduvai Gorge, discovered in 1911, in Tanzania, Africa. The gorge's volcanic ash erosion rift has layer after layer of fossils and bones dating back more than 2 million years. The earliest deposits show evidence of primitive hominids camp sites.

Wendy at Jebel al-Madhbah (Mountain of the Altar), 1993, identified by many twentieth century scholars as Mount Sinai where Moses, while leading the Israelites from Egypt, supposedly received the Ten Commandments from God.

Me, 1993, at the supposed site of Jesus' crucifixion in Jerusalem, Israel. The precise location of the Crucifixion remains a matter of conjecture; however, biblical accounts state it was outside the city walls, probably in the ancient place of public execution known as Calvary (Latin for skull).

Wendy, holding a Piranha, on the Amazon River, in 1998. Piranhas, known for their sharp teeth and voracious appetites, are ferocious predators that cooperatively hunt in large schools.

Me and Wendy, 1999, at Machu Picchu

The city of Machu Picchu (one of the New Seven Wonders of the World) was built on a mountain ridge above the Urubamba Valley in Peru fifty miles northwest of Cuzco as an estate for the Inca emperor Pachacuti (1438–72) and was never discovered by the Spanish conquistadors.

Me, 2000, bone fishing on Christmas Island, near Australia, world's largest coral atoll, with endless hard flats to attract cruising bonefish.

Scott, Sterling, and me on Christmas Island

Me, 2002, on the Great Wall of China (one of the Seven Wonders of the World) built in 206 BC, 5,500 miles in length.

Wendy and me, 2002, at Potala Palace in Lhase, Tibet. The palace was built at an altitude of 12,100 feet in 637AD and rebuilt in the seventeenth century to house the Dalai Lamas.

Wendy, 2002, above Omaha Beach in Normandy, France, where allies landed on D-Day, June 6, 1944, during World War ll. Over 425,000 Allied and German troops were killed or wounded at the battle of Normandy.

Me, 2002, at Claude Monet's (1840 – 1926), the French impressionist, home in Giverny, France.

Me, age 70, and Chris Reynolds, 2006, on north rim of Grand Canyon (one of the Seven Wonders of the World) the evening before crossing.

We descended five miles (dropping 5,000 ft.), hiked fifteen miles across (temperature in the nineties), and climbed five miles up to the south rim (ascending 5,000 feet) in ten hours.

Me and Wendy, 2007, at Angkor Wat, Cambodia (one of the Seven Wonders of the World). Angkor Wat was built in the early twelfth century as a temple for the Hindu god Vishnu. In the late thirteenth century, a Buddhist monk deposed the Indian king, the monks father-in-law, and converted the empire's religion from Hindu to Buddhism, which continues today.